Memories of a Big Sky
British War Bride

How tenderly we look back.
With what indulgent smiles
We remember our own young selves
Safe there, in the past.
Nothing can touch what we were.

—Millicent Ward Whitt

Memories of a Big Sky British War Bride

IRENE HOPE HEDRICK

TWODOT®

GUILFORD, CONNECTICUT
HELENA, MONTANA
AN IMPRINT OF THE GLOBE PEQUOT PRESS

A · T W O D O T® · B O O K

TwoDot is a registered trademark of Morris Book Publishing, LLC.

Text design by Lisa Reneson
All photos from the author's collection
Poetry by Millicent Ward Whitt is from *Say to the Moment* (Vermont: P.S., A Press, 1996)

Library of Congress Cataloging-in-Publication Data
Hedrick, Irene Hope.
  Memories of a Big Sky British war bride / Irene Hope Hedrick.— 1st ed.
    p. cm.
  ISBN 0-7627-3958-4
  1. Hedrick, Irene Hope. 2. World War, 1939-1945—Women—Great Britain.
3. War brides—Great Britain—Biography. 4. Women immigrants—United States—Biography. 5. British Americans—Biography. 6. Montana—Biography. I. Title.
  CT275.H5665A3 2005
  978.6'033'092—dc22

                                                                    2005023242

Manufactured in the United States of America
First Edition/First Printing

I dedicate this memoir to

My Mother
an *extraordinarily* good woman who passed away before I could say,
"I love you, Mother, Our Em, Me Mam"

My Father
musician, scholar, gentleman,
who knew that I was meant to be an *inordinately* good woman

My Three Sisters
who helped me grow up

and

My Children and Grandchildren
who have kept me young enough to write a memoir
at the age of eighty-five

Contents

Many thanks to

Linda Peavy,
consulting and developmental editor
and friend,
without whom these memories
might never have appeared in print

Peg Elliott Mayo,
anam cara, columnist, storyteller, author, artist,
lover of all things beautiful in their time,
and a true soul friend who has the same gluttony for words
as I do for chocolate

Dr. Simon Johnson
and Benton County Senior Citizens' Writers' Group
for their unfailing support, input, and friendship

Dr. Ann Staley
leader of "Reading and Writing Women" seminar

Debby Gremmels
for her many hours devoted to publicity research

Grandson Dan
and
great-granddaughter Kelsey
for their valued assistance with computer-art, photography,
and the Family Tree

Haydn and Barb, Hope and Gary, Dan and Les
for their ongoing faith in me

and
Hope Anne
for her dedicated work as proofreader and photographer

Prologue

After a silence, in which were gentle dreams, I asked of her, "What thing is this beauty? For people differ in its defining and the knowledge thereof, as they contend with one another in praise and love of it."
—KAHLIL GIBRAN

*H*er hair was boldly beautiful in the ugly room. The soft blue lights of Christmas danced along each strand as the comb caressed the black, black length of it, a raven's wing touching her shoulders. I could hear the clean squeak as her fingers parted the tresses, twisting and lifting them until everything lovely was eaten up and scraped into a tight black knot at the back of her head. It was neater that way, she said. There were a few straggling tendrils that loved freedom too much, and I laughed with them as they sprang away from their jailors.

I stared at all my secret places, looking for beauty in that ugly room. But that night even the flowers on the wallpaper stared back at me, pale and unresponsive when I tried to breathe life into their dead, flat petals and touch their velvet to my cheek.

I hated them because they had been beautiful, but now they were dead, and I locked them up with the blue lights in my mother's black hair.

I longed for beauty. I sought it in the scrubbed and polished floor that sang of marbled halls and crinolines, of twinkling buckles and dancing feet.

Red satin and blue velvet of my dream fabric swirled and faded in the tight black knot that was my mother's hair. Just that afternoon she had done the old red tile till it shone, preparing for a special guest who dropped in on most people this time of year. Some said he came in down the chimney, but I could never imagine anyone as beautiful as Saint Nicholas covered with soot. Some said he came only to good children, but I thought that wasn't fair because I always remembered that part too late. I was too big to cry, they said.

Before I could ask what Father Christmas would bring that year, my father's strong arms were lifting me up to his shoulders, and I was a giant walking through the doorway into the cold December night. He pointed to the star in the sky, a star bright as the light in his eyes, and when he spoke there were falling leaves rustling among his words. I caught them as they fell. "Let me tell you a story, Love," he said.

The words of his story whispered of three men who followed the star. Rich men they were, riding camels through the sand, camels with saddle-bags holding gifts for a king. I wondered what frankincense and myrrh were, but who could ask such a question when beauty was in the air? My father's voice robbed the saddlebags and gave those gifts to me, and I placed them, gently, among the blue lights in the braided black hair.

We might have gone back through the doorway then, back to the ugly room, but we didn't. Father walked toward the cottage next door and I became afraid, for ghosts and dead men lurked in the tall grass over there, and they'd made tut-tutting noises at me once because they didn't know what children were. Virginia creeper bearded the face of the house and shiny eyes of windows blinked at our intrusion. I held tight as he ducked low in the doorway and we went inside.

The old couple sat huddled at the hearth, as if, like the dying bit of fire, they too had almost gone out. They seemed not even to have the will to lift the poker and shake down the ashes from the glowing coals, and I knew the meaning of a word I had never heard. Despair was all around me. It was heavy in my hands as they slid down from my father's neck. It was heavy in my feet as they touched the cold floor. Hunger, and pain, and emptiness stared at me from their cold, pale eyes, and the wrinkles in their faces did not make a smile around their lips. I became an old, old woman as I sat with them by the fire.

"Merry Christmas," my father said, and they never looked up at him as they said the same.

Silently, gray ashes fell from the grate as the last wisp of smoke coiled slowly up the chimney, the smell of death riding its back. Still, the smile in my father's eyes would have paled a star, and his gentle "Merry Christmas" spoke to me the secret of life. I understood, in that moment, that charity can be given with an empty hand, and I felt wiser than the wise men.

Oh what gifts I could have given. The frankincense. The myrrh. Blue velvet and my mother's hair. If only I could make them smile! My heart was bursting with loving and giving, yet I had nothing but myself to give. The gifts were all locked up in my mother's hair.

I wanted to strip the flowers from the wall, petal by petal, without bruising their loveliness. I wanted to shake those frail old people and make them glad to be alive. I wanted them to leap up and dance with me till all the bubbles burst. But they didn't know how to see!

I could have turned them around three times and pointed them to the mystery that would open their eyes. But children don't teach games to grownups.

The star still shone on high, lighting our way back to the ugly room, and I became a little girl again, wanting a doll for Christmas. A doll with pretty blue lights in her long, black hair. And eyes that opened and shut.

And so it has been throughout my life. A searching for beauty. A longing after truth.

The cold, fish-blue eyes of that old man and woman, staring so fixedly into the dying embers of their life together, gave an eight-year-old child a grim picture of what the far distant future might look like when she became old and ready to die. I looked into my father's eyes, which were hazel like mine, for before that cold day I had thought he too was old, as most children believe of people taller than themselves. But no, his eyes were young and alive, alight with another kind of flame that would never flicker and die. Alive, too, with a mystical knowledge of life and love that gently shone from their depths.

I determined that I, too, should have eyes like my father's, even if mine grew dim and could no longer see the beauty that I sought. Yet only after many years of adversity and foolhardiness can I look into the mirror and say, "What took you so long!"

And so begins my story.

Part 1

Chapter 1

Life's aspirations come in the guise of children.

— RABINDRANATH TAGORE

*L*ooking back, I realize our kitchen in the cottage on Gatewarth Street at Sankey Bridges—an industrial town in Warrington, county of Lancashire—wasn't such an ugly room after all. Father's rocking chair was always there, waiting by the fireplace, the long leather razor strop hanging nearby, Mother's reminder that it could be used for more than one purpose. Not that she herself would ever dream of using it, nor was its use ever necessary, since the eyes in the back of her head would catch us on the brink of disobedience and a mere warning step toward the fireplace would be enough to stop our intentions toward mischief. The strop would disappear on occasion, to mother's chagrin, and while berating father for his absent-mindedness, she would send us scooting around the house to find it, in our secret hiding places—like in the Walking Day baskets hanging on the bedroom wall, which Mother never looked into since they were supposed to be empty until Walking Day when they would be filled with beautiful flowers for us to carry down the city streets, following Father's marching band in celebration of this religious holiday. Or we would hide it in the empty clothes washer in the shed down the yard, where Mother never went unless it was Washing Day, every Monday, and come hail or rain we wouldn't dream of hiding it on Mondays.

The teakettle was singing on the hob beside the fire, whose rosy glow spread warmth throughout the room. From the mirror atop the mahogany bureau, the fire's light reflected across to the far wall, making even that cold spot in the room a part of the cozy scene. Sometimes father would be in the mirrored image, his blowtorch stripping off old paint from the doors and cupboards so he could give them a satiny varnish.

Our mother Emily—or Em, as Father often called her—would say, " 'arold! You're going to set the bloody 'ouse on fire one of these days!" And he would just keep on blowing and scraping, a little smile touching the corners of his mouth. Father was a tolerant man who expected his four daughters to inherit that same trait from him. The larger portion of our character and personality, he decided, would develop from reading the classics, and I have never forgotten my days crouched beside the old Singer sewing machine, my world dissolved into the world of a girl named Anne of Green Gables. My father knew what he was talking about, for a burning resolve was dawning inside me that I should grow up to be just like her.

Our family was close-knit, and father gave us nicknames to show our togetherness. Our oldest sister wasn't just Eva. She became Our Eve. Doris, the youngest and smallest, he called Our Little Dot, and Joyce, two years younger and with a sunnier disposition than I, became Your Joy to outsiders, though Father called her Our Ike, or Ikey Moses to those of us at home. I suspect it was because he had wanted a boy when each one of his four daughters arrived. I swear I heard Our Ike come into the world laughing rather than crying, as she was always the one to bring out the smiles, bucking us up in times of trouble, sometimes by merely dancing round the kitchen table with the broom in her arms, while Our Little Dot climbed up on the table to accompany her, tap dancing to the only tune she knew, the old hymn "We Plow the Fields and Scatter the Good Seed on the Land." I can see them both now and feel so sad that Our Dot died from cancer in her early thirties, a few years after I left home, and I wasn't able to kiss her good-bye. The guilt wells up too when I think of Our Ike being the sole caregiver to Mother, who had always helped us all, in her later years, while I had sailed away from home with never a thought that Mother might need help herself one day.

As a matter of necessity, my nickname eventually became Our I, because father couldn't think of anything more befitting than the name he had already chosen for me at birth, Irene, from the Goddess of Peace, Irena. When I was old enough to understand the nuances children often attach to any name that isn't just plain Jane, I breathed a sigh of relief, glad he named me Irene rather than Faith, the name my Auntie May said would go so nicely with my surname, which was Hope.

It was often hope that kept us going. Hope and hard work. Thanks to Mother's strong will and iron hand, we survived through the first coal strike of the twenties, despite the fact that our cupboard was often as bare as Mother Hubbard's. A leaf from the book of Epictetus' Stoic wisdom must have hung high on Mother's branch of our family tree, because she would always make do if she could, and if not, "then we'll just have to do without then, won't we?" And do without we did, to the point that whatever was offered in the way of assistance by Granny Knight, Mother's answer was always, "Oh, no thank you, Mother. We have plenty."

What food we did have was magically expanded, stretched as far as elastic might go, to keep our stomachs filled and our spirits high. Potatoes were always on hand for chips, so all she would need extra to make cottage pie, sometimes called shepherd's pie, were a few scraps of meat with gravy made from the meat drippings, a chopped onion, and a can of peas. She would scrape from the bone the bits of beef or lamb the butcher's axe had missed, and brown them with lard or suet in the frying pan, then toss them, bone and all, into the waiting stewpot on the hob. She would make sure the large Spanish onion would set off her eyes to water—Mother would always welcome a hug from her four little women when the onion made her cry—before adding the finely chopped pieces to the pot, along with the peas, or carrots, and sometimes beans from a can.

While the meat and vegetables were slowly cooking in the big cast iron oven next to the hob, she would take up the boiled potatoes and mash them with a half a cup of milk and a pat of butter to make a potato topping. Once the stew had been thickened with a little flour, she would spread the potato mixture over its surface and then back into the oven it would go. Within a few minutes more, the crockery and silverware all set and waiting, that cottage pie with the potato crust would come out a beautiful golden brown, all bubbly underneath. Mother would sometimes forget to take out the bone before she put the lid on the pie, but no one objected to that, and besides, Father said the stuff in the joints, the marrow of the bone, was good for you. I took his word for it, but whenever I remembered, I would remind Mother to take out the bone so I could give it to the neighbor's dog.

Sometimes I would be so hungry I would sleepwalk to the kitchen cupboard downstairs. I told father I was afraid of falling down our steep staircase in my sleep, but he comforted me with the promise, "I'll sleep with one eye open so I can catch you then, shall I, Love?" In those days I believed every word my father said, but for good measure I dreamed up one more solution to the dilemma. I found a huge safety pin and pinned my nightie to the sheets every night, so I would wake up if I tried to walk in my sleep again. But morning would always come with a hint of breakfast, and maybe Mother would whisper, "Run home from school today and there'll be suet pud at teatime."

Whatever happened at school that day, be it fire drill, mental arithmetic, or poor Miss Jarman's face flushing red as a raspberry at the sound of knitting needles dropping to the floor as one after another of my classmates followed suit when I accidentally dropped mine under the desk while picking up a dropped stitch. We rather enjoyed needling her because she was easily embarrassed and too timid to chastise us. I didn't care about anything else that day except the suet pudding that would be awaiting us when we got home. I never cared what went into or onto suet pudding. It was an all-fulfilling bit of ambrosia to me, and I was delighted to receive the recipe in a letter from Our Ike recently:

> *Remember when we were kids, Irene, and Em used to mix packet suet with water till it was stodgy, pat it all together, roll it in a tea towel, fasten it up with a safety pin and boil it for a couple of hours then slice it up and serve it to us with Tate and Lyle's Golden Syrup over it. We loved it.*

Is it any wonder why food has taken such a big hold over my life and my memories when, throughout my childhood, food—or rather the sparseness of it—consumed me? I remember always being hungry, but Mother got around my whining with, "Go on with you now. Your eyes are bigger than your belly, so stop your blathering." Half an hour later she would feel sorry for me, take up the loaf of day-old bread (always day old so it could be cut thin to go a little further), pick up the carving knife, slice off a thinner-than-usual piece and make me a buttie jam. She would spread a bit of butter and a spoonful of Tate and Lyle's Golden Syrup on top of the slice and then fold one half over the other, slapping the two halves together with her palms before handing the buttie to me with the warning, "That's all you're going to get now before teatime, and it'll have to satisfy you," and then send me on an errand. I never was satisfied, but I was willing to wait as long as necessary after that.

On one such errand, Mother handed me the jug and sent me down to the neighbor's farm to fetch milk for the baby. I set off happily enough, swinging the jug loosely in my hand, the shilling rattling around where she had placed it, in the bottom of the jug so my hands wouldn't carelessly let it fall and be lost. All I could think of was how wonderful that milk would taste if only I were allowed to have some.

I often wonder how on earth I managed to achieve healthy adulthood without benefit of the standard requirement of vitamins and minerals, now considered essential to good health. Especially calcium. As soon as Mother had decided our teeth and bones would last us a lifetime, she would quit the breastfeeding routine and only the new baby (Our Little Dot at that time) would receive the nutritional benefits of cow's milk straight from the farm. Nobody gave a thought to the fact that it wasn't pasteurized.

Stamped on my memory for all time is the image of one tall glass of milk set beside my lunch plate on a school outing to Llangollen (pronounced Than-GOTH-len) in North Wales. It went down slowly and sweetly, and felt so smooth I could have sat there drinking milk for the whole day instead of climbing the hills with my classmates. But the memory of that moment stayed with me to the green-grassed plateau atop the orme, the little mountain that we scaled. There it became a glorious sensation of koinonia with the universe, a feeling over, above, and beyond the real, the routine sameness, of the world down below. I knew everything in the world I ever wanted to know and was master of it all. Oh, to keep the memory alive and live forever!

When my school chum Clarice Barlow and I grew brave enough to roll down the bottom 50 yards of the orme, across a patch that joined the meadow grass, this became an even luckier day. I landed on the level in a patch of gorgeous bright yellow marsh marigolds, and my teacher, when she finally got to the bottom, allowed me to pick one to take home with me for my pressed collection.

But I was older on the day I found the marsh marigolds, while I must have been only five years old on that long-ago day when I carried home the heavy jug full of milk for Our Little Dot. I loved flowers even then, and couldn't resist a cluster of red campions growing by the lane. I decided the milk would be safe if I placed the jug carefully on the grass beside me, and it did hold steady while I picked a few of the flowers, hoping Mother would like them better than she did the bunch of mother-die weeds she had thrown out the last time I picked flowers for her. Bouquet in hand, I reached down to pick up the jug, unfortunately tipping it a little so that some of the milk sloshed out. Guilt-stricken, I hurried home, dreading Mother's reaction. Sure enough, she demanded to know why the jug was not filled to the brim and asked if I had been swigging some on the way home. "You had no right to go off flower picking when you were supposed to come right home so I could feed Our Little Dot!" she exploded. "And, where, pray, is the sixpence change Mrs. Smith gave you?"

I looked in my hand, and it wasn't there!

Father rarely interfered with mother's questioning, but when I started to cry, he took my hand, looking hard at Mother as he reassured me, "Come on then, Love, we'll go find that sixpence. I bet it's hiding there in the grass somewhere by the flowers. Let's go look till we find it, shall we?" And away we went, crossing the railway lines and down the lane. Where the flowers were growing, we went to work on our hands and knees, feeling all around with our fingers and scraping the earth with our fingernails among the flower stalks and blades of grass. In no time at all, there was Father, holding up that silver coin for me to smile at.

We raced each other back to the house, father singing all the way:

I've got sixpence
Jolly, jolly sixpence
I've got sixpence
To last me all my life.
I've got tuppence to lend
And tuppence to spend
And tuppence to take home to me wife,
Poor wife!

Nobody could deny that Mother was an extraordinarily good woman, and with the promise or threat of Heaven or Hell—according to the merits of our behavior—she kept her family on a course of truth and honor that was straight as Robin Hood's arrow strafing the Sheriff of Nottingham in Sherwood Forest. Having decided that she possessed all the grace needed to finish her life on earth, she had left the church to fend for itself. She insisted, however, that her daughters be well prepared to become equally blessed, and so sent us to Sunday school. I rather enjoyed the adventure, especially one Sunday when we were studying the book of Proverbs. Many of them sounded familiar to me, and when the vicar asked my class who had written those guides for good living, I put up my hand and said, "I think my mother did!" The vicar smiled and said, "Your mother must be an extraordinarily good woman." I was so proud I ran home a little faster that Sunday to tell her what the vicar had said about her. I can understand, today, why she frowned and asked me to repeat the "ordinarily good" phrase I had used, but Father came to the rescue and explained that "extraordinarily good" was the phrase I should have remembered to use.

In those penny-pinching days when there was never enough to go around, Mother did her best to indulge father's somewhat gourmet tastes. I often wondered where Father had learned to enjoy fine dining. Perhaps his culinary tastes developed because his father was an adopted son in a very wealthy family, who might have passed along to his own children a taste for the finer things in life that he himself had once enjoyed. Grandfather Hope's early life of luxury had ended rather abruptly when, for reasons unknown, his adoptive family disinherited him during his youth and packed him off to Canada to finish his schooling under the direction of a tutor who, according to Grandmother Hope, absconded with the education fund once they arrived in Canada. Grandfather eventually returned to England, married Grandmother Mary Elizabeth, and died there when their six children were still young enough to need nurturing within family surroundings. With no means of income, his widow was obliged to farm out her youngsters with aunts and uncles. Since there weren't enough relatives to go around, Father was placed in the Blue Coat School. There, he probably received a better education than his siblings, despite the fact that he hated the orphanage life and would try to escape by tying his bed sheets together, anchoring one end to the bedpost just inside the window, then sliding down the sheet rope and onto the street below. "But," he said, "they always chased me down and took me back there." I could never hold the tears back when he told me that story.

I often wonder how Grandmother Hope felt when she had to "go into service," as they say in England, in order to earn a living. And I wonder, too, whether her earlier social status and Grandfather Hope's reputation as a musician might explain why so many of the upper crust of English families clamored for her services as housekeeper. Millionaire Sir John Moores, owner of Littlewood's Football Pools, hired her to run things at his mansion and to take care of his children. Barbara Clegg, John Moore's daughter, a popular television star in England, went to visit Granny Hope on her one-hundredth birthday, and Queen Elizabeth sent her a birthday telegram of congratulations. Famous film stars such as Tom Walls and Ralph Lynn clamored for her services, and the Lister family of Freshfield, with whom she was associated for a long time in her later years, paid all expenses for a grand funeral when she died at Aunty May's Freshfield home at 102. How I wish now that I had talked to her more often about her own life—including those years when Grandfather Hope was living and making music.

Those links to the past are gone forever, along with the food fads Father had acquired somewhere in his early childhood. But memories of Mother's attempts to honor Father's yearning for favorite foods are with me still. Digging out a few coppers from the biscuit tin on the top shelf, where she stashed the extra money from father's piecework—money she was saving for a holiday on the Isle of Man someday—she would send me off to the butcher's shop just down the road, with instructions to "fetch a nice quarter-pound cut of steak for your father's tea, and be sure to have him cut it thin, now." I hated to ask him to do that because I was very proud to be a Hope, and I felt as if I were begging for more meat than Father could afford to pay, from a butcher who owned far too much meat himself to ever feel one pang of hunger, and so would never know what it meant to do without.

I would slow down at Astill's pastry shop on the way home, running my hand along the name engraved on the brass window ledge and looking up above the window at the bold, black letters: CONFECTIONER TO HIS MAJESTY THE KING. I always imagined the royal pastry from their shop to taste better than pastry from any other confectionary shop in the country. I'd squint through the square, leaded-glass windowpanes, imagining the taste of the juicy fruit tarts, and the French pastries puffed up with rich vanilla cream tucked between featherweight layers, topped off with a shiny white icing. I spotted my favorites, cheaper by the dozen—sometimes a baker's dozen if Mrs. Astill was in a good mood—day-old Eccles cakes, a treat upon which mother would sometimes splurge on a happy occasion. They were round, crisp pastry boxes filled with raisins. I would dream, standing there, of my castle in the air, where I was some Lord's Lady, dressed in pure white georgette and a high, pointed hat with a billowing, long white veil. I would take lessons on posture and walking with my chin held high. I would ring for my upstairs maid to bring in watercress sandwiches, and tea in dainty demitasse cups like Granny Knight's fine china—just as soon as I became filthy rich and old enough to give a party for someone.

But Mother was waiting for her skinny piece of meat, so I would make up for time spent daydreaming outside the pastry shop by running the rest of the way home, rehearsing the answers to the questions she would surely ask: Had I counted the number of one-ounce brass weights to make up a quarter pound? Yes, I had always done that first thing, because they looked like the pawns standing up in Father's chess set. There were exactly four one-ounce weights on one side of the scale, I told her, and I had watched and figured out in my head again—sixteen ounces in one pound, one quarter of which would add up to four ounces, making up exactly one quarter pound of meat needed to weigh down the empty scale and make it level with the weighted side. Mother gave me another questioning look, and I went on to tell her how the butcher had put on a few more scraps from the cutting table, so the meat side of the scale then dipped down almost to the counter, and I knew Mother was getting more than her money's worth. "And what about the bone?" she queried, her voice rising a notch with her rising eyebrows as if I were to blame if the precious bone was missing. I unwrapped the package, letting the bone speak for itself, remembering how flushed my face had felt when the butcher gave me a wink and said, " 'Ere y'ar then. Just for the dog, Luv." He knew perfectly well that we didn't have a dog. He probably guessed the bone would go into the pot on the hearth, where the potatoes, carrots, and onion were waiting for the bone scraps that would turn those vegetables into soup. I was so busy imagining how good the soup would taste poured over the chips at teatime that it never occurred to me to begrudge father his bit of sirloin.

Father would make sure his girls got a taste of whatever specialty Emily could afford to make for him. His reason for giving one of us the top of the boiled egg that sat in his eggcup at breakfast was that he just didn't care for the top part of the egg, and that reason was good enough for me. I always shook my head when he offered a piece from his honeycomb of tripe, which he loved to eat sprinkled with vinegar. I had looked the word up in the dictionary at school, and I never could imagine anyone chewing on a cow's stomach. It gave me goose bumps. Trotters and brains weren't my cup of tea either. I could never see anything to pick off a pig's bony hoof, and the brains, well, I told father I already had my share of brains.

I never did learn the truth of the Gorgonzola, which Mother said had come from a reputable grocery store, the Co-op. Though she swore the maggots on that piece of pungent cheese were good for whatever ailed you, I believed with all my heart they had no culinary right to be there. I secretly suspected Jimmy Finn at the grocer's had turned a blind eye on those maggots, the way he had ignored whatever was clinging to Mother's loaf of bread the day he dropped it in the sawdust on the floor behind the counter. It was a solid, unwrapped, unsliced loaf, so he simply picked it up and dusted it off with a few flicks of his fingers. I never did tell Mother, because I would have been forced to take it back since I'd been fool enough to bring it home in the first place.

I rather admired Jimmy Finn, having decided he must be a mathematical genius as he slid the groceries along the counter, adding up the cost of each tin and packet in his head, to a total that was always totally correct. He didn't use a reckoning machine, but Mother always made sure his sum total agreed with her own reckoning. And that was in the days of pounds, shillings, and pence, where two ha'pennies made up a penny, twelve of which made a shilling, and twenty shillings equaled one pound. So, he added and carried over four columns of figures in his head, all as quick as lightning.

His brain must have been as big as an abacus, I reasoned, remembering how taxing mental arithmetic could be at school, especially Mondays after a weekend of freedom. In class, I was often the first to receive a question from the teacher. On one day in particular, Miss Jarman said, "Miss Hope, your problem this morning is to take away one farthing from one pound and tell us how much money you have left." That was a tricky problem for me, because farthings had gone out of circulation before I was born, and I saw no need to remember anything at all about them. Miss Jarman reminded me there were four farthings in a penny and asked me to come up to the blackboard to work through the problem. Just as I stood up, my sister walked into the room with the student register book, and Miss Jarman told me to sit down and, of all things, asked Eva to show the class how she would take one farthing from one pound and come up with the correct answer. I sat, red-faced, secretly hoping Eva wouldn't tell Mother and hoping Miss Jarman would drop dead. Eva quickly came up with the answer, but I forgave her for being so sharp when she bravely stuck up for me, looking up at that tall, old lady in steel-rimmed glasses with her gray hair scraped into a knot at her nape like mother's hair usually was. After figuring the problem, Eva put her stick of chalk down on the ledge below the blackboard and very clearly, so all my classmates heard every word, she said, "Miss

Jarman, why didn't you let my sister figure out the problem for you? She would have given you the right answer."

And so our family grew, in our togetherness, to survive whatever adversity life dropped at our door. We got along very nicely, thank you, in spite of scarlet fever and quinsy of the throat. Eva nearly died during an influenza epidemic in the late 1920s and needed to stay over at Granny Knight's house, where she was fussed over and pampered. I remember wishing I had picked up that bug too, so I could have stayed there with her.

Every year during the two-week holiday that was called teachers' rest, Eddie Perrin could be found measuring four pairs of Hope family feet to match up with the same size of shoe in his shop on the Green, next to the Pavillion Theater on Lovely Lane. Mother would parade us through the village square and wait patiently, sitting on the edge of her chair in Eddie's shop, while he came up with the right kind of shoe to meet her approval, and I can describe that kind of shoe in one word: serviceable. Tough enough to last all year round, and if Our Ike's shoes didn't have a hole in them by shoe-shopping time, Our Little Dot's feet would be obliged to suffer through the rest of the shoes' life wearing them. The remaining three pairs of cast-offs Mother would send to the Ragged School for poor children who otherwise would go barefoot.

Eve and I considered Dot, the youngest, just a baby who usually got her own way over us all. On this particular holiday expedition, Dot was sitting in her chair grinning like the Cheshire cat when Eddie approached, and, after stretching his aching back, started to say, "What would you . . ." when mother quickly broke in, "She will need good walking shoes, Mr. Perrin. She's in school too, you know." And Eddie smiled at her use of "Mr. Perrin," knowing it was to lend some authority to his name for Dot's benefit. Otherwise Mother would have used his first name like old friends usually do, and Dot would have been cheeky enough to do likewise. Dot shot Mother a mulish glare and tossed her head to Mr. Perrin, saying in her most ladylike English, "I'll have that pair over there! In a size three, please!" She pointed to an expensive-looking pair of soft, leather dress shoes with pointed toes and fancy, fan-shaped strap ends where the buttonhole slid over the button underneath. Mr. Perrin turned to Mother in confusion, but before he could raise an eyebrow to ask her permission to get the shoes, she was already saying to Dot, "Money doesn't grow on trees you know, young lady. And you'll be the laughingstock of the school in those fancy things." With a daring I could hardly believe, Dot left herself wide open for a belt on the bottom when we got home (though I doubted she'd receive one, since I seemed to be the whipping boy in the family, taking punishment that was due for my sisters' offenses, along with what I'd earned through my own exasperating misbehavior). She responded to Mother in a belligerent voice, "I don't care! They're to suit the wearer, not the starer."

"You can't beat that reasoning, Emily," Eddie said, smiling and trying hard not to laugh. "If you want I could probably let you have them half off, since you bring in a lot of business for me." Mother's pride turned her face red as Christmas, taking this as a put-down by her old friend, and with lips clinched together in a straight, red line she turned to deal with Dot's truancy. "Oh, very well, just this once, Doris. We'll manage somehow, but don't you dare come crying home to your mam, young lady, when your pinched toes start to hurt and that fancy crocodile skin gets all scuffed up on the playground." Doris decided to wear them home, rather than allow Eddie to wrap them up for her, since she was afraid Mother might change her mind about handing Eddie more money than she'd bargained for.

We left Mother, cash in hand, to pay Eddie for all those shoes, and I was glad enough to keep my distance for a while. Though I knew that she would not likely chastise Our Little Dot for her impudence, I also knew that should I commit one sin or omission during the rest of the afternoon, my head or my face would be the likely targets for the back of Mother's hand, as she let out her pent-up frustration from sitting on the edge of the shoe shop chair while her bold youngest daughter charmed Eddie Perrin and got her way about the shoes she wanted.

We four girls strolled next door and stood outside the Pavillion Theater, looking at the pictures posted on the front of the building while waiting for Mother to finish chatting with Eddie. Our Eve and I were fascinated by anything to do with the theater and drama. Father made sure to take Our Eve and me to see a stage play or a musical as often as possible. As I grew older, an especially fine act on the vaudeville scene, a stand-up comedy routine by Murgatroid and Winterbottom, became one of my favorites. The repartee between those two young men was so quickly delivered, you hardly had time to digest one story before they were in the middle of the next. Father, always considerate and ever aware of the hearing handicap that became evident in my teen years, would always ask if I could hear well enough where we were sitting.

On that autumn shoe-shopping afternoon, Eve and I stared at the movie posters and talked about the coming pleasures of Boxing Day, the day after Christmas, when Mother would fork up the pennies for us to go to the pantomime. I especially loved *Cinderella,* and there was *Dick Whittington* and *Babes in the Wood.* Eve and I argued whether *Pearl of the Ocean Wave* was a pantomime or an operetta. I chose operetta because there was mostly singing in every scene.

I loved Boxing Day, a tradition that probably leans back as far as the 400s but became a more formalized affair in the days when servants of the aristocracy had to work on Christmas Day and their employers gave them gifts of money and goods to repay them for sacrificing their holiday. By 1871, it was officially set aside as a bank holiday in England, a day on which citizens would treat their neighborhood deliverymen (I never did see a British deliverywoman back then) with a "Christmas box" (Christmas present in America) for their past year's faithful service delivering the post, the milk, the newspaper—or ice, if you happened to own an ice box—even on holidays when everyone else was taking time off from work.

On Boxing Day, the deliverymen would make their rounds, ringing the bell and being greeted by the master or mistress of the house. Father would always put money in an envelope for each and every deliveryman he could think of, and then make it a point to answer the door himself and hand over the envelope along with a word of thanks. This gracious custom on the day after Christmas is becoming outmoded however, because that is now also the day the big after-Christmas sales are being held, and even if the postman rings twice, he often won't find anybody home.

In those days, Mother was sure to be at home, since she always wanted to make scones and clotted cream with strawberry jam on that day, which was also recognized as the Feast of Saint Stephen's. While Mother puttered in the kitchen, Father would walk his four girls to the tram, reminding Our Eve (the little mother) to watch out for us all as we headed for the theater. I would sit in the plush theater chair, my eyes glued to the red velvet curtains piped in thick gold braid, pulled together to meet across the front of the stage, while the stage hands put up the scenery behind it. I can still remember hearing the orchestra striking up the overture to Act I, and seeing the beautiful curtains slowly sweeping aside, revealing the set and the players whose opening lines would set my heart racing.

Later, when the theater had sunk in status to the level of a picture house, I observed the transition from silent movies to the miracle of sound, with Maurice Chevalier's melodious voice singing "Every Little Breeze Seems to Whisper Louise" giving me one of my earliest notions of romance at twelve years of age. I was spellbound watching *Gigi,* and *Love Me Tonight* with that wonderful cast of C. Aubrey Smith, Charlie Ruggles, Jeanette McDonald (but no Nelson Eddy), and the girl from Montana, Myrna Loy. I will never tire of humming "Walking My Baby Back Home" and listening to another of Chevalier's hits, "Thank Heaven for Little Girls."

When Mother's call ended our wistful viewing of movie posters, we "little girls" traipsed home from Eddie Perrin's shoe shop on that long-ago day, with Mother chiding Doris about her fancy shoes every time she glanced back and saw her limping along behind the rest of us. "I'll tell you what, Doris," she began, "if this keeps up, you'll be wearing a pair of your sister's old shoes, and we'll just send these fancy ones off to the Ragged School." She meant it too—if Dot had continued complaining, she would have set those alligator shoes alongside our cast-off old shoes and sent them away with Uncle Fred, her younger brother, who supervised a group of young children there. I remember the place vividly even now, since Uncle Fred liked to take me along with him to play with the boys and girls in the games that he planned for them. Father would persuade me to go, because it would be good for the children if they had someone like me with whom they could play. I don't think Mother wanted me to go with Uncle Fred, because she would invariably have a chore for me to do when he asked, or say she needed to send me on an errand. I was glad enough to have her make such excuses, for I hated going to the Ragged School. Everyone there had such sad, sad eyes.

There were lots of sad eyes in England during my growing-up years. The first two decades of my life were full of strikes. There were two police strikes, a national rail strike, two national coal strikes, a shipbuilders' strike, an engineering strike, and in 1926, a general strike in support of the Trade Union Congress. Many of those strikes resulted in violent demonstrations, and at one point, more than two million people in Britain were unemployed, with most of them remaining so until 1936.

During the two national coal strikes, it was hard to sing along with Maurice Chevalier and feel romantic when rooms were chilly for lack of fuel. Though we could boast of having a fireplace in every room of our home except the scullery, when there was no coal to fill the grates, Father's ingenuity served to improve our circumstances. He would gather us all around him on a cold winter's morning, reminding us that necessity was the mother of invention, and taking us down to the river's edge to rustle up any flotsam and jetsam that might burn well enough to keep us warm.

Mother's ingenuity took a different turn. Her solution to the fuel problem revolved around her younger brother, our Uncle Jack, who was very proud of his station in life even then, and who, in later years, would boast about engineering the Royal Scot, the fastest train on earth, from John O'Groats on the northern tip of Scotland to Lands End, where the white cliffs of Dover still guard the southern coast of England. The idea of a Chunnel being dredged under water, to facilitate a trip on wheels to the French coast at Calais, was then a mere whispered dream. When Uncle Jack would boast about the Royal Scot, Mother used to say, "Don't pay too much attention to your Uncle Jack now, he's something of a braggadocio," and I loved that word, even though I guessed it had the same meaning as braggart. I loved it because I loved my Uncle Jack and was all ears whenever he was telling a story. As I became older I learned there were quite a few fastest trains on earth beside the Royal Scot, though Uncle Jack's train did make the longest non-stop run—300 miles, between Crewe and Troutdale—and was capable of reaching a speed of 80 miles an hour.

Back when I was very young, during the coal strike years of the 1920s, he drove a pufferbilly coal-fired freight train on a small railway line that skirted the farm at the end of our street. Once in a while Mother, with her eye on the kitchen clock, would say, "Put on your coats now. Uncle Jack will be by any minute." And she would scoot us off pell-mell to pick up the sack of coal, a miracle lying as though it belonged there on the railway embankment. I never wanted anyone to see me dragging it home, so I persuaded my sisters that I would do most of the pulling if they agreed to go the alley way, so there wouldn't be all those nosey people to stop and gawk at us with that knowing look in their eyes.

The most startling thing about writing a memoir is the shocking discoveries that pop up out of nowhere as you're traveling through time, and a sack of coal trips you up in an alley, stopping you in your tracks to wonder if one of your shortcomings might have been a false sense of pride, given your thieving ways. But then, after all, didn't Mother make us do it? It wasn't really our fault. We were just children! And as we grew older, we four girls would talk through the dubious deed out of sympathy for one another's moral scruples, and we would come out smiling every time, certain that

God loved us too much to send us to Hell for such actions.

There was one happening in my young life, however, that would have horrified my sisters, my mother, my dear father, the rest of man and womankind, and God Himself, had I whispered its terrifying secret to any one of them. I would rather have died than tell. Instead, I shoveled it, with all its dirty appendages, into that cubicle of the mind called amnesia, and there it lay dormant—until it sprang to life again seventy years later, through a hole meant for a toad.

I was making toad-in-the-hole, an oven dish from an old recipe of fried sausages nestled in mounds of puffy popover dough that my mother used to make for us—if we were good. I was using the old recipe and daydreaming of times gone by, when I used to make this dish for my own children, remembering how they loved *Wind in the Willows* and the outrageous adventures of Mr. Toad of Toad Hall, their favorite character. I smiled, about to pop a tiny toad into its bed of dough, and I was up and away, rowing down the river with Ratty and Moley, wallowing in my reverie, when out of the blue, the kitchen started moving to another address, a strange, yet familiar, kitchen. Suddenly there I was, standing at a much older table, its scratched-up legs revealing a history of little children's restless feet. Whatever distress the tabletop had suffered throughout its apparently lengthy service was covered up by a snowy white Irish linen cloth, a little frayed at the seams. The clock had stopped ticking and my heart started beating its time. A tiny, fried sausage toad was clutched in a hand much smaller and younger than mine, and only I knew that the sausage would never reach its hole in Mother's toad-in-the-hole dish that sat in the center of that table, in the old cottage at No. 3 Gatewarth Street.

I had run home from school knowing that Mother had made toad that day for lunch, and I was impatiently waiting at the table for my sisters, who had lagged behind. Mother's eagle eye spotted a hole in the dough without a sausage snuggled inside and she hastily came to the conclusion that since I was the first one at the table, I was the one who had snitched it. I winced, hearing the words "disobedient," "greedy," "selfish," and all the "thou shalt nots" we were supposed to know by heart. She made me write all ten of those commandments ten times over that night, just to make sure I knew what the rest of them were, should I decide to break another of them.

Father had walked in on the toad tirade and had turned mother around to face him, speaking softly but with such authority on that day seventy years ago. "Em, you're going to knock the spirit out of that girl if you keep that up. Leave her alone!" And I wondered what I would look like without a spirit.

Even so, I was feeling anything but contrite and didn't want to go back to school. But Mother insisted I would feel better once I got there, her usual remonstrance and the standard remedy for anything from an earache to my ingrown toenails. If I get there, I muttered to myself, and for the first time in my life, I disobeyed my mother and set out on an adventure that led to my keeping a terrible secret to myself for almost the rest of my life.

As soon as I was out of earshot and eyesight, I ran for the farm at the end of our street, to the path leading around the fields to the woods, where my secret place was hidden behind the blackberry bushes. I outran a gaggle of giggling geese chattering, "Watch out! We're not as silly as they say we are, you know. We're going to get you!"

I had forgotten it was Wednesday, butchering day, and when I neared the farmhouse, there was Mrs. Smith, the farmer's wife, slaughtering one of the little pigs. My heart jumped at the strange, piercing squeal and the sight of blood spurting high in the air as she slit the throat of a piglet. I ran quickly on, past the stinking midden with its sodden, steaming fodder ready to be fed to the little pigs who didn't cry that day, and I held my nose and my tears all in the same moment.

I knew where the stile was by heart, and I eagerly pulled the brambles apart, treading carefully up the steps to the top and jumping down the other side of the hedge. Grass and chickweed covered the old, worn wagonwheel ruts in the path, where cow pads had dropped long, long ago. I had never before met another soul, man nor beast, there in my secret garden.

Under a canopy of hawthorn beauty, boughs bending lovingly to send corymbs of their tiny flowers showering confetti on my head and shoulders, I walked in beauty in veils of white, a bride walking down a cathedral aisle, with a posy of daisies clutched in my hand. I was drenched in a wild perfume called hawthorn, too precious to be stoppered in any bottle. I heard the cuckoo echoing around my world and wondered where she had laid her egg that year and who had done her mothering. Celandine and silverweed spread their sunshine through the shadows on the grass, and I spotted the speedwell too, blue as the sky showing now and again through my Sistine ceiling of hawthorn beauty. I would come again, soon, to pick the first wild roses growing along the ditch, mindless of the thorns, and I would ask myself again, who on earth would have given the stately bladder campion such a sorry name, and why. I would come again in winter and see the trees unfrocked, yet draped in a blanket of snow.

On this spring day my secret garden had never been so warm. So still. My world, my mother, had gone away, and I was safe.

I was sitting on the grass at the edge of the path, absorbed in picking off a daisy's petals one by one—he loves me, he loves me not—and I neither saw nor heard them as they sneaked up on me, three of them. They were belting each other with long, limber hawthorn branches, which they had stripped of their beautiful blossoms and were thrashing around in a don't-give-a-damn manner. I stood up to let them pass by, wondering how on earth they had found the stile. One of them was poking my arm with his stick.

"Let's play," he said, and I was too afraid to say anything before they were pushing me, lobbing me from one to another, sending me reeling and tottering until I fell over the edge of the bank and went rolling down to the ditch. They followed, laughing and yelling, and I was afraid they were laughing at my navy blue bloomers, which must have been showing under my gymslip.

One of them was shouting down, "Sit on 'er, Reg. 'Old 'er down!"

And Reggie did, spread-eagled over my chest and looking down at my face, an ugly look in his eyes. As rough hands grabbed my wrists and ankles, I thought they were going to throw me in the stream. I was afraid I would drown or die of fright and go straight to Hell, praying it might be a better place than this, because I knew they were not done with their playing yet. I heard someone screaming for her mother and hoped mine would never find me there. She would say it was all my fault and that I was old enough to know better than to go around with scruff like them. She had already called me a thief that day.

I kicked and struggled, trying to keep my bloomers and my gymslip where they belonged, but my head was suddenly jerked around to one side as if it might break off, and I felt something warm and gristly, something that might have been the tough, bristled stalk of the comfrey growing along the ditch. I know now what it must have been, that thing poking in my ear, but then it was just something that hurt and burst inside, seeping blood down my neck and into the back of my white school blouse collar. I drifted in and out of the dark, feeling as if I were clenched in the jaws of a grizzly bear intent on pounding my head into the ground until I gave up the Ghost. By the time I stumbled to my feet, hurting and hysterical, those ruffians were racing down the path, calling me names, trampling my daisies, thrashing the hawthorn blossoms with their sticks, and heading for a stile that wasn't hidden anymore.

I wanted desperately for an angel, or just anybody but them, to come along to hold me and stroke my hair, to tell me it would be all right come morning. But no one came. The inside of my head was throbbing with each deafening pain, which came with the sound and fury of waves rising and thundering to their death as they smashed against a rocky coast. I didn't want to put a dirty finger in my ear, but I did dare to pat the lobe of it with a wet comfrey leaf and found, to my relief, that it wasn't blood at all that dribbled from my ear, so at least I wouldn't have to explain blood-stained clothing to Mother.

I knew a lot about the flowers I gathered, and when my mind sobered up again, I told myself that the sticky stuff I was wiping off my neck must have been sap from the comfrey stalk. I kept on wiping my arms, my legs, but when I reached down to my knees a sickly feeling went shivering through me. My bloomers . . . they weren't there! What would Mother do if she found them missing! I labored up the hill, stifling my sobs, but cried out in relief as I reached the top. Those boys had taken off with my bloomers, and there they were, hanging on a branch on the far side of the lane. I sat on the turnstile at the railway crossing for a while, watching for the school children to come home, so that I could run home ahead of my sisters and hide somewhere.

The next day Mother looked out to see Reggie in our backyard, his hands in a stranglehold around my neck. She was outside the gate before he knew what hit him, the stiff-bristled broom flaying the air and landing with a whack across his bottom. All the while, she screamed at me, "What on earth did you do to make him choke you like that? He almost did you in!" She asked me that question over and over, and when she stopped asking, I must have stopped remembering.

I never went back to my hawthorn lane, as far as I can remember, and I wonder now how such a thing could ever have happened in that beautiful garden, where the secret has stayed hidden for more than seventy years. I wish with all my heart I'd had courage and good sense enough to run home to Mother. Whatever she could have said or done would, in retrospect, have served me better than trying to deal with the oppressive feelings of guilt that play the devil with me, now that revelation and remembrance have come in my old age. I realize now that if what had happened in the wooded lane— that dark secret forgotten long ago, perhaps repressed by fear—had been disclosed to someone older and wiser, rather than left to fester in the silence of amnesia, I might have understood then, as I do now, that I wasn't to blame for that repulsive, ignorant, and insensitive act. My only fault lay in being too naïve and innocent to know that a girl alone in a secluded place is easy prey for boys with dirty hands and even dirtier thoughts.

 ˙ And now, here they all stand, naked before me, begging forgiveness in their old age. But it's impossible to forgive without forgetting, isn't it? I did not ask for second helpings of this no-good, indigestible day in my child-hood, so I might just as well chuck it in the stinking midden and let it go. The pigs will know what to do with it! And once again I will only remember being safe, there in the past. Yet there is no way to rebury that part of my life, and I am forced to acknowledge the incident and its impact upon my life during all those years in between, the forgetting years when I kept that dark secret bottled up tight, until it fermented and finally blew its cork.

 What role has that buried incident played in the sequence of my life's unfolding? What happened to my psyche in those moments frozen in fear? Did my mind, my mentality, my soul, become all twisted up in a psyche knot pinned up with my mother's black hair? Will all this introspection now reveal that I am back there still, a child at eighty-five?

I, the undersigned, Do hereby certify that the Birth

Irene Hope

4th May One thousand nine hundred and twenty

WARRINGTON. *WARRINGTON.*

I was a gift for my father, born on his birthday, May 4, 1920.

After I was in "The Land of the Free" in 1945.

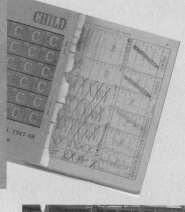

MINISTRY OF FOOD

RATION BOOK
(CHILD) 1947–1948

Surname HEDRICK

Initials I. R.

CHILD

Ration books — during the war years, more precious than gold.

Father played the part and loved it.

My grandmother, source of wit and wisdom, Mary Elizabeth Hope.

The employees of Unilever in an operetta.

Another show — "overtime" for Joseph Crosfield & Sons.

A charabanc trip — (left to right) Grandfather, Grandmother in foxes and plumed hat, Irene.

Chapter 2

A rich child often sits in a poor mother's lap.
—DANISH PROVERB

Aside from that one long-buried incident, I was happy enough as a child in Sankey Bridges, where we lived amid the cotton mills, the two wire companies, Rylands and White Cross, the White Cross Lead Paint company, a tannery, and the Unilever soap factory, then Joseph Crossfield & Sons, Ltd., and now the worldwide Unilever giant.

When my father was younger, the staff at his orphanage had placed him in an apprenticeship to learn the roll-turner trade for two years, after which he was employed as a roll-turner at the Whitecross Wire Works—a job in which some close measurements and other elements are gauged as the coils of wire go around and around the roller.

Sankey Bridges was within range of the smokestacks of a few industrial plants, but we could get away for a breath of fresh air once in a while in the surrounds. The River Mersey was accessible to us by virtue of the railway crossing at the bottom of our street, and the river was also a nice walk along the Sankey Canal a few blocks away from us down Liverpool Road. This stretch of water was the route for small barges carrying cargo to the huge ocean-going vessels sailing the Manchester Ship Canal from Manchester to the port of Liverpool. Watching one of those vessels sail majestically through our town from a few blocks away always puzzled me because I couldn't see the water for myself.

Yacht racing day came only once a year, but you were certain to see the Hope family there at the Ferry in full regalia. Father in his band uniform, Mother in her high-necked, white lace bodice and long black skirt—regal as any one of the ladies with their parasols who were there to cheer on their yacht-owner husbands—with a pretty pout and a well-rehearsed shout. We four girls in our pinafores, panama hats, and serviceable shoes were princesses as we mingled with them in the lobby of the Ferry pub.

Father would stop in for a pint there on other occasions too at the building along the river, and the four of us would take turns standing on a small platform where there stood a huge captain's wheel. "All brass and polished oak." That's how they used to make 'em, Father would tell us on every visit there. We would take turns as captain, sailing our very own ship.

On this stretch of the Mersey, the river may have once been used to ferry people and goods from one bank to the other side of the water, but all that remained of the tiny landing place in the 1920s was the public house called "The Ferry."

Yacht Racing Day at The Ferry was very special to me because Father and his band were always there to take part in the ceremonies. Mother would remind me to be polite and not grab a seat in the row of deck chairs sitting along the riverbank, but I didn't care about chairs. All I wanted to do was sit in the grass where the daisies grew on the edge of the bank and wait, watching a fish flipping up a fin now and then, listening to the birds squawking above me, just soaking up the sun until I could see white sails stretching around the bend, and the leader of the yacht pack proudly waving his hand in a winning gesture.

When all the sailing vessels had been secured, the Yacht Club Cup presented to the winner, the participants congratulated for their efforts, and everyone involved honored by the mere mention of his name, I could at last sit and listen to my father's prize-winning band, the high point of the day, always, for me. There was no music in the world that could compare. The yacht race, the ceremony, the cakes and tea and entertainment over, no one moved until the notes from Father's tenor horn sounded the end of a beautiful day, with everybody standing, hand over heart, singing along with the tenor horn,

God save our gracious King,
Long live our Noble King.
God save the King!
Land that is glorious,
Send him victorious
Long to reign over us
God save the King!

I don't believe anyone raised in England, man or woman, could ever forget those words, because they were sung in respect for our country and the monarchy on every blessed opportunity, public or private. Whether some sang merely to air their talents in public or from a burning desire to be patriotic, I always thought it was the law that I had to stand and pay homage to the King. Even at the picture house, as the lights went on at the end of a show, the Odeon organ would bring the audience to its feet while this tribute to the King was being played. I was afraid to leave the theater before that final note was sounded, lest a bobby be waiting outside to take me straight to jail.

Closer to home there was always the stinking brook and its effluent from the White Cross Lead Paint company to contend with. For the most part, we were unaware of the long- and short-term consequences of the air we breathed daily, but I remember Mother's words to her four daughters concerning the dangers from such chemicals as lead. "Now then," she would warn us, "when you have to go by White Cross make sure you have a hanky in your pocket so you can cover your mouth and nose. And don't take one breath until you're past the whole building." I never needed to be reminded—it was worse than the stinking midden down at the farm.

I would even dare to cross the dangerous Liverpool Road and walk on the other side just to avoid the overpowering smell. Could it be that Our Little Dot failed to run fast enough past the place? She died at such a young age from cancer, and I suppose the mortality statistics from the region might suggest lead pollution as a possible cause of her illness. Although most of the worst polluting industries are no longer operating in that area, a recent Internet check of employment opportunities near Sankey Bridges revealed that industry still offers the most jobs there. Now, however, most of the positions are for environmental solution specialists and healthcare lead solution specialists, those who deal with the lingering effects of the industrial enterprises upon which the economy of our town was built.

Despite the air pollution problems of Sankey Bridges, I would say the environment of our cottage on Gatewarth Street on the outskirts of town was healthy in ways that offset the pollutants of our neighborhood industries. Never a day went by but my father would say, "Are you happy, Love?" And just his asking made me so.

Had I complained that there was nothing to do, like children nowadays do, even before the price tag has been soaked off another new toy, Mother would have shoved a block of pumice stone in my hand and said, " 'Ere y'are then. You can get a bucket of water and go scrub the front step. That'll give you something to do!" I hated the harsh grinding sound the pumice made on the cement step, so I didn't complaint of boredom very often.

We all respected Mother as the real disciplinarian of our household, and we certainly had a healthy regard for those eyes in the back of her head, which were always seeing whatever mischief we might be up to and discouraging us before we could yield to temptation. But let me tell you what I never told the rest of the family: What I respected most was Mother's third eye—the one that nobody else could see or thought existed. I am able to offer memories of this third eye to you only because those memories came flooding back when I came across a faded old photograph of Mother just today.

Judging by the tailored suit, the collared white blouse, her hair waved back from her face in a bob and showing just enough of the white earring to give her an aristocratic aura, she must have been in her early sixties. In spite of the cracks across the one-by-two passport image, it's obvious that her face was still in good shape at that age, with no telltale lines from time and hard work. Her beautiful brown eyes were serenely, yet purposefully, fixed on the world with the same determination of spirit she had when trying to bring me up a lady.

Looking at her clear gaze in that photograph made me more certain than ever that there was an extra-special eye she kept hidden deep within, an eye that cast a protective spell over her children, an eye that seemed always capable of viewing what seemed catastrophic and tragic to others with the thought of how she might change things no one else believed could be changed. The first inkling of the power of this third eye came to me early one cold wintry morning as I stood by the fireguard—the wire and brass contraption that kept us from getting too close to the hot coals and the sparks they sometimes spit out. I was hanging on tightly to the guard that morning, not because I was afraid of catching fire, but because every time I opened my eyes, there was nothing there. "Mam!" I was screaming at the top of my voice. "I can't see! There's nothing there. Everything's gone black."

She was there in a flash, gently prying my fingers from the fireguard and moving me backwards till I felt the edge of the rocking chair as she sat me down in it. "Now then. You just sit there and don't worry. Don't move and I'll make you a nice 'ot cuppa tay and a spot o' Granny Knight's ginger wine. You'll be right as rain by the time you start for school, you'll see." And I believed her. Maybe she had read the tea leaves in my cup again, and maybe she was asking God if he would care to help, and he had given her a quicker answer than he ever seemed to give me when I asked for anything. But I believed with all my heart that everything was going to be all right. In the few minutes it took to drink my cuppa, Mother had managed to bring my eyesight back where it belonged. A teaspoonful of ginger wine down my throat to stave off the cold wind, and I was on my way to feeling better when I got to school.

Father had given this family eye of Emily's the name "Faith" ever since Our Little Dot was run over. She was only six years old but had already been crossing the highway safely with the rest of us on her way to school for several months when the accident happened. Mother's timeless caution to the four of us had always been, "Stay together now, and don't be late," but this time Doris had lagged behind without our noticing, and we were way ahead of her on that fateful day when she was left standing on the sidewalk, afraid to cross the road without our help.

A lorry carrying a heavy load suddenly swung around the bend where she was standing on the sidewalk, and sideswiped Our Dot, leaving her unconscious. The first Mother heard of this was from an onlooker, who had run the several blocks to our house and screamed from the front door, "Emily, your little Dot! She's been run over by a lorry. She's lying there, just lying there not moving, Emily. Flat as a pancake!"

We three older girls slept in Mother's big bed that night—the only time I can ever remember our being left alone—while our parents were at the hospital, watching over Our Little Dot, who was still unconscious. Mother stayed there day and night, while Father went back to work and Auntie Lil—wife of Mother's oldest brother—came over to take care of us. We were allowed to see Doris, even though she stayed in that condition for six long weeks. I would hear Mother, as she smoothed Our Dot's hair away from her forehead, saying, "It's going to be all right now, Love. It's going to be all right. I'll see to that!" Mother could just plain see it with that wonderful third eye that Father called faith, and when Dot finally opened her eyes, she turned to mother and said, "You're still here?" Mother simply said,

"Yes, I'm still here, Love, and I'll be here all night, but I have to go home in the morning and do the washing." And just that quickly she turned her energies to the more ordinary tasks that lay at hand.

When mother would hang out the washing to dry in the top garden, she would allow us to sit on the top rung of the turnstile that bordered the railway crossing, so that we could watch the trains go by. And as I sit here today, an old woman computing my life, I am remembering the lines from Robert Louis Stevenson's poem, "From a Railway Carriage." I would sing the rhyme along with the music coming from the wheels as the train ran the rails:

> *Faster than fairies, faster than witches,*
> *Bridges and houses, hedges and ditches,*
> *And charging along like troops in a battle*
> *All through the meadow the horses and cattle:*
> . . . .
> *Here is a cart run away in the road*
> *Lumping along with man and load;*
> *And here is a mill, and there is a river:*
> *Each a glimpse and gone forever!*

No, Mr. Stevenson—not gone forever. Your words will bring them all back to me forever. Such were the joys I found in my life. The pufferbilly was real, and you took me along for the ride while I sat on the stile. I'm off again now, as far as I can see, and the year has reached 2003!

Even though we had Mother's permission to sit on that stile so close to the tracks, the fence on the other side was forbidden territory, since its whole purpose for being there, according to Mother, was to protect little children from falling into the stinking brook. And we'd have no one to blame but ourselves if we sat on the top railing of that fence and fell into the water rushing all that muck to who knows where. But Mother was right there with her stoicism—and that amazing third eye—saving Our Eve when she fell off that fence, in spite of the warnings she'd had about the poisonous effluent the water carried from the White Lead Paint Company nearby.

Well, somebody actually pushed our poor Eve so that she fell, headfirst into the stinking brook, sinking under the water as it carried her along, surging toward the tunnel that was ready to swallow her up. I was bigger and stronger than Our Eve, though two years younger, and it's likely I could have held my own against the rushing water. But not poor Eve, for the current had taken her along far too fast for the rest of us to run down the hill to the mouth of the tunnel. As Eve came closer and closer to being swallowed up forever, we were all pointing and screaming at three lads who were playing along the water's edge, near the entrance of the tunnel. Suddenly they were thrashing through the filthy water, bending down with hands outstretched, ready to grab any part or parcel of her and drag her away from the gaping mouth of the tunnel. As I held my breath, praying that she hadn't already drowned, the boys managed to catch her skirt and snatch her from the water.

Somehow they dragged her up the steep bank and squeezed her between the end of the fence and the stone wall of the tunnel. I could see her hands at her throat as if she were choking, and ran over to help the boys. Two of them made a seat by grasping each other's wrist with one hand and holding their own wrist with the other hand, and some of the other kids lifted her onto the makeshift seat. I took one look at Eve and raced home, fortunately as close as the end of the street, shrieking, "Mam, Dad! Come on quick. Our poor Eve nearly drowned and she looks like a big, black dog."

"Oh God! I told them to stay away from that bloody stinking brook," Mother was saying as she flew past Father like the wind, and reached the garden gate to see Eva slumped between the two boys. "She's not breathing!" she declared, and ordered the boys to get her inside and lift her up onto the kitchen table. There was nothing at hand that resembled a lifesaving object, so Mother did what she always did. She made do with what she had, and stuck her little finger into Eva's mouth to crook out whatever she felt didn't belong there. Then, tilting back her head slightly, she opened Eva's mouth and gently pushed two more fingers inside, far enough to the throat to make Eva gag and throw up whatever else was lodged further down.

Finally, Mother heaved a sigh, "She's breathing again. You'll be all right now, Love. Don't you fret. You'll be fit as a fiddle come mornin'! Just you wait and see!" And she set about making it so. " 'arold, go stoke up the fire. Joyce, we'll need that kettle of hot water on the hob, and make me a cuppa tay while you're at it. Irene, go and tell those nosey parkers at the door to go home and mind their own business. Then come back and help me with this mess and get your sister into bed."

The boys, whose names we never knew, had long since gone, though they will remain heroes in our minds forever. The neighbors at the door were all whispering, "She could die, you know, with all those chemicals and muck inside her little stomach." But Mother soon took care of that too, with a heaping teaspoonful of cod liver oil.

Joyce, Our Ike, was the only one in the family who didn't benefit from Mother's third eye. She never seemed to need it, and Mother would tell us Joyce was so lucky that if she fell off the roof of the Grand Clothing Hall, she'd be fortunate enough to fall into a suit of clothes. The rest of us accepted that statement as truth, because whenever Joyce's friend Dora got a present, Dora's mother would gift Joyce with an exact duplicate, as though they were twins or at least sisters in the same family. I remember Joyce receiving a beautiful bicycle on Dora's birthday, and when it was time for Dora to learn what time it was, Joyce received a brand new watch, too.

While I sometimes envied the presents Joyce received, I didn't mind those two particular gifts at all—not because I felt gracious toward my sister but because I simply never wanted to know what time it was anyway, and I couldn't ever manage to stay up on a bike because I had what they called a vestibular imbalance in the right ear.

I found my balance by exploring the worlds open to me in the books

I read from my earliest days. We didn't learn a lot about life from experience when we were young, since my father sheltered us, saying he'd rather we learned from good books than from running the streets.

I never had very many books of my own, but there were school and library books at hand, all filled with wonderful heroes and heroines who would help develop my own personal character. I read Charlotte Bronte's *Jane Eyre* and took on her enduring patience. I read Jane Austen's *Pride and Prejudice* and talked to father about the good and the evil in both of those traits, wondering, in time, whether the two words had interchangeable meanings. I devoured Louisa May Alcott's *Little Women,* measuring the experiences of those four sisters against our own. And I was so moved by seeing the first motion picture of *Little Women* that when the tiny bird flew up from the windowsill as poor Beth lay dying, I cried all the way home from the pictures and couldn't stop the flow of tears, even for tea.

Back in those days of my youth, I built a lot of castles in the air in which to house my impossible dreams. Whenever our mother thought our dreams were out of all proportion to our means, she would invariably simmer down our enthusiasm with her proverbial wisdom and tell us, "You're looking at the world through rose-colored spectacles. Settle down and see life as it really is if you don't want to come crying home to Mother."

I would feel guilty every time Mother mentioned the word spectacles—rose-colored or plain—but nothing could ever induce me to confess how I lost the thick, steel-rimmed glasses I had worn for over a year. I must have been about six or seven when a school nurse decided I should be wearing glasses. There was nothing rose-colored about them. They were hideous, or at least I thought they were. They became even more unsightly to me when Our Eve lost her own spectacles one night when she'd sneaked them up to bed to read by the gaslight, and upon wakening the next morning, they were nowhere to be found. Mother searched the house with a fine-tooth comb, but when they didn't materialize she scraped up enough to buy Eve a fancy horn-rimmed pair. Eve managed to read without glasses until her new ones materialized, giving me the bright idea that I, too, should be able to read without the aid of spectacles.

I was too young to actually think of any underhanded scheme for getting rid of the hated glasses, but when the opportunity presented itself, I didn't fight the impulse. One day when the backyard gate was locked, I dared to climb up and over the top and jump down on the other side. As I did so, my spectacles fell off my nose, onto the cobblestones leading to the back door. I don't recall actually seeing the glasses lying there on the cobblestones—both lenses shattered and the wire earpieces twisted out of shape—but even without the benefit of the broken spectacles, I definitely did see Mother. She was lying on the ground, not moving. I left the glasses where they were and dashed over the patch of grass to where she lay.

From the looks of the chamois cloth and the bucket of water spilled on the ground besides the broken stepladder, she must have decided to wash the windows since it was a nice day. I almost fell on her, I was so anxious to get down on my knees to wake her up. I kept trying to open her eyes and kept stroking my hand across her face, until she finally looked at me with a puzzled frown, saying, "What happened?"

I pulled the ladder along the wall, close enough to Mother so I could help her turn around and grab hold of a lower rung for support to hoist herself up from the ground. It was a very difficult thing for her to do since she had such a large stomach then, and I wasn't too much help in the process, but she finally limped into the house, me limping along with her, and she kept a good eye on me while I made us a pot of tea without making a mess. Thus everything turned out all right, except for the glasses, and I was very proud when Father came home and told me I had probably saved Mother's life. Later on, when Our Little Dot was born, he told me I had saved her life as well, since Mother had been expecting her at the time of her fall.

It was two years after I'd broken my own glasses before Eva's old pair was found. They had slipped between the skirting board and the wall by her bedside, and Father had found them when he was fixing the boards. By that time my old glasses had also been replaced—much to my dismay, for there would be no horn-rimmed spectacles for me. I was always the po-faced, ugly duckling of the family, plain as a pike-staff and twice as ugly because of those steel-rimmed spectacles that weren't thick enough to hide the resentment I felt for having to wear them.

Family photos show bobbed black hair, my mother Emily's hair, parted down the middle with a donkey-fringe cut high up to my hairline to keep it out of my eyes. Father would say, after a couple of pints at Granny Knight's piano, his long fingers finding the right keys by ear, the whole family enraptured by his voice rising and holding those grand notes, he would say, with a critical look at me, "Looks like you cut her hair with a bloody basin, Em." And I would glance over at our lovely Eve—who had so many privileges because she was the oldest and stayed at grandmother's home and received the bounty of her generous spirit much more often than the rest of us—and wish I wasn't such a tomboy.

Grandfather Knight, was a seagoing man who had sailed all the way around the world twice. Gran had put the lovely mementos he'd brought back from strange, foreign countries on display in a glass case in the center of the living room. Everyone seemed always to be on tenterhooks that I would drop one of those treasures some day, and I told myself that was why Granny liked Our Eve best. And then, just when I was feeling sorry for myself, I would pick up the sepia photo of me in the silver frame grandmother had on her sideboard, and see reflected in the glass my hair shining out from the center part in a halo that glowed with the same blue lights that were in my mother's hair. It was the one redeeming feature I could see in myself. The rest of me was an ugly duckling, longing, yearning, to become a swan.

In my longing I would turn to another kind of beauty, the kind I would find when I picked up *Anne of Green Gables*. Within those pages dwelt my *anam cara,* the soul friend after whom I was determined to fashion my own life. She was a companion and a role model of which my father heartily approved, as were the four girls in Louisa May Alcott's classic. When he would sing his favorite song, "My Little Gray Home in the West," Father would look around the circle of his own "little women," and we knew we were loved with the same kind of passion and openness with which he embraced all of humanity. He said to me one day, "Trust everybody till you find them out, Love," and I don't believe he ever did find anybody out.

When the weather was nice, Mother trusted me to go posy-picking by myself. The excitement of roaming the fields and woods, and maybe finding a wild rose bush along a hedge, or water crowfoot growing in the pond near the trees where the wood anemones were hiding, meant more to me than Mother's mince tarts. It was the purple loosestrife, elusive as the Scarlet Pimpernel, which was never pressed into my wildflower books, no matter how hard I searched. I finally gave up my obsession to find it when I learned that it grew in boggy parts of England far away from my own countryside. Friends now tell me that beautiful flower of my childhood spreads a carpet of royal purple across the fields of Vermont and New Hampshire, where it is classified as an invasive weed.

Before I was twelve I had collected 250 wildflowers, all scientifically identified, labeled, and pressed into three large drawing books. When I let my sister Eve take them to her secondary school to show her class, she hadn't the heart to say they weren't her own work, and she won the Greening Roberts prize for the most scholarly presentation. She was awarded two volumes of *Wayside and Woodland Blossoms* by Edward Step. When Mother heard the story of Our Eve's waywardness, it took her just two seconds to set things straight. She said, "Now, Eva, you just hand those books over to your sister, right now! You know and I know very well that she is the one who earned them—along with the honor that goes with the prize." And, reluctantly, Eva gave up the books. They are seventy-two years old now, and I'm hoping one of my grand- or great-grandchildren will want to have them one day.

Actually it's a wonder Mother didn't make Eva return them to the judging committee and confess her deception, as she'd made Eva do on her first day in kindergarten, when she'd picked up a stray penny on the desk in front of her, brought it home, and asked Mother if she could spend it on candy! Mother took her right back to school to stand in front of the class and tell them what she had done. That must have been a humiliating experience for a little girl, especially our sister. I remember, years later, as we were reliving childhood experiences, including that particular one, Eva soberly warning me, "Don't ever steal, or lie, or cheat, Our I." That day must have left a deep impression upon her mind as she returned the penny to its true owner.

As a gifted student, Eva was chosen from her elementary school class, along with girls from other schools, to sit for an examination. If she excelled over the other entrants, she would be entitled to a free scholarship to enter the four-year academy of higher learning situated in our city. Eva matriculated into this four-year academy, to the delight of Father, Mother, and my sisters. Mother gave a whoop of joy when she learned that uniforms and athletic equipment, such as hockey sticks and tennis racquets, were included in the scholarship money. My excitement stemmed from Father's encouraging words: "I wish we could afford to send Our I along too. She's bright enough to learn Latin and French along with Our Eve, but," he added, putting his arm around my shoulder, "maybe you'll be chosen to sit for next year's scholarship, Love." I held back the tears, and set my hopes on that.

Finally, it was graduation week at Evelyn Street Girls' School, and many of my classmates were glad enough to be done with their schooling and excited about going out into the world to find the perfect job, or the perfect young man or woman with whom to begin a fairy-tale union. My own excitement came from thinking that now that I had completed the lower grades with honors, I would, at last, be able to follow in Eve's footsteps and begin my upper-level studies.

Clearly, there was no doubt of my being ready for the next learning adventure. A day or so before graduation, Miss Norman, our headmistress, called me into her office and handed me a small book, saying, "Congratulations, Miss Hope, you have won the class prize for scholarship, and I present you with this book of Shakespeare's tales for young readers, as told by Charles and Mary Lamb." Then she handed me an award label, adding, "You may put this on the front page." I took the label and, while thanking Miss Norman, licked it and put it on the page, not realizing that in my excitement I had pasted the precious label upside down and on the last page rather than the first. Miss Norman merely smiled and said, "I know you will keep on writing and I'm hoping that one day you will write your own book."

I thanked her again and turned to leave. "Wait," she said. "There's one thing more I have to say to you. Perhaps you aren't aware of this, but school laws say that elementary students must stay in school until they are fourteen. Since you are only twelve, you must remain in Form for two more years until you come of age."

I was thunderstruck. Two more years in the same grade just because I was too young to graduate? Why then had I been pushed into school as a four-year-old and encouraged to skip a whole grade, if only to repeat all that I had learned so conscientiously? I held back the tears as I left her office and headed down the hall, Charles and Mary Lamb clutched tight in my hand. Yes, I would write my own book one day, and I would write about the shock and disappointment of what should have been one of the happiest days of my life.

Two years later, once again graduating at the top of my class, I was allowed to sit for the examination that would qualify me for a scholarship similar to Eva's. I sailed through the exam with flying colors and the highest marks, and waited eagerly to wear my school badge and learn to play hockey. But it wasn't to be! The chairman of the Board of Education told Mother, he was sorry, but when they allowed me to sit for the exam, they weren't aware that a scholarship had previously been awarded to a member of the

Hope family. So although I had qualified to attend that school, my parents would be expected to foot the bill.

Mother's immediate response was her final one: Impossible! I would have to content myself with whatever schooling I could find for myself after the final year of my elementary education, which was to be at the new Bewsey Street School. Gone were my dreams of playing advanced sports like hockey and tennis, creating science projects, and the various other higher education offerings that Eva's school offered. And gone, too, were any hopes of studying Latin and French. But, as my mother had taught me, I simply got on with what life offered, believing in her promise that things would be better when I got to school.

In addition to these disappointments, I went through the typical insecurities of coming of age in an era when no one talked about confused feelings for the opposite sex. Thus, though I remember a certain time when the comforting arms of love were begging for acceptance in a body going on thirteen years, Cupid's darts would fall far short of any sexual exploration. In later years I was called a cold fish by more than one persistently amorous young man, and I wondered what a hot fish might have done in my place. Kissing was daring enough, and I was certain that was all *Anne of Green Gables* would have done, had she found herself in the same predicament. Going all the way, at least as cousin Dorothy tried to explain it to me one night, seemed like an impossible feat and an act far different from all my romantic dreaming had led me to expect. I tried to imagine exactly what that act might be like when I went to bed on the night after her explanation, and ended up scaring myself into a fever and a frightful nightmare in which I was being mauled by a bear.

Coming of age posed still other problems for me. In those days I didn't wear a brassiere, and for a long time I was too embarrassed to mention to Mother that I needed one. She would have asked me why, and I would have had to tell her that some of the boys from the upstairs classes had giggled and pointed at me. I started to walk with my shoulders hunched forward to squeeze back those noticeable protrusions, until one day Mother caught me slouching and straightened my shoulders where they belonged, with warnings about the need for proper posture. As I stood straight and tall before her, she got the picture. "My, you're blossoming out!" she said. "You should be wearing a brassiere, couldn't you see that? Didn't you know that?" And then, "We can't afford brassieres," she mumbled to herself. "But let's see what we can find." And she rummaged around in the big chest of drawers, finally pulling out a long piece of flannel material and telling me to find a couple of large safety pins from her sewing box under the bed.

"Now turn around and get out of your blouse," she went on, slipping the two pins between her teeth as I slid out of the too-tight blouse. I caught the cloth as it was tossed over my head, mother holding on to the two ends behind me as I pulled the makeshift garment down and under where it might fit. It looked nothing at all like a bra should look, even after it was pinned tightly together at the back. I was afraid to turn around and see myself in the big mirror. I must have looked like a squeezed up roll of toilet tissue. I started to cry, knowing, but not daring to say, that Our Eve was wearing a bra, and Mother said, "Now what are you sniveling at? You'll feel better once you get to school."

A man might never understand something so personal as a young girl's first bra, but I know without doubt that every young girl in the world would have cried just as loudly as I did that day—except, perhaps, those living on the pages of *National Geographic,* who were too innocent to know there was an unwritten law that said the rest of the world's young women must cover up their budding breasts so boys wouldn't stare and giggle at them.

I loathed the sight and the feel of that flannel thing with the big safety pins, and I would throw it in a corner of the room every night when I undressed for bed. Still, it was there, always there, taunting me. And it was hovering over me in the nightmare that came after Cousin Dorothy spilled the beans on going all the way. In the nightmare I wasn't actually wearing the thing. I wasn't wearing anything, but had become tangled up with that same grizzly bear, his cold, silky nose sniffing at my hair, my ear, my bare breasts; his long, sharp claws gripping my shoulders.

I don't recall ever having to shower after school sports activities, so there was no need to undress in front of other girls, and I could hug my secret shame close to my chest. However, I did take part in plays that required changing costumes now and then. I practiced some slick cover-up maneuvers and became adept at removing the garment I was wearing after first figuring out how to slip into its replacement. Actually, since my class-mates were all older than I, they didn't pay a lot of attention to what I did or said, and I was not inclined to confide in any one of them, except for one close friend whom I loved dearly: Clarice. Mother wondered why Clarice had no other friends until I told her that she had just moved into Bewsey Street School from a school in another city. Mother made one of her few compliments: "Well, she's a lady, then." I thought so too, and we worked on school projects together and didn't have the urge to join in the other girls' conversations where the never-ending subject was boys. Had Clarice ever observed anything unseemly about my appearance, she would have politely turned her head and pretended not to notice.

Though I looked with longing at every brassiere ad that I saw, I still had to wear the thing till the day I left school and found a job. A bra was the first thing I bought from the allotment I was allowed to spend from my wages. I was free from bondage at last, but I carried the memory of that humiliating garment all the way to America and right up through the era of the Maidenform bra. Maidenform became a popular brand of brassiere in my early married days, when some clever ad-men dreamed up a snappy slo-gan using the theme "I dreamed I was at the Ritz (or some other posh place) in my MAIDENFORM BRA," and showing a picture of an eye-catching, well-rounded young woman, her upper torso clad only in her Maidenform and a happy, self-satisfied smile. I hated her, remembering my unhappy days wearing the thing.

Seeing that advertisement so many years after the humiliation of the thing triggered another bad dream, in which I am on the school playground, ready to return to class and standing in line with the rest of the girl students at Bewsey Street. The headmistress is monitoring us, waiting for the toll of the bell to march us back to our classrooms in orderly fashion. Suddenly I hear Miss Norman's voice, not low and gentle as it always had been with me, but loud and shrill, practically shrieking the words, "Miss Hope! What on earth is the matter with you? You can't come to school looking like that. Go inside right this minute. Go to my room and I will be there to deal with this."

I swing my head around and hear the laughter getting louder and louder. The other girls are giggling, some of them looking horrified and holding their hands over their mouths. They are pointing at my bare chest, at my new, perfectly rounded beautiful BREASTS.

I dreamed I was back in the schoolyard—with no Maidenform bra!

At this stage in my life, I look back and seem to have been overly obsessed by that make-do thing, which Mother made me wear while I secretly longed for a real, shapely garment like the other girls wore. And it's no wonder! I'm sitting here at my computer, nearly seventy years later, dumbstruck at the innuendos coming back to me—this time not from a dream in the night but from real feelings of shame I faced in broad daylight! Some classmates were lined up and waiting for the bell to ring at the new Bewsey Street School, where fourteen-year-old girls and boys from Evelyn Street were finishing up their elementary years. The teacher on playground duty was following orders to choose six girls who would compete for the honor of becoming Graduation Day beauty queen. The teacher beckoned to one girl, who was much smaller than I, with golden hair and a nice smile. Then, after passing glances up and down the other lines, exercising her expertise to know beauty when she saw it, she started up my row, pulled me from the line, and said, "Go stand over with the other girls, but stand up straight, Miss Hope. Hold your chin up and do straighten your shoulders." She sounded like my mother.

I became panic-stricken when I heard how the judging would take place. The new school was very modern, with glass-fronted classrooms facing the quadrangle of lawn. The boys' quarters were on the north and the girls' quarters were on the south, and various other common rooms made up the rest of the square, so that everyone in the school would see me as I slouched from room to room in line with the other contestants and the accompanying teacher, who kept reminding me to stand up STRAIGHT!

The other girls looked all shaped-up as we stood side by side and the students raised their hands for the teacher to count the votes. All I could possibly look was all trussed up. I was thankful that not one of the boys gave me a second look, but even so, the overall voting pegged me as one of the queen's attendants. The school staff provided material for long, formal dresses, which we were expected to make on the school's sewing machines. Mother would never let any of us use her old Singer, so I wasn't an expert. But I caught on as to how to put the tissue pattern on the lovely purple satin, cut out the dress pieces according to each piece of the pattern, then fit the pieces together according to directions, and guide them under the machine's foot. Eventually, all the pieces were sewn together. I thought I looked fairly presentable, considering this was my first homemade dress. The whole procedure, however, became a nightmare to me, since not even being chosen as a queen's attendant could persuade me that I possessed one bit of the beauty for which I had longed. This was not, of course, the sort of feeling I could ever have confessed to my mother.

But then, as my father once whispered to me after Mother had been particularly cross with me one day, "Our mother has no soul, Love." It shocked me to hear Father say anything about Mother that I didn't know already. He explained that the soul was a beautiful, unseen part of us all that governed our thoughts, our minds, and our behavior in the name of goodness. And it was a very necessary thing to possess. I didn't dare ask whether soul had anything to do with the spirit he so often told her she was knocking out of me.

My spirit remained unbroken, despite my ugly duckling self-concept and the disappointment of being denied the scholarship I'd earned. Making good on my promise to apply myself to my remaining study time at Bewsey School, I felt well prepared to make my own way in the world, and graduated with excellent marks at age fourteen. That very year, I found employment at a department store, where I earned a modest wage, plus a discount on all merchandise sold there.

Always, though, I was drawn to the idea of working for Lever Brothers, Ltd., manufacturers of soap products. Lord Leverhulme treated his employees royally, providing recreation facilities with hockey fields, tennis courts, bowling greens, and cricket grounds. A ballroom and theater were added, and employees and their families were encouraged to participate in the events that took place there. Though Father was not employed at the factory, he had friends who were, and somehow my sisters and I were invited to participate in the children's theater productions—operettas, pantomimes, and other shows—that were funded and sponsored by Lever Brothers affiliate, Joseph Crosfield and Sons. At three shillings and sixpence per ticket, our proceeds from the week's performance went toward a holiday for retired employees at the boarding house the company owned in Llandudno, Wales.

Thus the stage became our stomping ground all through our growing-up years. Suddenly we found ourselves rehearsing for bit roles, chorus line routines, and songs in musicals we had seen as children—*Dick Whittington; Cinderella; Pearl of the Ocean Wave; No, No Nanette;* and others on the tip of my tongue. We spent long weeks working on our routines, so that we might put on a polished performance for the two-week teachers' rest holiday in autumn. Meantime, Mother spent days and weeks sewing costumes for the entire cast—another possible reason, I suspect, for our being allowed to participate in the theater, along with the children of employees.

Suddenly the day of performance would arrive and I was in my flower-girl outfit below stage, ready and excited to have the cosmetician make up my face. I used to love that moment when I would sit on a high stool with an apron around my neck, an ugly duckling waiting to be transformed into a beautiful swan. Crimson lipstick and deep blue eye shadow were blended in where they belonged over a skin-tinted base, which was darker than my naturally pale complexion. I knew that moments later, I would be facing the glare of footlights looking alive, rather than a pale, wan ghost who might scare away the audience. I became agog with anticipation as the sound of notes wafted up from the pit and the company's orchestra tuned up their instruments, creating a cacophony of sound that took my breath away. Here a bassoon booming, there a bass fiddle floundering, cymbals clashing in between, violins reaching for—and catching—the high notes to heaven, muted trumpet butting in a bar or two, as up and down the scales they rambled, and all the while, the piano tinkled along its solitary way.

And then a moment of silence before the conductor lifted his baton and the overture began. I knew no words to describe the ecstasy of that haunting musical flight of fancy, but even now, as I write, the sounds come waltzing back. I see myself standing on the stage, waiting for the overture to end and the opening bars of the chorus to begin. I am there, once more, singing my heart out as the red velvet curtains part to show a full house of expectant people willing to listen, to laugh, and to cry with us. What child could ask for more?

We were sometimes jealous of Our Eve, though. Born an actress, she was! Comedienne, tragedian, old woman, young man—whatever the character demanded, she became. The audiences loved her and showed their appreciation by showering her with flowers and candy on closing night. She knew her sisters loved her too, and she would willingly share with us whatever she received.

Later on, Eve's natural talents earned her roles in Lever Brothers' adult plays and operas, and again the whole family became involved in one way or another. She took me along for support when she auditioned for a part in a one-act play, *The Last War*, written by Norman Holland, an executive of the Lever Brothers' factory. I sat in the front row of the theater with fingers crossed, in hopes that she would land the leading role. The readings, except for Our Eve's, were rather dull, and I was wishing they would come to an end, when I saw the director, Mr. Worthington—who also directed our hometown branch of the soap company itself—motioning in my direction. I felt embarrassed because I couldn't hear what he was saying, but he repeated the words close up and lent a hand for me to climb onto the stage, saying, "Would you like to read the lines that are written in red for me?"

I nodded, speechless, and waited for my cue. I read the lines clearly, enunciating the words properly and with emphasis where it belonged. I was confident and ready—until I scanned ahead while awaiting another cue, and saw the name Chopin, one of Father's favorite composers, whose name I had made a hash of pronouncing when I first said the name. "His name is SHOW-pan, Love," Father had said. And now, here he came swirling into my view again, and I had to pronounce his name correctly! I began repeating to myself, "Show-pan, show-pan, show-pan," and I would have missed the line altogether had not Eva poked me with her elbow. I caught my breath, started the sentence, and, to my horror, out came the humiliating "Chop-in" of my childhood. Eva poked me again and whispered, "Show-pan."

Mortified, I carried on, reassured by kind Mr. Worthington's "Don't worry. That happens to all of us at one time or another." I so badly wanted to scream, "I know Chopin. I listen to Chopin. I love Chopin and his 'Minute Waltz,' and I really, really do know how to pronounce his name!" But I held my tongue, realizing the futility of shouting out any such defense, which could only be seen as a lame excuse for ignorance. Even today, whenever I listen to my album of Chopin waltzes on my old-fashioned turntable, I smile and say, "You still bring beautiful music into my home whatever your name, Mr. Chop-in!"

The day after the audition, Eva was named to play the leading role of serpent, as she deserved to be, and I got the surprise of my life when I was named for the Lioness part. Mr. Worthington had chosen me for that important role, even though I had only recently joined the company. Rehearsals for *The Last War* went smoothly, and I wish I could remember the dialogue, but sixty-eight years is too long to remember trivia. I can, however, remember the broad scope of the well-intentioned plot, which was based upon the proclivity of the human race to destroy itself. I do remember, too, the final scene: I was still growling my lines as the lioness, our Eve was still the serpent twined around a tree (apple, of course), and the lowly microbe was still there. The conclusion, in short, consisted of an angel reading some kind of proclamation! To what crowd he was proclaiming, I couldn't imagine, since everybody else but the three of us had supposedly died and only the lowly microbe was still there, in case he was needed.

By this time Eva had been working as a chemist in Crosfield's laboratories for two years, ever since her graduation from secondary school. Though I was glad enough to have gained a cashier's job in a department store at only fourteen, I continued to dream of becoming a Crosfield's employee too, determined as I was to take part in the firm's many recreational and cultural programs. Thus I took the first job opening that was offered to me there—scrubbing soap racks all day long and sometimes helping the male employees with their piece-work. I would help them lift six-foot-long, heavy slabs of soap onto a table that was fitted at one end with a cutter, the strong wire partitions of which would cut through the slab, turning it into pieces the size of hand soap.

It was heavy, tiring work, with not much time to stop and take a breath, since payment for piecework was based on production and brought in extra money beyond the regular paycheck. The more they produced, the more they were paid. I worked as hard and fast as they did, determined to be considered an equal partner up to the task at hand, even though my own paycheck was simply figured as the acceptable amount to pay a fourteen-year-old girl who had no previous experience at scrubbing soap racks.

As time went on I was promoted to the laboratories and put in charge of the storage room, from which the chemists checked out chemicals and other supplies. When the chief chemist's secretary announced she would be leaving after six months to be married, I was promised the position on the condition that I would attend business college at night and become proficient as a stenographer—learning to type at a high speed and to take down Pitman's shorthand at 120 words per minute. I was excited at the opportunity to attend college, even though my classes would be limited to the company's specified subjects.

Studying those secretarial courses took up only two evenings a week after working hours, so I thought I might as well use up the other three weekday evenings to attend the Lancashire Institute of Learning, where I enrolled for English literature and German courses. I completed the Business College curriculum, a year's course, in six months, and started on the demanding job of being secretary to a chief chemist and his staff of a dozen or so men and women, including my sister. The High German language courses I had taken purposely came in handy, since I had control of the library where my office was situated, and I was able to assist staff and other employees in locating German authors and their works. I was barely sixteen then and kept at my job till the day I sailed for America, eight years later.

I must admit that gaining a position with Lever Brothers at such a relatively young age had given me a bit of boldness. Though I was still living at home, I had, after all, been out of school and working for three years. Understandably, I was tempted to push my limit with my parents, especially concerning curfew. Father usually gave Mother full rein when it came to the matter of house rules and our attitude toward them. But I vividly remember one evening when Mother had had all she could take. She locked the door and went to bed early, leaving Father to wait up for me. People were more trusting in those days and not many locked their doors, even at night, so it was most unusual for Mother to lock and bar our door—and not against strangers, but against the return of her own daughter. As I turned the knob and realized it was locked tight against my entry, I remember the feeling of desertion and isolation that swept over me. I was a castaway, not good enough to stay inside the family circle. I knocked lightly, afraid of what might be awaiting me inside.

Father, who was still waiting up even though it was early morning by the time I got in, heard the knocker and opened the door. Mother hadn't been able to sleep either and called down to Father, "You can let 'er in 'arold. Lay the law down to 'er now. She'd get the back of me 'and, she would, if I came down there."

Putting his arm around my shoulders, Father whispered, "Come on now, Love. At two o'clock in the morning, your body is at its lowest ebb and needs to rest. Your mother expected you home long before now." I didn't need to try to explain or excuse my lateness. I knew Father understood that if a sixteen-year-old girl had brains enough to organize a formal affair for her fellow workers, she shouldn't be punished for staying till the last waltz was over, now should she? Mother never stopped to consider any reasons why I might break her rules. The back of her hand ended any argument of right versus wrong on my behalf. Strangely enough, I don't ever remember seeing the back of her hand hitting any other one of my sisters across the face. At eighty-four, I'm beginning to wonder why this was so and whether my mother ever really liked—or trusted—me. Was there something in my nature that caused her to feel I needed a harsher discipline, a tighter rein? Did she somehow transfer to me her own feelings of guilt concerning her being six months pregnant with Eva at the time she married my father—a secret I discovered only through reading their marriage certificate, which I ordered during the final year of writing this memoir?

The first performance of Mr. Holland's *The Last War,* a trial run at the company theater, was well attended and enthusiastically received, giving us hope of winning the coveted cup when we competed at the yearly drama festival, against players from Port Sunlight and several other Lever Brothers' firms throughout the country. Our Eve and I were especially delighted upon learning we would be celebrating my premiere performance at the Fortune

Theater on Drury Lane in London, where the likes of Lawrence Olivier and Helen Terry had taken their bows before the footlights.

We had studied about London in school, but Uncle Jack's stories of his train runs to London were much more enjoyable. He would tell us about the people, people not unlike ourselves, whom he had met there. When he heard our Eve and I were actually going to the big city he told us, sotto voce, that Londoners were not too friendly to foreigners, and to be careful. "In fact," he said, "when the Irish were coming over here and landing jobs alongside the London laborers, those Cockney lads so strongly resented working beside them that they devised a clever way of putting rhymes together that the Irish would never understand." Eve and I were fascinated when Uncle Jack told us that "up the apples and pears" meant "up the stairs," and a girl in Cockney rhyme would be camouflaged with a twist and a twirl, but sadly, when we started making up our own secret codes at home, Father didn't approve of our messing with the English language.

London was awake and awaiting as we arrived that morning so long ago, eager to see and be seen. The whole entourage of cast members, stage crew, and a couple of company executives who rode in Mr. Worthington's car, were greeted at the hotel like long-lost cousins. The name of the hotel, I am sorry to say, along with other names of other places only marginally relevant to the telling of my story, is a faded blur in my mind. I remember it being in the Theater District, close enough for Eve and me to wander over to Drury Lane, where the costermongers were dragging flower carts alongside the fishmongers and other cart pushers, all begging you to buy in a singsong chorus as you walked across the court. A little old lady, shawls tied under her chin to ward off the cold wind, left her stationary spot and came close up to us, wafting a bunch of violets temptingly under our noses, singing "Who'll buy my violets? Just smell my pretty violets. Only tu'pence a bunch, luv. You buy my violets?" She wore clogs and a long, dark skirt covered with a white apron, along with what looked to be a man's jacket, all tattered and torn. Her smile, I'm sure, was a practiced art as she pinned the bunch of tiny purple flowers onto my coat lapel and whispered, "They'ull bring ye luck tha' knows, Love!" The smile stayed with me, among the violets, until they all wilted and I had to let them go.

Of course, one didn't go to London without seeing the sights, because nobody would believe that you had been there. No family members had traveled along with us, so Mr. Worthington suggested we make the tour as a group. Riding around the city on the top level of London's bright red double-decker buses, we found time to visit St. Paul's Cathedral. There, up inside the magnificent dome, I whispered a few words into the famous wall, and Our Eve, with her ear pressed to the portion of dome across the void, heard every word I had said. I wondered if Sir Christopher Wren, the architect who had designed that famous structure, was still hovering around its hallowed hall, listening in.

We were impressed, too, by another building almost as sacred, the Old Lady of Threadneedle Street, more formally known as the Bank of England, an institution whose worth in gold was whispered around the world. We lunched at a famous pub, alongside the best reporters on Fleet Street, all of whom left with a full stomach of pork pies and stout (those who drank it had Guinness, of course; mother would have had a fainting spell if she'd thought her girls had imbibed). We sailed in an open boat along the River Thames, listening to the awesome bongs of Big Ben chiming out the hour, and glided by the Houses of Parliament where our guide reminded us Guy Fawkes and his cohorts had plotted to overthrow the place—along with King James I himself, who was due to speak there on the fifth of that November. But even the best-laid plans go up in smoke when the match doesn't strike. The king must have said, "Off with their heads" for the mere plotting of this heinous crime, and every fifth of November thereafter, we would all burn Guy in effigy in a bonfire, while feasting on roasted chestnuts and hot baked potatoes, with fireworks buzzing overhead.

Such were our London amusements that long ago day. But the show must go on, and go on it did in that beautiful Fortune Theater on Drury

Lane. Tier after tier of balcony seats, filled with London theatergoers, circled the walls. Our Eve and I glowed in the limelight of that performance, enjoying ourselves immensely, in spite of the fact that the playwright's view might have been more frightfully accurate than we were all thinking. *The Last War* hinted, indeed, at just how inhumane humans could be to one another. In that season of 1936, with Germany's Hitler on the edge of yet another war steaming toward a holocaust, Neville Chamberlain's approach to diplomatic relations under his umbrella of peace accomplished nothing to persuade a power-hungry maniac to behave like a gentleman.

The play's dark theme aside, we were in the best of moods on the evening the coveted cup was presented to us at a prestigious banquet in a posh hotel. Was it the Ritz? Or the Waldorf Astoria? As one grows older, one can't be bothered with trivialities; names of places, even famous and important places, have become unimportant in my life. Anyway, in the seventy years that have gone by, I myself am still standing, while both those grand hotels may have long since gone the way of all old buildings, down in the dust.

What I do remember, vividly, is that our happy gang of prizewinners, along with the losing companies' competitors, had received an invitation to dine with the founding father of Unilever, Lord Leverhulme himself, and that the elegance of the occasion was fit for a king, though his majesty wasn't in attendance. Even though at that time in my life I didn't know the difference between damask and a demitasse, I didn't miss a beat of that wonderful evening!

Lest I make a wrong move, I buried my face behind the menu, which to my dismay was written in French. Eve saved the day for me, and with a rather superior air to show off her knowledge of the language, she picked up her own menu and rattled off a few words: *table d'hôte,* the chef's choice, which meant I would be eating *de boeuf,* or beef. "Guess what's for dessert?" Eve asked, looking up with a smile. I had already spotted that one on the list and managed to translate its title, so it was my turn to smile. Didn't everybody know that cherries jubilee was a flamboyant presentation of cake and cherries soaked in *Eau-de-vie* (brandy) if you please, which the waiters would set alight on their trays and parade them, high above their heads around the room. The dish was created by a French chef, Auguste Escoffier, in honor of Queen Victoria's Golden Jubilee in 1897. I must have read all that somewhere, as I had certainly never tasted cherries jubilee before that night.

The soup had not yet been served when one of the dozen or so waiters lining the mirrored walls stepped out of line, sidestepping chair legs and their human counterparts. He minced his way through the maze of tables, a look of haughty servitude painted on his face and a spotless white serviette lovingly draped over the sleeve of his black dinner jacket—waiting to be flipped out to serve the slightest request from his lordship. His image reflected from those four, mirrored walls was like a plethora of penguins with sore feet. My sister broke my thoughts into shivers of apprehension as she nudged me and said, "He's coming to our table." And he most certainly was. I nervously wondered if I had made a faux pas somewhere along the line of introductions to his lordship, or if his honor had noticed a petticoat showing or a ladder running up my tights. It was not often that a commoner dined and supped with the aristocracy. In those days formality overshadowed any hint of familiarity, and I felt somewhat uncomfortable in my little black dress with not a glimmer of glitter about it to show I had any right to be there.

And there the waiter stood, hand outstretched, and I almost swooned as he took a slip of paper from the silver tray and, offering it, bent down and whispered in my ear, "You are Miss Eva Hope, aren't you?" My sigh of relief could have blown out the candle in the centerpiece, and words failed me as I shook my head and pointed to my sister. She grabbed the note, stared in disbelief, and exclaimed, "I've been invited to sit with his lordship!" Waving the waiter aside, she pushed back her own chair and sailed majestically over to the head table to take her place of honor behind the potted palms.

I was left high and dry to contemplate the dozen pieces of cutlery and a like amount of various pieces of crystal, from which to sip the drinks that were right for each and every course on the menu. I felt a strong desire to hide under the table before I fell off my chair from raising three glasses of cheer in toasts to the king, even though he wasn't there. I suppose our founding father, the most eminent lord, had taken a fancy to our Eve for her portrayal of the snake slithering round the tree in the Garden of Eden. His admiration for her acting was understandable, for the applause was enough to bring the house down. But it is more probable he had simply fallen madly in love with Our Eve, since she was the image of Deanna Durbin, one of the most beautiful movie stars of the era.

The plant pots had been cleared away in case his worship wanted to rest his elbows on the table, and I could see Eve. The fork in her left hand hovered midway to her mouth, her right hand grasping something like a megaphone—which I guessed was an ear trumpet—trying to act as a lady accustomed to conversing with the crème de la crème, and at the same time maintaining her equilibrium and dignity. Our Eve rose to the occasion, as always, managing a difficult situation in a manner befitting her dramatic accomplishments. And so did his lordship as he stood and praised her per-formance, his beard scratching a gusty kiss on her cheek while handing her the winners' trophy on our behalf. Of course she took the kind of bows befitting a queen of the stage, even daring to blow me a kiss in recognition of my presence. All I had to do was sit back, tuck in, and say nothing more than, "Pass the salt, please."

All in all it was a grand celebration and a fabulous meal—one far from the fish and chips to which we were accustomed. When the dinner was all but done, that same smiling waiter who had brought Eve the note wobbled over to my table, silver tray held high, ready to serve the flaming dessert. And he had the audacity to wink at me. The next time he made the rounds, a new serviette folded over his wrist, he asked, "Black or white, madam?" I had no idea what he meant by black or white, but thought I had better choose one of the two since the wine was making me sleepy. "White, please," I said, and was glad I made that choice when he picked up a pitcher filled with hot milk and poured in half a cup before filling the rest of the cup with black coffee. I flashed him my best smile, along with another sigh, as he went on with his silver pots to the diner next to me. I took another sip from my cup of white coffee, but all I really wanted by that time was our little cottage on Gatewarth Street and a nice hot cup of Mother's Mazawattee tea.

Our Eve was an instant star that summer night of 1936.

A new century has already begun, and I am still waiting to be discovered. And no, I have still not stopped dreaming.

Chapter 3

*To call war the soil of courage and virtue is like
calling debauchery the soil of love.*
—GEORGE SANTAYANA

$\mathcal{I}$ was nineteen in 1939 when the Second World War began hovering over us, wreaking havoc in our land with loss of life and property. By 1940 the sky was literally falling as the Germans began blitzing British cities, especially those with industrial operations. Men were called up for military service, many of them merely boys, and all of them trained to kill or be killed. Millions were killed and more millions wounded in the futility of war. We thought it would never end.

Women were being conscripted into the service of His Majesty the King, and to help the war effort in munitions factories. I was naïve enough to want to go into the Land Army, where the young women wore such becoming uniforms. The only enemy I would have to face, I reasoned, would be a bull, and I could hoe the garden rows and eat the peas without having to shell out precious coupons to buy them.

In the end I could do none of the above, because my civilian job was listed under a "classified" category, "Laboratory Worker." Thus, my war effort was confined to civilian duty on the home front, where, as a fire watcher, I patrolled a designated area two nights a week, armed with a steel helmet, a gas mask, and a stirrup pump intended to put out incendiary bombs that were dropped by enemy pilots upon their targets of munitions factories, military command posts, and any other strategic installations.

The remaining evening hours were spent at the headquarters of the local Home Guard unit, which was made up of men who didn't qualify for active duty and were assigned to guard the home front. I was also expected to learn about poisonous gases and first aid and do my share at the YMCA, where servicemen of all branches and countries contributing to the war effort spent their leisure hours. I washed a lot of dishes and flipped a lot of pancakes in those war-weary days, and was comforted by the sight of all those uniforms, evidence of forces for good united against a common enemy.

We didn't pity ourselves, but took ourselves lightly most of the time. As father used to tell me, "Don't fret so much, Love! Do as the angels do! It's because they take themselves lightly they can fly so high. Don't go worrying about things you cannot change all by yourself."

Flying high as we worked to win the war didn't mean that our hearts were flighty. Or empty. Or that we didn't love our country. You can't possibly take the horror of war lightly, but you can take yourself lightly through it. The pain of a thing is real. The suffering, we bring on ourselves.

The propaganda of war led one to hate the enemy, and it was easy to hate *en masse* when that hate was directed at a whole country we had never seen rather than at someone's father, a mother's son, or a young girl's sweetheart. It is much easier to hate than to love, and it is much easier to hate an enemy when you see enemy bombs striking a children's playground, scattering little bodies and pieces of bodies across the grass. The pilot of that plane, which was camouflaged as a British Spitfire, dared to fly across the English Channel in broad daylight to destroy a paper mill. And he missed! As such atrocities continued, it was easy to hate—until and unless you could find it in your heart to understand that one pilot was neither a country nor a cause, just some mother's beloved son who was forced to fight an enemy he didn't make.

Like my friend Harold, who, conscripted and rifle-readied for landing on the beaches of Dunkirk, confided to me his dread of a bayonet coming at him. That was seventy-five years ago, and I can still see the fear in his eyes as he made his confession that day he received his marching orders to be sent "over there," a fear he passed on to me, one that returns at the slightest whisper of the word war. I never saw him again. His parents received the dreaded "missing in action" telegram, and I never knew how he met his fate. The life that once was came back as just a number carved on some unknown faraway grave. I pray that he rests in peace.

Though this was a time of fear as well as loss, we couldn't let the fear itself be the death of us. Walking home from our volunteer duties late at night, in the dark of blackout, Our Eve and I would talk.

"Whatever would we do, Our I, if the enemy were to drop down and storm our house and tried to you know what?"

"What what?" I wanted to know. She knew I was goading her into saying the word.

"Rape us, you dozey bugger. There! I said it. Now are you happy?"

War taught us about survival and about bearing the burden that was thrust upon us. Survival meant waking up after a short sleep, stroking a hand over your face to see if you were still there, and staying awake the rest of the night listening for sirens that were now quiet. Survival meant doing without when you had already done your share of that the day before; it meant depending upon one another in the community.

We quickly learned that the fundamental things of life apply in war. A sense of humor was a necessary staple in our family now, and feeling sorry for yourself was never tolerated for long. "Self-pity and self-importance," Mother would say, "will be the death of you." And pretty soon we would hear her singing, "Pack up your troubles in your old kit bag, and smile, smile, smile." So we tried to live lightly, doing what we had to do seven days a week, and on Saturday nights, dancing under the stars, beneath the glass roof of the dance hall. We danced lightly through many a weekend till another misguided missile hit the wrong spot on the map—this time the dance hall roof—shattering glass and plaster over that beautifully polished floor. Luckily we had warning from the sirens in time to send the dancers scurrying into the underground shelter, where we waited out the bombs singing, "Oh the Yanks are coming! The Yanks are coming! And they won't go back till it's over over there."

Then in 1941, a huge sigh of relief was heard throughout the land. The word was spreading around. "Have you heard? It won't be long now! The Yanks are coming . . . the Yanks are really coming!" And we worked with lighter hearts as they swarmed across our shores to set up camp and plan their strategy to help us win that bloody war. They were very, very welcome in spite of the few who called them overpaid, over-sexed and over-here. The 509th Supply Squadron of the American Air Force settled in at Burtonwood, a suburb of Warrington, much too close for Mother's comfort, since she had four daughters.

Of course the young girls, including my sisters and I, welcomed the presence of these handsome Americans with open arms, in the absence of the Englishmen who had been snatched from under our noses and sent overseas, some never to return. If Mother would only give her permission for us to date just one of these Americans, we confided one to another, wouldn't there be cigarettes, cosmetics, and stockings that looked like silk rather than sackcloth? We were obsessed by the lack of such items, as essential as they would be in the unfamiliar world of sophistication where our dreams and schemes were leading us. Things like that matter when you are young and insecure, eager to be welcomed into a brave new world where you have never felt you belonged.

They mattered to Mother, too. She welcomed the young Americans into our home, and it eventually became a halfway house between the base at Burtonwood and the city center where the YMCA was located. We didn't have much in the way of entertainment to offer our young saviors, but they seemed to make themselves at home, and Mother always had the chip pan at the ready to serve them up a plate of chips. We would all pitch in, peeling and slicing the potatoes at the last possible minute before popping them into the pan, so that they wouldn't dry out and blacken if they were left standing.

Every so often she would warn her four daughters, "Don't go getting serious with those young men now," and by that she meant we weren't supposed to date them singly. But who could resist a night at the pictures now and then, with a packet of cigarettes or a candy bar thrown in? What Mother didn't know didn't hurt her one bit, so we reasoned. Her attitude softened somewhat after Our Joyce got a job at the Burtonwood base and began to invite the American airmen with whom she worked to come to our house for a cup of tea. After Mother came to know them as "nice young boys," she had a change of heart about our dating any one of them alone, though she still made it clear that we were not to get serious about any of those American soldiers.

But there came a time when things did get serious for me with one of those handsome Americans. I met him at the YMCA on July 21, 1942, and he came week after week to sit there, drinking coffee and watching my every movement as I worked the counter or cooked in the kitchen as a home front volunteer. The third time he asked if I would go out with him, I said yes. But it wasn't the fatal attraction of sex that led me to agree. I just couldn't deny the pleading look in his hazel eyes, and I pushed Mother's warning to the back of my mind. He was kind and attentive, and I began to entertain fanciful dreams of a fairy-tale future together.

He wasn't like the English boys I'd dated in that he didn't seem to have any qualms about defying convention. On our second date, to see a movie, as we walked down the steps in the more expensive area—the loges—he whispered, "I brought something for you. Let's sit here for a minute." I didn't want to be seen sitting in the aisle at the pictures, but I took a chance that none of my friends would be watching a Tom Mix cowboy movie. Besides, the lights had already been dimmed and the audience would be too engrossed in the plot to care, so I sat down beside him, uncomfortable about the whole situation.

Nudging me with his elbow, he said, "I brought two of them. Here." And he pushed something into my hand. I was hoping it might be chocolate, or cigarettes, chewing gum, or anything else other than what is was—a huge turkey drumstick! My eyes stopped blinking as the smell of food reached my nostrils, and as he bit into his drumstick, I followed suit with my own. I didn't give a damn about cowboys chasing Indians across the screen or about those in the audience who might be wondering what we were doing sitting in the aisle. It was the most daring thing I had done in my whole life, and looking back, I've come to realize that my companion's sense of unconventionality probably had a lot to do with my attraction to him. At any rate, I will never forget my first taste of American turkey, that delicious bit of contraband, courtesy of my airman's work in the mess hall.

That night I took Raymond Hedrick home to meet my parents, feeling light-headed and full of fancy for my new beau. After all, he had introduced me to my first cowboys-and-Indians movie, and I'd laughed when he told me he came from Montana and that's what all Montanans did every Sunday afternoon. When I invited him into the house, Mother stayed in the kitchen while Father made conversation with him in the parlor. Father was very polite, but asked him many questions before saying goodnight. When I closed the door and walked back into the parlor—and while mother was still in the kitchen, out of earshot—Father said, "Our I, no man is an island unto himself, we are told, but John Donne never met your young man, did he now? Be careful, Love. In time he will turn everyone away from you." I just couldn't believe my father had said those words—Father, who had never before found anybody out.

Though Father's comment startled me, the idea of marrying my airman and setting off for a life in the Rockies was increasingly attractive to me. I suppose I had some sense that whatever mending my future husband needed could be accomplished through my tender love and care. I had, after all, seen my mother devote herself to my father's every need—and all to the good, it seemed to me.

I never, of course, said a word to either of them about other experiences beyond Tom Mix that my Montana man wanted to introduce to me. I had never seriously welcomed sexual involvement—as little as I knew about it—as a necessary and integral part of a relationship between another and myself. I had long been considered a cold fish on first dates, and I had begun to believe I was one. But my present beau seemed obsessed with trying to persuade me to become otherwise, talking of love and marriage and leading my reluctant body along as well as he could, yet always with only minimal interest on my part. Sometimes I wondered if I were missing out on some beautiful, mystical experience, but quickly perished the thought, remembering Cousin Dorothy's words for the wise.

I thought for years that it was Mother's insistence on proper behavior that kept me cool and resistant to passionate advances, but once I remembered that long-repressed incident in my secret garden, I began to think that those deep-down, murky feelings of repulsion came from the body bullying I'd experienced that day, an experience that kept me too fearful of a repetition of that violent act to welcome those tingly feelings of desire that sometimes crept over me. Today as I think back over such a terrifying and traumatic introduction to sex thrust upon me as a child, I realize why my mind channeled the energy and urges of my emerging sexuality into a heightened passion for the pursuit and attainment of beauty. My greatest arousal came from the discovery of an opening blossom, my ecstasy from the aroma of wild roses caught in a tangle of briars and honeysuckle vines.

Though I had dated many young men before meeting my Montana airman, the only time I had come close to feeling the kind of physical excitement my friends seemed to experience with such frequency and ease was on the night of my twenty-first birthday. Turning twenty-one meant more back in 1941 when that birthday was considered a milestone, a threshold to adulthood, even for those of us who had been out of school and in the workforce since completing our elementary education. For this special occasion, Mother had baked a cake and bought a bottle or two of wine. Just the thought that she would really bake a cake, just for me, sacrificing her wartime rations and her precious best butter and demerara sugar, made me feel giddy even before the champagne popped its cork.

Indeed, as I walked toward home that evening and stood by the canal, waiting for the bridge to rise up and let the barges through, I felt as if the gourmet sugar itself had been tossed high into the air for me to catch and enjoy. The bridge was actually a section of the main road, built over the canal and spanning the distance from shore to shore. I loved the strange sensation I felt when it was time for the bridge to be lowered down again. It seemed as though it was standing still and I was slowly moving up to meet it.

To make it a real birthday party, Mother invited all my closest friends, including newlyweds Marge and Cyril. She made a huge platter of fish and chips, and insisted on doing the washing up after the meal herself, saying she and Father would listen to the war news on the wireless in the kitchen, while the rest of the party retired to the parlor—a smaller room but cozy enough, with its fireplace and Father's favorite reading chair.

The wine flowed and we danced, crowded into whatever space wasn't taken up by the fireplace and hearth, the upright piano Father had bought for me, knowing I loved the classical music he loved to play, the chintz-covered settee and matching chair along the window wall, and the lovely, long-legged table whose curved legs led up to a square top just large enough to hold an aspidistra plant, which must have been as old as the table. Even though its growth seemed a bit stunted, it never wilted, never shed its leaves, and never died, at least not while I knew it. It was stalwart and sturdy like Mother, and it stood up that night to the party noise and the music from Father's RCA Victor gramophone with not a leaf astir. On that special night, the treasured gramophone ground out platters of World War I melodies rather than the voices of Caruso and the Street Singer that were my father's favorites. We danced the night away to wartime music like Vera Lynn's lovely rendition of "The White Cliffs of Dover." And we all joined in singing "The Yanks are Coming" and "When Johnny Comes Marching Home Again, Hurrah, Hurrah!"

We played silly parlor games, most of which involved kissing—even though some of the rules didn't call for kissing—and before long the games had ceased and the kissing continued, escalating into other levels of longing. As conversation gave way to other forms of communication, we took turns winding up the gramophone to keep the music scratching out its audio camouflage for the benefit of my parents, who had long since nodded off in the kitchen or made their way up to bed. Couples were cuddled together on sofas and chairs, and other bodies were sprawled across the carpet. I am not sure whether the champagne would have led me down the garden path that very night had not the hubbub of the party dwindled into whispers and the music played itself out just at the right moment for me to hear the long moaning wail of the air raid siren's "All Clear," telling us that German bombers had been busy in our skies.

We had been so oblivious to everything but the music and momentum of the party that we hadn't even heard the earlier short blast of warning to rush to the bomb shelters. We had learned from experience that if the spitfires didn't respond in time, the British ack-ack guns nearby weren't sufficient to stand up against German bombers hurling missiles from above. We had foolishly risked our lives for a birthday cake and a glass of wine, and we were lucky to survive, even if it was only to see another day of war.

Though some felt we might as well stay on, since we'd already made it through, the wail of the siren had cast a somber spell and soon couples began leaving. Within minutes of the last departure, I heard the short wails of the warning sirens and tried to calculate who would have had time to get home and who would have been caught in the predawn attack. I was most fretful for Marge and Cyril, who had the longest way to go on foot, and my worries were not unfounded. As the sirens went off, they were walking arm in arm, Marge tottering along as fast as her high heels would allow, when a missile came whistling down.

"Dive! Shrapnel!" Cyril shouted, and they hit the pavement together just as a time fuse on the shell's bursting charge exploded its ammunition. The balls of fire were hitting all around them. And then there was silence.

"Oooohh," moaned Marge.

"Are you hurt, Love?" Cyril whispered, as if the enemy were right there, holding them hostage.

"No, I'm all right. It's my coat! It's ruined!" she said.

Though I wasn't there, I can imagine the scene from their account of it. Shaken by her close call, Marge was crying uncontrollably, wailing over and over, "My coat, my beautiful coat! The fur . . . it's ruined, Cyril." He consoled his young bride as best he could, but she confided to me later that she would never forgive the Germans for ruining the lovely fur coat Cyril had used all his coupons to buy for her! When Mother heard the tale of woe, she said, "Oh well, he drives an M.G. doesn't he now, so he must be well off. He can just buy her another coat, and no harm done!" Actually, Cyril was the sports reporter for the *Manchester Guardian*. He was a few years older than Marge, and I stood somewhat in awe of him because he was a journalist, and a good one at that.

Marriage was in the air. A war was on and who could wait for tomorrow? In the way of the young, I went on with plans to marry my American, and neither of my parents expressed any objections, despite the words of warning my father had spoken the night I first introduced him to my Montana boyfriend. My friend Marge, along with my three sisters, would serve as bridesmaids, and the wedding was to be held on September 11, 1943, at St. Mary's Church of England at Great Sankey. I had always felt at home in the old church at Great Sankey, and have fond memories of stained glass windows and pews that had been hand polished to a soft shine by the ladies of the congregation. The rows up front, closest to the altar, were marked with brass plates bearing the names of the prominent families for whom they were reserved. I would run my fingers over those names and wish that I, too, could sit in a row that had my name engraved on a brass plate, a row that was there just for me.

Instead, those names, to my childish thinking, were a command to "Stay Out. Trespassers will be prosecuted." I respected the warning, since I had no desire to trespass on hallowed ground, as I had once done when the vicar caught me walking outside near a sign that said, "Keep off the grass." Anyway, I preferred to sit in the last pew, where nobody could see me if I nodded off during the long sermon. Incidentally, the ancestors of those same prominent members of the Penketh borough seemed to stand sentinel outside of St. Mary's as well. Resting on the front lawn were their imposing headstones, adorned with heralding angels and sentimental obituaries carved into the stones.

Once the church and date had been chosen, I took care of all the preparations and formalities myself, hiring the photographers and making sure the bridal bouquet would be lovingly put together by my Aunt Mary— wife of mother's younger brother, Fred. Mary, who "had a way with flowers," owned a small florist's shop on Bridge Street. I requested yellow tea roses for my bouquet, and golden, glorious chrysanthemums for my bridesmaids' flowers, imagining how well their color would look in contrast to the white, floor-length dresses Mother was busy sewing for each of them.

Though Mother insisted on coming along with me to choose the wedding dress, I didn't tell her until we were inside the shop that I had previously paid a couple of pounds to the proprietor to put away an elegant gown. Fortunately, she approved of my choice and was easily satisfied with the promise that she could choose the wedding tiara and train. The dress was made of georgette, a thin silk crepe of very fine texture that was named after Mme. Georgette de la Plante, the French modiste. The gown's only adornment was a delicate outline of butterflies embroidered around the skirt in gold silk. On the day of the wedding, Mother insisted on finding good luck charms—one a fancy, pink satin garter to roll above my knee, and the other a lucky thr'penny bit that she would hand to me after the ceremony.

I had started my planning in late June, and I had been so completely focused on my September wedding plans that I had paid little attention to anything else. Therefore I was stunned when Father came home on a day in late summer with news that his doctor had said he must spend time away from us all at a sanatorium. Though he had seemed a bit tired that spring, and over the summer had been bothered by a persistent cough, he had never complained about his health. Looking back, however, I realize he must have suffered in silence for many months before the physician took the X-rays that revealed a spot on his lung, which would require weeks of treatment at a sanatorium.

I looked up the word sanatorium in the dictionary, which told me that he would be staying at either: 1) a health resort, a high altitude summer station in the tropics; or 2) an establishment for the treatment of the sick, especially one using natural therapeutic agents, i.e., a tuberculosis sanatorium. Our town of Warrington was no tropical spa, nor was it located high up in the mountains, so I knew the second definition must apply. The sanatorium Father entered was on the outskirts of the city, a barren-looking place where the patients lay on outdoor cots to breathe in the natural therapeutic benefits of fresh air. That was it—the sum total of his treatment. I never discerned any other kind of therapy.

There were one or two distant relatives who voiced their disapproval that I should even think of going through with my wedding plans with my dear Father being so recently hospitalized, and I almost changed my mind at the last minute. But Father would have none of that. "Go ahead with your plans, Love. I insist. Your Uncle Harry [Mother's oldest brother] will walk you down the aisle. Just tell yourself that I would never consent to give you away, even if I were able to be there." Then he paused and his eyes grew serious. "Just remember, Love, that if you are not happy over there, I will spend every penny I have to come and bring you home." Taking him at his word,

I threw myself into the final preparations for the wedding, resolving to take plenty of photographs so that he might almost feel that he had been there.

With only a few weeks remaining before my wedding day, I received a call from the vicar, asking me to drop by the vicarage to answer a few questions he had about reading the banns, the public announcement of a proposed marriage that is read in church, preparatory to the marriage ceremony itself. The purpose of the custom, so Mother had explained, was to allow me the chance to change my mind if I were still uncertain, or to allow any interested party to come forward and say why I should not be married to my Montana airman.

My cousin Dorothy, who had earlier told me about going all the way and whom my mother had described as a promiscuous young lady, said she would come along to the vicarage with me since she had once visited the place herself. She stayed out on the lawn as I went into his house. The room into which the vicar led me was paneled in old mahogany, with shining floorboards and an oriental rug thrown here and there, including one that protected the beautiful planks in front of a chintz-covered sofa. The sofa stood under a bay window and was decked with soft, velvet cushions. The bookshelves, also mahogany, glowed softly, like father's blowtorched, varnished cupboards and doors. My gaze never left those handsome leather-bound books that seemed to beckon me to open their covers and devour the stories on their gold-leafed pages.

The vicar and I sat facing one another across a mahogany table. The interview was straightforward enough and when his questions were answered, he closed his appointment book, rose from his chair, and walked over to the bookshelf, bending low to pull out a rather large volume, which he then carried over to the couch by the bay window. He beckoned for me to sit beside him as he thumbed through the pages of the book, and then nonchalantly pointed out to me a graphic photo of two nude bodies intertwined.

"When a young lady is married in my church, I expect her to learn how to please her husband before I ask them both to take the church vows," he said.

Surely he can't mean he intends to be the one to explain all this to me. A minister? I had never allowed any man, including my intended, to even talk about such matters, much less touch me in an inappropriate way. Mother's veiled warnings about little bastards—and perhaps my buried memories of the incident in my secret garden—were sufficient reasons for keeping myself pure and inviolate, a virgin awaiting my wedding night.

Yet here was the vicar himself, sliding closer to me on the couch as he began to talk about the best positions, pointing to more and yet more couplings. I felt sick; hot and confused and ashamed at having to look at those provocative scenes, afraid of what was happening. And then I thought of Mother! What on earth would she think of me sitting through this charade? The last picture I saw had a pillow under the two bodies, and I closed the book, ready to rise and leave as hastily as I could without showing the embarrassment the vicar didn't deserve to see.

"Don't go—I'm not done yet." The man beside me placed the book in my lap, reached for a pillow, and leaned toward me, saying, "Just lie back, easy now, and raise up a bit so I can put the cushion under and show you how it's done."

I had heard enough. The book in my hands became a weapon, and I found myself thrusting one of the sharp corners of that hard cover into the nearest part of him—his big, fat thigh. Managing to swipe away the hand that tried to grab my skirt, I left him there and ran down the hallway and out the front door. As I made my escape, I was thinking that Mother might be proud of me for being so bold—but knowing, deep down, that she would more likely ask why I had egged him on, and him being a minister, too.

As I practically ran down the steps, I could hardly wait to tell Dorothy what had happened, for surely she couldn't have suffered through that kind of counseling without warning me! But before I had the chance to share my terrifying experience, she met me with the question she'd been eagerly waiting to ask: "Well, did he show you?"

The following Sunday, the assistant minister announced that he would be conducting church services for several weeks while the vicar was on a leave of absence, one that just happened to extend past my wedding date, September 11, 1943. Considering the trauma I suffered on that evening, I've wished many times that I'd somehow found the courage to tell my mother what had happened in the vicarage that day and how afraid I was of my wedding night because of that experience. But the invitations had been issued, the banns had been read, and there was no turning back.

The wedding itself went as smoothly as I could have hoped, with everyone looking lovely and everything going off without a hitch. Oddly enough, the thing that comes back to me about that monumental event in my life was not the moment the groom and I stood at the altar to speak our vows and be declared man and wife, though the vows themselves have sounded in my ears ever since. Instead, the one feeling that overwhelms me as I look back on that day is a deep sense of gratitude for family and friends and neighbors, whose warmth and love and sharing gave me a sense of belonging to where I was born and raised. Most of all, I feel even now an appreciation for all the sacrifices made as so many people donated their precious wartime supply of coupons so that I could have such a posh wedding.

The gift of Mrs. Delaney's three-tiered cake was one such wonder that was hard to believe. That good woman must have saved her meager rations of margarine and sugar for weeks to have enough to produce such a cake. The eggs must have been given up by quite a few generous people, since rationing amounted to only two eggs per person, per month. My cake was beautifully decorated with frosted roses along the edges of each tier, and sitting on the top tier was a miniature bride and groom of the kind you see on cakes even nowadays. Honoring British tradition, Mrs. Delaney had brought along small white boxes, lace-doily-lined, to hold pieces of cake from the bride's table. The boxes were given out to be placed under the pillows of the young ladies present who were "still looking." I would probably be still looking myself, even after I'd found the man I planned to marry, had I not been granted official permission to wed one of America's own. Yes, I was actually required to write a letter to my fiancé's commander, requesting that I be allowed to marry him!

Soon after the reception came to a close, we bade farewell to friends and family and boarded the train for a honeymoon in Wales. I had fallen in love with the Welsh countryside on that long-ago school trip to Llangollen, and so persuaded my new husband that we might enjoy honeymooning there. I made reservations at the Royal Crown Hotel, hoping that he would enjoy a little peace and quiet away from the crowded air base supply depot.

The Royal Crown was a jewel of grand proportion. In the lobby, the long narrow windows were draped with heavy velvet curtains of royal blue, each panel tied back with gold tasseled braid. The drapes shut out some of the light from a September sky that would have made the room seem a trifle smaller but more bright and inviting to arriving guests. White lace antimacassars covered the backs and arms of comfortable-looking easy chairs upholstered in a paler blue than the blue of the drapes. The chairs were grouped in twos and threes around the room, and people were sitting around small tables, each one laid out with a delicate china teapot and matching cups and saucers, along with plates of cucumber and watercress sandwiches. Potted palms and aspidistra leant elegance to it all and allowed some privacy for quiet discussion. The thick carpet underfoot diminished noise to a hum as we approached the desk to announce our arrival, and we were welcomed, not as royalty, but with due respect.

Three hearty meals a day were served by half a dozen waiters who bounced around the table with an eager air of anticipation. When the first course had been served, they stood along the wall, each with a serviette over his arm, tray in hand, and chin set at an upward slope with an air of superiority, like trained seals waiting to bounce over at a diner's slightest glance in their direction. During our first meal at the Royal Crown, my husband

Our Eve in her bridesmaid gown.

My mother's brother Harry gave me away.

The wedding party: Uncle Harry, Marge, Joyce, Orville (Eva's husband), a friend's child, Ray, Irene, Eva, Doris, Granny Knight, Mother, and Mr. and Mrs. Delaney.

Our Dot, Our Eve, and Our Ike.

"Stepping lightly into marriage"

Manning the oars on the River Dee. Ray on our honeymoon.

CABIN.
Mauretania 1945
SECOND SITTING.

Table No. 57

Seat No.

Name

Passengers are requested to hand this card to the Table
Steward when taking their seat at first meal.

Admission to the dining hall aboard the Mauretania, 1945.

Mrs. Delaney's Wedding Gift.

Doris, Joyce, Mother, and Eva on a visit home.

might as well have been back at the base supervising his mess hall staff, rather than dining at an accredited hotel whose staff were all superbly trained and aiming to please. He took up his soupspoon and looked it over with an eagle eye for foreign objects, then began polishing it with his napkin while tossing a supercilious sneer at the line of waiting waiters. The one assigned to our table came hurrying over to ask if there was a problem. I was so embarrassed I couldn't bear to look him in the face, and so excused myself and headed for the powder room till the waiter had departed. I had never been a party to that kind of behavior before. Yet I was the one who took on the burden of guilt, which my new husband merely shrugged off when I questioned the insulting act. I wondered how he could have done such a thing on our wedding day.

I wondered, too, at my own ignorance in the realm of wedded bliss, for later that evening, after a glass of Sandeman sherry, we embarked upon a wedding night that bore no resemblance to the beautiful, first-night performance of the romantic drama I had vaguely visualized. I had been anxious about this moment for weeks, because the only male human body I had ever seen had been the ones pictured in the vicar's book, and in those scenes body parts were well-veiled, especially the male reproductive organ, which was always in some obscure position between the male model and the young woman beneath him. There might have been other, more revealing photographs, but nothing I remembered seeing had looked anything at all like the appendage supposedly intended to invade my body.

To make matters worse, I was having my menstrual period and could not imagine initiating our sex life under such circumstances. I mustered the courage to say, "Can we do this tomorrow?" But the words fell on deaf ears. Within moments I was terrified, hurting, and tried to tell him so. But he wasn't listening! In some strange way I felt as if he didn't know I was even there.

So I entered into the sacred act of marital bliss with the word "obey" ringing in my ears and a pregnant awakening of the first and foremost wifely duties.

The rest of the week's holiday left memories of good Welsh lamb and mint sauce, and an array of other meals far better than I had been eating since 1939. The days dragged by, however, broken only by renting a boat to row ourselves down the River Dee to Horseshoe Falls, and on past the Home of the Ladies of the Vale—a mansion full of beautiful antiques, with lawns stretching down to the water and yew hedges carved into imaginative shapes of other fauna and flora. I asked if we might stop for a tour, but my husband didn't think it would be worth stopping to look at what he called a tourist trap.

The only picture house in the village was closed, there was no TV in those days, and it was slowly dawning on me that my husband and I didn't have very much at all in common. Having lived much of my life hoping, often praying, for a better day tomorrow, I was only beginning to realize that tomorrow didn't come tailor-made especially for me.

The honeymoon finally over, we returned to England to take up our new life together—but not at my old home in Sankey Bridges. Mother had previously warned us, "You won't be living here, you know. That would be the worst possible place to start a life of your own," and she really put her foot down hard with the statement, knowing we would probably be begging her to take us in if nothing else was available within our price range.

Rather than shell out more than we could actually afford for a place of our own, we accepted an invitation to rent from Margaret Dolan, a daughter-in-law of my godmother. She offered us a bedroom with kitchen privileges, and we'd be "keeping her company" in her home while her husband was serving overseas. Margaret Dolan was a very pleasant woman who opened up her heart as well as her home to us, and I could see what a burden it was for her to know her husband was fighting the enemy overseas where all the action was.

Our stay there at No. 40 Malpas Drive in their semi-detached home was pleasant enough. Margaret was a good cook and we pooled our rations. My husband occasionally brought home a box of egg powder to be reconstituted and scrambled, and with vegetables and fruits from the garden we didn't go hungry. Voluntary war work took much of my time after regular working hours, but I occasionally found a free evening to work on my embroidery projects. None of my family ever visited us after we were married, even though we lived only a mile or so from them. We would stop by to say hello to them, however, once in a while.

The most beautiful moment in our stay with Margaret Dolan was the day I answered the doorbell to see a handsome man in uniform standing on the doorstep asking, "Is Margaret home?" Margaret had heard her husband's voice and came bounding down the lobby and into his arms. I can't remember if he had been reassigned to home base or was home on temporary leave from overseas duty, but it was one of the happier moments that occurred during the war.

I kept reminding myself how lucky I was that my own husband had not been sent over to the front lines, even though things didn't seem quite right between the two of us during the thirteen months we lived in the Dolans' home. I rationalized that it must have been the lack of privacy, even though Margaret was very considerate of our presence there, and I told myself that things would improve once we were living alone and settled in a home of our own.

While I had long been accustomed to spending time with friends, both at my parents' home and at events sponsored by the laboratories where I worked, the only time my husband and I ever socialized during those long months was when I could persuade him to go dancing. He did not have a good sense of rhythm, but I wouldn't have cared about that, had he not perpetually scowled at me as if it were my fault that he wasn't a good dancer. The thought never occurred to him to learn a few steps in the right direction, and the years ever after have shown that he never intended to do so.

His intentions on other matters were equally clear: The demands of sex, no matter what day of the month it was, made nightly couplings a rit-ual as regular as Mother's washday—except that dreaded chore, washing day, happened only on Mondays. Even after a year of marriage, I could still not understand what was so romantic about this thing called sex. It simply had no place in my search for beauty.

Part 2

Chapter 4

They change their climate, not their souls
who rush across the sea.

—HORACE

$\mathcal{I}$t was raining when the telephone rang that January evening in 1945. A hard, insistent rain. "Are you there?" I said as I answered, and an American voice came back, tinged with amusement, "Of course I'm here! This is the American Embassy calling. Am I talking to the person whose husband's serial number is 19070704?" No name, only a number linked to my identity and that of my spouse.

When I assured her that I was that person, she continued, "Listen carefully please, because the information I am about to give you will be brief, for security reasons, and is to be shared with no other person—relative, friend, or employer." The driving rain pelted the roof with relentless energy, accentuating the words being clipped so precisely through the earpiece, words that were to change my life forever.

"You will be allowed two pieces of baggage. Mark them 'V-2.' You will be allowed to carry only 100 pounds in traveler's checks, and you will report to the American Embassy in Liverpool at 10:00 A.M. tomorrow. Please be prompt,"—all of this delivered in a tone suggesting, "Your country will be counting on you to keep your mouth shut. You know there's a war going on!"

There had been whispers that this was the way I would hear the news I had been expecting ever since I married my American airman. All this time I'd been waiting with hopes of his getting leave to go home to America with me, a blushing bride at his side; waiting to see those streets paved with gold, the chicken in the pot, the two cars and a boat in our garage; waiting to be welcomed by my new American family into their gracious home, overlooking a lake surrounded by snow-capped mountains; waiting for all the things with which my husband had fueled my daydreams for the two long years we'd shared the tiny, rented room in Margaret Dolan's home.

My father had been full of dreams of going to America someday. When I was a child, he would sing to me, tears in his eyes, Nelson Eddy and Jeannette McDonald's, "When it's Springtime in the Rockies," and tell me of a mighty land with shining mountains shouldering up to a sky forever blue. He spoke of brave pioneers, their wagon wheels carving ruts through virgin soil as they made their way across the continent to start a new life out in the West. I couldn't wait to see it all.

My father would dream until he died, but my dream was about to become a reality.

Even so, the words "tomorrow," "embassy," and "V-2" struck like buzz bombs. Tomorrow!

It's not that I hadn't tried my best to be ready. Months earlier, in London, I had gone through the rigmarole of preparing for immigration under wartime protocol: the fingerprinting, the intrusive questioning, and the indignity of having to stand in line and strip for the smirking medics, while they checked to see that I was physically fit for departure. I felt the bidding might begin at any moment to see which one of us naked wives would bring the highest price.

"Is all this scrutiny really necessary to get a passport?" I had dared to ask. I was given a churlish look and a quick retort: "Don't you know there's a war going on!" My question had been asked more from embarrassment than from ignorance. Of course I knew only too well that there was a war in progress and that every action, every comment might be used as propaganda by the enemy against our country and our servicemen and women at war with them. I also knew better than to press for an answer as to whether my husband might be accompanying me on this long journey, for I understood that an Englishwoman's desire to emigrate to America at the same time her husband went home on leave was of no consequence whatsoever to those in command of troop movement.

And now this phone call—with no mention of whether my husband and I would be departing together, and every indication that I would be making this journey alone, that his leave must have still been tied up in red tape, while my application had gone through with flying colors. There I stood, facing a journey into the unknown, with no knowledge whatsoever of the route I was destined to take, I who had never traveled alone more than a few miles away from my hometown of Sankey Bridges, Warrington, Lancashire.

Even as I stiffened my resolve and tried to convince myself that I could make this journey on my own, I was flooded with questions. How on earth could I possibly have time to quit my job at the laboratory and call all my friends to say goodbye, all without actually telling any of them that I was going anywhere, let alone where I was going, or why?

And, on a more practical note, how on earth could I possibly fit everything I loved into two suitcases marked V-2? I turned first to that task. Not much space was needed for clothes, since the twenty-four coupons allotted every six months never covered everything that needed covering. The camel's hair coat, which had cost eighteen of those coupons a year earlier, looked as bedraggled as the hair still on the camels that clomped and sweated their way across the Sahara, but it would just have to do. It was the only coat I had, and it would be bitterly cold sailing the high seas in January. At least the forest-green Robin Hood hat with the long pheasant feather was stylish enough to take the eye up and away from the old scuffed leather brogues with their fringed tongues and fancy, acorn-tipped laces.

I consoled myself by thinking of the freedom I would have to buy whatever suited me once I reached my new home. I wrapped what was left of my meager wardrobe around the family photographs I took from the mantelpiece in the parlor, then added whatever of the other much-loved treasures I could squeeze into the suitcases. With both suitcases bulging, I looked up with longing at the 48 x 24 portrait of Mother hanging on the kitchen wall, and wished with all my heart I had room for that reminder of her presence. I would miss her, even though the respect I felt for her was somewhat tinged with fear, not only because she was the sole disciplinarian in our household but also because all her senses were so very keen, especially the extra ones.

I was convinced her foresight came from those eyes in the back of her head, hidden in that glorious mass of shiny, black hair that she would wash in rainwater from the barrel that caught the drippings from the eaves. Those furtive back-of-the-head glances followed me everywhere. Though the deep, brown eyes smiling out from her serene, confident face seemed relatively benign, there was a certain sovereignty about them. The way she stood there, surveying her kitchen kingdom, bespoke the strength with which she ruled it. Yet despite the starch in her lace-embroidered bodice, the tailored black suit and pompous foxes slung haughtily around the royal neck, there was no doubt that the strong, capable hands tucked out of sight inside the dainty fur muff, were ever and always ready to reach out and embrace the whole wide world with compassion—and to tackle any job that stood in the way of her accomplishing that.

The biggest job assigned to my mother was my father. You see, Father was put on earth to love and be loved, and Mother thought she was put beside him to make sure that he did and was. I can hear her now, telling for the umpteenth time—with another dash of exaggeration thrown in—the story of how Father spent an evening scraping a sack full of tiny new potatoes and shelling a pail of peas that would go so well with her mint sauce at the next day's dinner, for which she was serving the Sabbath leg of lamb.

Then, same as every Sunday, he had slipped on over to the Black Horse Pub, which was conveniently—albeit unfortunately—located right across the street from our house on Gatewarth Street, and whose doors had just opened, as always, right after church. As usual, the "quick one" had dawdled into two or three, since, "A fellow's obliged to take his turn buying a round or two now, isn't he?" By the time my father was making an unsteady entrance through the front door, singing "My Little Gray Home in the West" in the most glorious notes his tenor voice could muster, the leg of lamb lay dying in its juices and put to rest with the Yorkshire pud, the new potatoes had grown quite a bit older, and the peas had dried hard enough for a peashooter.

Mother's lips pursed up a little as she said, "That's another ten shillings down the drain, 'arold, that could have been used for more sober occasions." Whereupon my father, a lover of words, a maker of music, the gentlest, most sensitive of souls, sat down, took off his shoe, and threw it right into Mother's face—the face looking down so accusingly at him from the portrait hanging behind her on the wall, the portrait in the gilded frame for which he had paid two pounds to prove to Emily that money was no object in his adoration for her. I was stunned to see such a reaction from my dear father, the man who had asked me every day of my young life, "Are you happy, Love?" and just by his asking had made me so!

The last day I saw him alive, a week before my wedding, he had repeated to me, "If you're not happy over there, Love, I'll spend every penny I have to come and bring you home!" I had gone alone to see him that day, and I close my eyes and am still standing there, staring at a face that had lived life with such honor and dignity, the face of a scholar whose respect for another's dignity included not only a chosen few, but all of humanity. He had stayed by my side through thick and thin. And he lingers still!

I was the one who took care of the paperwork, including the death certificate—which contained not one mention of the word tuberculosis. Instead, the cause of death read, "Carcinoma of the Lung." We could have brought him home from that miserable place, to be there for my wedding and to spend his last days with those he loved, had we but been informed of the misdiagnosis. Instead we had left him in that distant sanatorium, out in the cold, to die alone.

For some unspoken reason, after Father died, his four daughters started calling Mother "Our Em," the nickname Father had given to her. Or "Emily," her proper name. Looking back in time, I believe now our reasoning stemmed from the desire to keep Father's presence there for her. She seemed to handle his passing with her usual stiff upper lip, and she didn't cry as people sat silent around the fire, waiting for the funeral hearse to arrive, a semicircle of mourners, as many as could fit inside the kitchen. There we stood, family, friends, and the close-knit members of his prize-winning band, all in somber black, staring fixedly at the glowing coals as if he might come sliding back by way of the chimney, like Saint Nicholas. Mother had come to sit beside me, close to the fire, and I felt a strange stirring inside as she reached out her hand and clasped it over mine. It was stone cold! And it was shaking. She leaned a little closer to my ear and whispered, "I can't go, Love. I just can't go! Don't let them persuade me. I'll just stay here, by myself, at the fire."

I whispered back, "Don't be silly! I'll be here with you."

No one questioned, no one stared back as they went, one by one through the doorway, to climb inside those big, black limousines. They simply understood. In spite of the circumstances, I felt a comfortable satisfaction as we sat there, hand in hand, Mother and I, moving only to stoke the fire. My mother needed me, and everybody else could leave her here with me while they went about doing the expected thing and went through the rituals of burying a body. My father would understand our choosing to remain there at home. In fact I felt his presence there with us, nodding his head in approval.

It was he who had taught me to love literature and music and art, and in his honor I knew I simply must find room among my other treasures to pack the leather-bound edition of Lamb's *Tales from Shakespeare*, the class prize I had won in 1932 for being the head girl at Evelyn Street Girls' School, though I was only twelve at the time and a full two years younger than my classmates. Oh, and the two volumes of *Wayside and Woodland Blossoms* by Edward Step, the prize my sister Eva had won when I let her take my collection of wildflowers to show to her class.

And I couldn't forget to pack the tablecloth I had sewed from yards of Irish linen, soon after my wedding—the four pieces of linen I'd feather-stitched together to make a square, the edges of which I'd hemstitched in drawn threadwork. As the day approached when I would leave the country, family members and friends who I might never see again had taken time to write their names on the cloth, in pencil, ready for me to embroider with multi-colored silk thread, knowing however far away I might be, their names would bring them back to me.

Sunday, January 30, 1945. Suitcases bulging, the long pheasant feather on my hat pointing the way to no man's land, my unwilling feet snug in the serviceable old brogues—stout, coarse shoes, Mother's choice—I shuffled my way along the Liverpool sidewalks alone, as instructed, and felt like a displaced person about to be cast out of her country. Then suddenly, there was Lime Street, where the railway station was located, and I knew where I belonged immediately—with the group of women standing with a suitcase (undoubtedly marked V-2) in each hand, all lined up for loading into a military lorry bound for the port where our ship lay waiting. The ocean liner *Mauretania* was the only ship berthed at the dock where we were unloaded from the lorry. Seeing her brought to mind other ships from the Cunard Line of beautiful pleasure cruisers, vessels whose pictures I had picked up here and there to satisfy my curiosity about the way Father had described our long-anticipated passage to America, the elegant staterooms we would find aboard, the food, the games, the entertainment, and other pleasantries we might look forward to. Before that January day, the only ship I had ever boarded had taken me to the Isle of Man, home of the tailless Manx cats. I was only eight years old when Granny Knight took me with her on her annual holiday to the island, and why those cats should be famous for *not* having something was beyond my comprehension.

Not until I saw the white cross that was painted on the *Mauretania's* side, did I begin to suspect that crossing the Atlantic aboard a hospital ship would be no holiday trip to the Isle of Man. Surely the enemy couldn't muster sufficient meanness to torpedo a ship on such a mission.

There was no piping ceremony for our ungainly group and no captain to welcome us aboard and show us to our quarters. I dejectedly found my own way to one of the staterooms that had been retrofitted to receive the war brides, rooms with four double-decker bunks lined up on two of the four walls, and wooden benches lining the other two.

As soon as I marked my territory by stashing my V-2s on the top bunk of the bed farthest from the doorway, I retraced my steps to the ship's rail, looking down at the docks where curious onlookers stood, waving goodbye to yet another ship leaving a dock for parts unknown. A wave of the hand without an audible word of farewell must be something of a letdown, but it was impossible to hear what those below were shouting over the surrounding noise, so I just stood there till the sun went down. No lights were lit, and the blackout swallowed up the crowd below, along with land and sea, all in one big gulp.

That night, I tossed and turned on the narrow bunk, my mind meandering around the turn my life was taking, a turn that seemed not of my own choosing. Now that I was no longer "Our I," I found myself fretting that I might never again find the comfort I'd known in that old rocking chair by the hearth in our cottage. Had the throes of war and the surreal existence of the past six years befuddled my mind and played havoc with my heart? Had I been swept off my feet by a Prince Charming on a white horse, only to find myself spinning around, alone, on a carousel hobbyhorse with no sign of a brass ring?

Had I made a choice without considering the consequences?

Looking back, I wish I'd had the company of my unborn son in those days of empty arms. He became my source of inspiration almost from the moment of his arrival. When he was old enough to talk back and was entering adulthood as a psychologist, I asked him how I could make the right choice between a couple of alternatives that were bothering me. He gave me one of those looks that sons reserve for their mothers when they ask a stupid question, and he said, "Mother! No one has ever made a right choice. You simply make a choice, and then you make it right!" I was grateful for his wisdom.

He told me of the psychiatrist Victor Frankl, who had survived the Nazi death camps around the same time the *Mauretania* was carrying me across the Atlantic to America, "the land of the free." Even when all of Frankl's possessions were taken from him, including his grandfather's watch that he so treasured, he later wrote in *Man's Search for Meaning,* "The last of the human freedoms is the ability to choose your attitude in any set of circumstances." Jean-Paul Sartre, the French author and philosopher, tells us, "We create ourselves by virtue of the many choices we make." Down through the years, the words of these three wise men—Frankl, Sartre, and my oldest son, Haydn—have led me through the joys and sorrows that have made me the person I have become.

But I was not yet that person back in January of 1945, as I dozed on the ship's narrow bunk and tried to picture my husband as I'd left him back in our spare room. He was merely a blur in my mind's eye at first, but then the blur came into focus—a mass of hair, the color of chestnuts, giving a glow to his pale complexion. Clean-cut features indicating a sincere and trustworthy character, "upright" as Mother would have put it. His eyes were hazel, like my own. And this attractive, upright young man was, according to my father, destined to turn everyone I loved away from me. After Father's death I'd resolved not to think any longer about his somber prediction, for in that war that seemed likely to go on forever, there was just today and the need to live today as fully as possible because nobody, not even my wise and loving father, could possibly have known, back in 1943, what tomorrow and tomorrow and tomorrow would bring. But now, on the brink of my departure from my war-torn native land, Father's solemn prediction concerning my American beau came rushing back to me.

I awoke with a queasy feeling and rose with trepidation, shoving my arm into my old camel's hair coat and climbing the stairs to the upper decks. The weather, I saw as I walked off the stairway and onto the top deck, was a pea-souper, with fog as dense as the blackout erasing the last image of my homeland. I ventured a step or two toward where I thought the ship's rail might be, hoping I could shake off the feeling that had come over me, when a hand touched my shoulder.

"Where on earth do you think you are going at this time in the morning, young lady?" I could make out a steward's cap as the hand tucked itself under my elbow, guiding me back to the stairs, I supposed, and he went on to say, "You'd better go back to your cabin and get ready for breakfast."

"I just wanted to find out how far we had sailed in the night," I stammered.

"Well, I can tell you it wasn't very far," he said, with the hint of a laugh in his voice. "All we were able to do was just sit here, right where we were last night, and roll with the tide. I'm afraid we're stuck here till Doomsday if this fog doesn't clear up soon. This is the largest ship that the tugs can maneuver out of the harbor, and they would never dare try it in weather like this."

We were fog-bound for a couple more days, which seemed like many more. I was a stranger, already adrift in no man's land though still only a few miles from my hometown, for no one back home realized we were still in port. In fact, most didn't know I was even missing, since I'd been sworn to secrecy under strict military orders that forbade any communication with the outside world. Soon enough we would be sailing across the stormy Atlantic, where we'd be chased by submarines and obliged to conduct lifeboat drills every day.

While I maintained a cordial relationship with the fifteen other women who shared my "stateroom," I didn't particularly enjoy sitting on those hard benches and swapping stories relating to our marriages, especially since several of the girls always managed to move quickly into the realm of sex. Thus I chose to pass the time away by spending most of my hours in the makeshift hospital rooms with the battle-scarred men who were on their way home. They would tease me, as they taught me to play pinochle and cribbage, swearing that Montaaana was the baaaack country and all I would see would be sheep and snow and cowboys chasing Indians. Even with all their teasing, I gathered that the streets in America really were paved with gold, so long as you learned how to turn a penny into a dollar bill, and that there really could be a chicken in every pot and two cars in every garage, as long as you learned how to pluck the chicken and grease the cars.

And I also learned that they all had the same uncle, a stern but genial fellow named Sam. A few tears were shed amongst us as they brought out pictures of their loved ones, wives and families, some of them showing snapshots of a child born after they'd marched off to war and so had not yet seen. My heart bled for them, even as I tried to stifle my own nostalgia for a home and family I sensed I might never see again.

When an enemy sub dared to give chase despite the white cross so plainly marked on our side, the importance of those bothersome daily lifeboat drills became very clear to us. Whether the enemy had chosen to be merciful, or whether our captain was simply an artful dodger was never quite clear, but we were glad enough to escape with our lives.

There was a gift shop aboard which featured luxuries we hadn't seen for years, and one or two of the brides went wild with their emigration allowance, buying Max Factor and Coty and things beyond the bare necessities that had been our lot since 1939. I was very tempted to buy this and that right along with them, but was sensible enough to realize the cash in my pocket still had to take me across a continent. I suppose I was a soft touch though, because I did part with some of my precious money when a bride headed for Wisconsin confided she'd been a little reckless buying gifts for her new relatives and had nothing left to help her reach her destination.

My own biggest temptations came in the dining room, where I failed miserably at trying to resist anything that might cause me to put on weight—and this despite the annoying nausea that plagued me each morning, nausea I blamed on the rolling sea, since no other reason crossed my mind. One unfortunate girl had become violently seasick before we ever set sail, and her condition kept her bunk-bound, existing on crackers and water and a few bites of whatever we brought her from the captain's table. I considered myself lucky to have had only a tinge of *mal de mer.*

More than once I found myself standing at the ship's rail, looking out over that great expanse of water, my thoughts in limbo. I wanted to go back to what was old and comfortable, afraid as I was to go on to what was new and strange. But ultimately I went below and asked the pilots in their hospital beds to tell me all about their homeland, the country for which they had risked their lives and to which they were now returning, the burnt-flesh smell of war still hovering around them. They talked about their big cities and their little towns, their families, their relationships, and more than anything else, they spoke of all the freedoms they enjoyed in America, compared to the freedoms longed for by other peoples they had met up with around the war-torn world.

To a man they said, "Gee, it's good to be going home," and their actions as we sailed into New York harbor on February 4, 1945, a date I have quietly celebrated to myself for over sixty years now, made me believe them with all my heart. At the sight of the familiar skyline, those who could hobble around began throwing crutches in the air. Others were wheeling their chairs around in crazy circles and heading for the ship's rail. They hugged one another, and some of them cried.

I had rolled with the waves through nights of agonizing doubt as the ship's bow cut through the monstrous waves of the icy Atlantic waters, taking me ever farther away from a loving family, security, and the comfort that goes along with belonging where you are rooted. In time, the pain of separation will fade, I told myself throughout that long journey. But in the end it was the exuberance of my fellow travelers, and their obvious faith in their country, that gave me new hope that the life I'd chosen would be a good one after all.

That feeling was amplified a hundredfold when I saw their Statue of Liberty, the symbol of the freedoms they treasured, the lady with the torch whose spirit had inspired the sacrifices they'd made to preserve those freedoms. "Give me your tired, your poor, your hungry masses, yearning to breathe free. The wretched refuse of your teeming shore. Send these, the homeless, tempest-tost, to me: I lift my lamp beside the golden door," the Lady promises, "and I will make them free." And with that bedraggled mass of patriots returning home on the *Mauretania,* I too cried partly out of longing for my beloved father who was not there to share that long-awaited moment with me.

The ultimate joy anticipated by those servicemen—reunion with their families—was delayed a little longer as we were herded onto Ellis Island, the interrogation point for entry into the U.S.A. The original name given to the island by the local Indian tribe was Kioshk, or Gull Island; later, when Dutch settlers discovered oyster beds there, they called it Little Oyster Bay. In the 1790s, when executions were carried out there by means of hanging criminals from a gibbet, or a gallows tree, the place was dubbed Gibbet Island. Only after Samuel Ellis claimed it during the American Revolution did it become Ellis Island.

I've since learned that over the past few decades, Ellis Island has become a mecca for tourists, housing a modern museum of the island's immigration history, including ships' lists of people who traveled to this country in earlier times. Tours of the island are offered, along with exhibits of clothing and luggage worn and carried by those coming to this country, fascinating material for those who are eager to walk where their forebears walked and learn of their family's heritage. I was one of twelve million immigrants coming into America in the early 1940s, so my name and entry date must be recorded there for posterity. After all, America did let me in, and onto, the sidewalks of New York, a free spirit in search of wings.

At the time of my arrival there, Ellis Island was little more to me than a huge, old building, filled with noises and echoes, crowded with people, a way station where I was obliged to sit on a bench, frozen between time and space. There were piles of paperwork and questions to be answered. We were held there for quite a long time until, in that same state of limbo, I vaguely remember being shuffled aboard the ship once more, where the servicemen lined up on one side of the top deck, the immigrants on the other. I stood at the ship's rail, watching the roll of the waves until we glided slowly into port. The pier was alive with eager people, mostly women with anxious faces, their eyes lit up with expectation, heads swiveling from side to side, searching intently—for nothing but death was positive in 1945—through the mass of uniformed men, whose hopes for going home were about to be realized.

Suddenly the gangplank assigned to war brides slung down to meet an empty quayside, soon to be crowded with V-2s and their owners, exhausted women with vacant looks on their faces. All I could think at that memorable moment in my life, sitting on a suitcase marked V-2 that had already accompanied me over 3,000 miles away from home and into the vast unknown, was, "Now, what do I do?"

I glanced over at the other gangway, where men in uniform were jostling one another for room to run, hop, wheel, or jump into the waving, outstretched arms of their loved ones. Cheering, laughing couples kissed and kissed again; elderly men and women reached for their returning sons and daughters; large families bunched around one of their own; and I wondered if a long and lanky young man to my right, the one hugging a toddler so tightly in his arms it seemed as if he would never let go, might be one of the many returning heroes who were swept up in the joy of holding a son or daughter for the very first time. Lost and uncertain of my own course of action, I was tempted to walk over and approach one of those many rejoicing people to ask, Where should I go? Tell me. Point out my way. Anywhere!

I fought back the urge to intrude, reluctant to interrupt their joy with such a self-centered, down-to-earth question, and instead followed one of the English girls who looked as though she knew where she was going. It was to Customs, where out in the open air, loads of luggage had been tossed on the ground and suitcases were lying open as uniformed officials checked their contents for contraband. I followed her to the end of the queue of frustrated travelers, and waited impatiently for my turn to declare whether or not I had hidden anything away. Finally my own V-2s were thrown open and carelessly ransacked by one of the men while I stood there, still in a stupor, a wad of traveler's checks for a train ticket clutched in my hand, knowing only that I was standing on streets of gold with not much of it in my pockets, wondering what on earth I would do next.

And then I saw one smiling face. I'll remember it forever. The man came over to the baggage area and pointed to my luggage. "Do you need some assistance?" he asked, and my "Oh, thank you! YES!" must have seemed out of all proportion to that simple question. As I accepted the card he offered me, I let out another sigh of relief, for he was a Red Cross representative. He took me under his wing and escorted me back to his headquarters, where I sat for several hours while he tried to book a train reservation to Montana. Though he soon discovered there were no reservations readily available, he explained that the ticket office had promised seating for me the following day.

Quickly assessing my look of dismay, he asked whether I had money enough to stay overnight, and when I shook my head, he phoned in a lodging reservation anyway, at some hotel, the name long since forgotten, the cost to be taken care of by the Red Cross.

Before phoning for a taxi to take me to the hotel, he signed a document to prove to the station's ticket master that I had a guaranteed reservation made through the Red Cross. With this document, he said, I could be sure they would honor the confirmed reservation and allow me to purchase a ticket.

Today I would be delighted by the chance for a one-day visit to the Big Apple, seeing the sights, the shops, the shows. But there, on the sidewalks of New York almost sixty years ago, home was still the England I had forsaken, and my dreams of a home in faraway Montana, the Land of Shining Mountains dreamed of by my father, were still a long way from being realized. New York City was a strange and somewhat terrifying new world to me. Hailing a taxi with the grace and aplomb of film star Paulette Goddard would have been difficult enough, even in the best of times and in a familiar city. Only a fool or a foreigner would try to hail a cab on the wrong side of Madison Avenue! I wasn't born a fool, but neither was I born and raised in America, so I certainly felt like a fool when I realized that the right side of the road to travel on in America is the right side of the road, not the left. It's a wonder I hadn't been killed by my innocent mistake!

Though my husband had always been noticeably tight-lipped concerning his siblings and the rest of his family, just prior to my departure from England he had mentioned that his older brother, Ted—who was also an enlisted man—was stationed in New York City and living at the YMCA. On the chance that he was still there, I decided to call the YMCA number, eager to talk to someone who at least knew my name. It took much longer than I'd expected to search through the thick telephone book for a number—several numbers, as it turned out, since I quickly learned that there was not one but several YMCAs in New York. I persevered and finally located Ted at one of them, but only after I'd finally realized that "Ted" was short for Theodore! He came to my hotel right away, and we had dinner there together. It was a pleasant, but hurried, meeting, since his time was as limited as mine, but I was sufficiently impressed by him to be truly sorry I couldn't accept his invitation to stay long enough for him to show me the town.

Six decades is a long way back to remember incidents surrounding the purchase of that railway ticket, and I've long since forgotten what it cost me. I do remember finding a bank with a sidewalk window open for business even on a Sunday, and I quickly cashed in my American travelers checks in the amount of 100 pounds sterling, the total sum a military wife was allowed to take outside of England during the war.

At that stage of my journey I was weary, homesick, and ready to burst into tears at the very thought of making a mistake in my travels and becoming truly lost in my brave new world. I became angry at myself for my inadequacy, and for not insisting my husband provide me with a better idea of what to expect in America—his homeland—instead of letting him brush me off with, "Oh, travel in America is easy!" I was angrier still that I had not pressed for more details about his home and family, for I was becoming more and more anxious and jittery at the idea of living with his aunt and uncle, rather than his immediate family. Why weren't his mother and father eager to welcome their new daughter-in-law? And why hadn't someone, anyone, from his family been willing to take the train across country to meet me there in New York? Fears of traveling alone for yet another 3,000 miles, to God-only-knew where, were eating away at my dogged determination to prove to myself that I could make this trip on my own.

Chapter 5

No matter how many miles a man may travel,
he will never get ahead of himself.
—GEORGE ADE

*G*rand Central Station was all hustle and bustle, seemingly in a state of confusion, with conductors' whistles tooting for passengers to board their trains, people running to catch the ones meant for them, and the Red Caps grabbing up your suitcases and asking where you wanted them to go when you were still wondering exactly what it might cost. With eyebrows raised in a questioning look, one of them picked up my bags. I gave him a five-dollar bill and pointed to a ticket counter on the far side of the station floor, keeping an eagle eye on the V-2s as I followed after.

Without looking up from his record-keeping so that I could have read his lips—my hearing loss had been triggered by infections that began in the wake of that long-forgotten day in my secret garden—the ticket master mumbled something I presumed was, "Where to?"

"Missoula . . . Montaaana, please."

Putting down his pen, and glancing up at me with a quizzical look on his face, he repeated the question with emphasis, "Where?" On the third try he finally got it and before I could recover my composure, he was asking,

"Round trip?" Intent on saving myself further embarrassment over my accent, my head was nodding yes to the question before he had gotten the words out of his mouth. Had I stopped to think for a second, I would have known he meant "return ticket" and in plain English my answer would have been, "Single, please."

That hasty nod of the head was an expensive one for me, and I kept the return portion of the round-trip ticket to Montana as a memento of my initiation to the easy but costly way to travel in America—though it has since been lost in the shuffle of moving possessions from home to home over the years. Added to the expense of that unneeded return ticket was the five dollars I had foolishly tipped the Red Cap, a lot of money in those days, considering that I could have purchased ten gallons of milk for that amount. Then, too, there had been no time for me to weigh the value received for American goods and services against the value of similar items I was accustomed to getting with the British pound sterling.

"Coach Class" was marked on my ticket as the means of travel for the first leg of my journey, the trip to Chicago. Upon my arrival there, I would change to a Pullman train bound for the far West. When I boarded the train in New York City, I found American "Coach" to be on a par with "Third-Class" travel in England, but with more legroom and walking space. British train cars in that era were designed with a line of single, enclosed compartments running down one side of the car, with each compartment featuring two benches that faced each other. An outside door positioned between the two facing benches in each compartment led to the station platform, while a door on the opposite side opened out into a corridor that extended the full length of the car. During the war, especially, I hated having to travel third-class, for overcrowded trains meant people were jammed into the benches in those compartments, elbows poking your ribs and eyes measuring you up and down across the couple of feet that separated their seat from yours. The reticence of the English to chat with strangers added to the discomfort, and if you attempted to open up a book or the daily news to cover up your embarrassment, your own elbows would, of necessity, be glued to your sides.

The coach on the American train I boarded was fitted with two rows of double-occupancy, straight-backed seats that ran the length of the car and were separated by a central corridor. I was glad to see that there were windows along both sides of the car and plenty of space between the rows to get up and move around. At first glance, all the seats seemed to be occupied, but I managed to get situated in an empty one by a window, which I peered through with great expectations.

Unfortunately, the scenery along that first leg of my trip presented a rather dismal picture of America the beautiful, for the train whistled its way along the wrong side of the tracks, as it were, skirting the more scenic routes that a car might travel. Waking up from a nap, I happened to glance out the window as we were pulling out of a station someplace on the edge of the Midwest, and saw a large red structure with a snow-covered roof. As the train switched its way through a maze of interlocking tracks, I strained to see whether there might be people living in any of the buildings, but decided they must have been barns for the horses and cattle roaming around. Then I caught sight of a smaller, whitewashed structure with a fenced-in yard. Smoke curled up through the chimney, and I guessed that this must be the farmhouse where the owners of the animals lived. The house looked well settled in, and I caught a flash of bright yellow curtains as I twisted around in my seat for a final glimpse. Only happy housewives put up bright yellow curtains. Would that be the kind of cozy home waiting to welcome me?

My reverie was interrupted when a woman behind me touched my shoulder and asked in a distinctly non-British accent, "Would you like a banana? It will be a while till we get off at Chicago."

After six long years without my favorite fruit, would I ever like a banana! I thanked her profusely, apparently surprising her, for she said, "Why, you're more than welcome."

Peeling back that yellow skin made me smile, for how many times had I joined my sisters and friends in a rousing course of

Yes! We have no bananas!
We have no bananas today!

That old vaudeville song had taken on new meaning for those of us who'd been without that delicious fruit for so long, but there was hardly any way to have explained my feelings to the woman whose generous gift had ended my long period of deprivation.

Still savoring the taste of banana, I closed my eyes and dozed until the train was toot-tooting into another big city and the conductor called, "Chicago, Gateway to the West."

At first glance Chicago's Central Station looked big enough to hold all of England and its population. It was probably 400 feet long and 100 feet high from floor to ceiling. It was not only cavernous, but dimly lit, with windows too dirty for any light to come through. It was also noisy, and like all railway stops in those days without air-conditioning, the air was thick, smoke-laden, and smelly. We arrived there at mid-morning, and I learned to my dismay that it would be late evening before I could board the Pullman train heading west. Though I'd been told in New York that I simply must visit the Shedd Aquarium during my layover in Chicago, I had already decided I couldn't afford to venture outside, since I was still hanging on to my cash for the rest of that never-ending trek.

The waiting area in one large portion of the station contained a solid block of not-too-comfy, polished oak benches bolted to the cold, cement floor. I sat down on the end of one of them, V-2s at my feet, longing to see a familiar face and hoping that the markings on my suitcases would arouse the curiosity of a passing stranger with whom I could strike up a conversation. But no one stopped to ask what V-2 stood for. Even so, I sat there with my answer at the ready, eager to be recognized as a living, breathing human being rather than just another piece of baggage. Oh, I'm not quite sure, my mind was rehearsing, but it probably stands for Voyage Number Two! That cryptic reply would make them sufficiently curious to keep them talking, wouldn't it? I continued to visualize the scope and extent of my conjured-up encounter. Who knows, I reasoned, maybe I will make a lifelong friend!

Then I suddenly remembered passing a section of the station that had been cordoned off from the rest and marked SERVICEMEN'S LOUNGE. Though the lounge hadn't been occupied when I passed by, remembering that sign sent thoughts other than my own self-serving imaginings to come tumbling down. Servicemen! Military maneuvers! Security! Secrecy! Mum's the word! Would not my new homeland be engulfed in security measures similar to those implied by the V-2 code on my suitcases? Would I, by reason of leaking information about my own voyage, be endangering the lives of servicemen like those brave men on board the *Mauretania?* How foolish of me to even think of making small talk about my suitcases when I knew so well that "loose lips sink ships."

I sat in silence, watching the faces passing by, intent upon getting somewhere, and eventually melding with the throng of travelers coming and going. You could spot the people who'd debarked from trains from their expectant looks and their eagerness to embrace those awaiting them. The faces of those waiting to depart reflected my own anxiety and impatience to be moving on.

I could also easily pick out the railroad employees. The ones that I counted were all wearing black bowler hats, hats with a high crown and a straight narrow brim running horizontally to meet the crown at its lower end. A bowler hat sat on the head somewhat like a teapot without a handle. All the men were mustachioed, and all were wearing some shape of black trousers, sleeveless black vests, and sturdy-looking shoes. Stiffly starched collars hugged their necks, with a narrow black bow tied at the front of each shirt, giving the men the aura of diplomatic dignitaries. Even though I guessed some of them were foremen, some managers or clerks, and some assigned to the dirty work of running a depot, it was impossible to guess who was who. They all wore white shirts!

My father had dressed in a clean white shirt every day of the working week for his roll-turner job at the wire factory. On weekends he would wear something sloppy, like an old shaggy sweater or his Harris tweed jacket with leather patches protecting the elbows, but every work day called for a white shirt. Consequently, you could find Mother every Monday washday, rain or shine, sleeves upturned, her strong arms plying the old worn dolly-peg in the tub of hot, soapy water. She had elbow grease enough to make her whites turn out pure as the driven snow and prepared for the long ironing process she undertook every Tuesday.

Today, I own a couple of steam irons and other electrical gadgets to get the creases out of my laundry, though thanks to modern fabric blends, I rarely find any creases, even though my clothes are shoved, unfolded, into storage drawers. Mother, for most of her married life, never catered to all that newfangled rubbish, so the creases in Father's white shirts were ironed out with an old-fashioned flat-iron, which she heated on a grid over the burning coals in the kitchen grate. For a long time she had spurned Grandmother Knight's offer to buy her a gas iron that could be plugged into the gas jet in the ceiling, saying, "Gas costs money, and we use too much of it as it is. We can't afford to use up any more." With a thick kitchen towel wrapped around one hand for protection—and a quick sniff of disdain sent in Granny's direction to tell her she could manage very well, thank you—she would pick up the hot, heavy iron by its handle and test its readiness by sprinkling water onto its flat side from an old glass condiment bottle with a perforated stopper. If the water bottle wasn't handy, she would improvise with a bit of spit. If the water drop sizzled, the iron was ready. With a satisfied smile, as if saying to herself, *Well, then, let's get on with it, Emily,* she would set the hot iron on a trivet, pick up a shirt from the pile of laundry, and set out to prove her capabilities. Granny Knight would just sit there by the fire in Father's chair, forever rocking and twiddling her thumbs.

Ever aware of her duty to teach her daughters the skills they would need once they had homes of their own, Mother rolled up her sleeves and called me into the room, along with Our Eve. "It's about time I taught you two the correct way to iron a shirt." So saying, she first made sure there was no rust on the flat of the iron, then set it on the grate to heat, tested it with that telltale drop of water, and set it on the trivet. She then held up one of Father's shirts, gave it a light sprinkle from the vinegar bottle, and advised us to "tackle the toughest pieces first and the rest will come easy."

Her directions were clear and concise as she smoothed the garment onto the felt pad that protected the surface of the kitchen table—the only ironing board I ever remember her using. First, you must do one sleeve at a time, starting at the cuff, which you will press on both sides. I watched with careful attention, knowing my turn would come one day and there would be no room for error. Keep the iron moving now, so you don't singe your father's shirt. And I watched as the iron flew back and forth over that bright, white surface. Then go on to iron the front and back of each sleeve.

Quickly, smoothly, the flat iron sailed along each sleeve in turn. Then you do the same with the collar. When both arms and collar were wrinkle free, she picked up the shirt, flapped it down again and smoothed it into shape, front panels meeting together where they should, arms outstretched horizontally. All it needed to resemble a scarecrow was a straw hat. Though there were pauses in the action while the iron was reheated, Mother's careful instructions continued on apace. When the demonstration of a perfectly ironed shirt was concluded to Mother's satisfaction, she held the shirt up for us to admire.

Even after that lesson in ironing, Mother continued to attend to this chore herself, and I was perfectly content to let her do so, staying clear of the house on Tuesdays lest I be called in to take my turn at the task. But my freedom from ironing suddenly came to an end, all because Miss Snoddy—the home improvement teacher at Evelyn Street Girls' School— had given me one of her pretty necklaces as a prize for showing the class the right way to iron a man's shirt. After earning that honor, I found myself in sole charge of the ironing every Tuesday afternoon, with the exception of Pancake Tuesday—the day before Ash Wednesday, when ironing was left behind and the ladies would run races, flipping pancakes.

For years my mother had steadfastly refused Granny Knight's offer to buy her a gas iron, but she finally relented and accepted that gift—on my behalf, of course. The gas iron came with a thin tube that plugged into the gas jet in the ceiling, a jet I could barely reach by kneeling on the parlor table, where Mother had decided the ironing could now be done, since there was no longer a need to stand close to the kitchen fireplace and since she could reclaim her kitchen table for her own use.

While Granny Knight's gift was well-intentioned, I hated that new iron because heating by gas was much more efficient than heating the flat iron on the kitchen grate. The result was that the iron reached the scorching point very quickly, meaning I had to constantly test the temperature and adjust the gas so that the clothes wouldn't burn from too much heat. As I sprinkled the clothes with water from the vinegar bottle, I would let a drop or two drizzle onto the flat of the iron to test how quickly the water would sizzle. If the iron was too hot or too cold, I had to climb up on the tabletop, reach up high, and adjust the jet.

All went well with the new system until the day Our Little Dot came in, unknown to Mother, to help me. I was atop the table, on my knees, and didn't see or hear her as I reached up to adjust the force of the gas. The next thing I knew, I was on the floor, with Mother bending over me and scolding, "Why didn't you take Doris out of here?" In the same breath she was saying sweet and soothing things to me, while stroking my hair and trying to stop my screaming.

Once I calmed down, Mother explained what had happened. As I knelt on the table, Doris—who was barely tall enough to reach the tabletop—had picked up the iron, found it too hot for comfort, and set it back down . . . on the back of my calf. I tried to look at the burn but couldn't turn my leg around far enough to see the back side. Mother described it for me: The pointed half of the iron had left an image of brown scorched into my skin. She applied what we called the bluing bag, the bag she used to whiten the clothes, to my wound, saying, "There, there. This will make it all better."

I have no idea what the bag contained that would "make it all better." I only know that it didn't. I suppose the bag might have contained some liquid or powder akin to modern-day bleaches like Purex and Clorox, and my mother hoped it would have some miracle cleaning or medicinal value, since it took out stains from the clothing. Hers was a do-it-yourself medical practice, for the magic word doctor was hardly, if ever, used in our house. Though I survived the day and many more after, proudly showing off my trademark as an ironer, Mother insisted on tackling the ironing herself again until I was "old enough to know better."

My reverie was interrupted by a train whistle, shrieking a warning into my one good ear. A glance at the station clock assured me I still had an hour or so to wait. The hands of the clock overlapped at twelve. It was lunchtime, though I had no money for food. I stood up and stretched, consoling myself with the thought that I might at least have a nice hot cup of tea to calm me down, as mother would say. So, stashing the V-2s underneath the bench where I had been sitting, I started in the direction of the shops that lined the far wall of the station, away from the benches and their occupants, most of them apparently travelers like myself.

There were a few who looked as if they didn't belong in the waiting room, men with unshaven faces and a hopeless look in their eyes, which hinted that they were there because they had no other place to go. Deciding I'd just have to trust that these bedraggled human beings were not hungry enough to steal a person's luggage while I went in search of a cup of tea. Yet I had walked only a few steps when I turned around and walked back to slide the V-2s out from under the bench. Taking one in each hand, I somehow found enough strength to carry them the length of the waiting area, for I had been a fool to leave them behind at the risk of losing everything I had in the world.

It wasn't exactly what you would call an English teashop, I thought, as

I placed the V-2 bags close to an empty stool at the counter, but I hoisted myself up on the stool, propped my elbows on the countertop alongside the row of elbows already there, and asked for "a cuppa tay." The waitress set a cup and saucer on the counter and handed me something that looked like a sachet bag hanging on a string. I looked around to see if anyone else had one of those things and the waitress said, "Is something wrong?"

"You must be mistaken, Miss! I asked for a cuppa tay!" It was one of those Lancashire colloquialisms that hang on with your heritage. It becomes a part of you, and in spite of Father's insistence on proper English, a cup of tea is not a cup of tea until it's a cuppa tay. The phrase has a cup-of-love connotation. It's a kind of get-together phrase, one brimming with invitation and expectation of warm, friendly relations. The phrase is intrinsic to the English language and used so often that I wouldn't be surprised if it were at home in Buckingham Palace. The waitress filled my cup with steaming water, pointed to the bag, and whispered, "It will be tay if you dip that there bag into this 'ere cupper."

My research today tells me that hand-sewn tea bags made from silk muslin were patented as early as 1903 and first introduced commercially in 1904 by Thomas Sullivan, an American merchant who shipped them worldwide. But if tea-in-a-bag was ever served in England prior to my departure, I neither saw nor heard of its existence. If Mother ever used tea bags, she must have stashed them in the tea caddy on the top shelf or out of sight in the bottom of the old brown teapot sitting on the hob by the fire. But I don't really think she would ever have stooped to making tea with a bag. The English are proud of their teatime customs, and of the time and effort involved in the ritual of brewing a real nice, hot cuppa tay. It is an art unto itself.

The tea I was drinking in the Chicago station left me inconsolable. It didn't warm the body up one bit, but did give me a little comfort thinking of Mother. Whenever I would come down with a cold or a fever, she would say, "Lie yourself down now, and I'll make you a nice hot cuppa tay and a basin o' pobs." She would fill the old black kettle with cold water and set it to boil on the hob. On the other side of the grate was the black cast iron oven with the shiny steel trim, built close enough to the fire to cook the basin of pobs—the poor man's bread pudding—that Mother would slide into it soon as the kettle began to sing. From the moment she began those loving tasks, I began feeling better. Though simple in composition, my mother's pobs were a basin of ambrosia, created from a half loaf of dried bread that had been softened with hot water and canned condensed milk, then sweetened with sugar, enriched with a few currants or golden raisins, and topped off with a sprinkle of nutmeg. Angel food to a ten-year-old!

By the time the pobs were sizzling and the water in the kettle had come to a full boil, the brown earthenware teapot had been rinsed with a little boiling water from the kettle to acclimatize it, so to speak, and then put into the pot one shake of tea per person, with an extra shake from the tin "for the pot."

"No need for measuring," she would say. After the boiling water was added to the teapot, the lid plonked on, and the pot set on a trivet to brew for a few moments, the pot would then be carried to the table, where it would sit under one of her beautiful hand-crocheted tea cozies. When our cups were poured, we sipped to find that she had managed yet another perfect pot of tea—all without measuring.

The secret to her perfection lay, in large part, in the fact that only the best type of tea was spooned from Mother's black, lacquered square tin that Grandfather Knight had brought from some place around the world. And the very best brand of tea, Mother said, was the one you would see advertised on billboards up and down the country, showing a little old lady in her rocking chair sipping a cup of Mazawattee Tea. Whenever I passed by one of those huge pictures, I would nudge my school chum and whisper that Grandfather Hope had painted that little old lady, for, you see, both my grandfathers were intricately tied to my appreciation of a good cuppa tay.

While the tea poster was my personal favorite, Father preferred the painting Grandfather Hope had done of the muscle man flexing his arm and holding a glass of beer under the caption "Guinness is good for you." The excuse he made for drinking Guinness was that it contained a lot of iron, which the body used up daily.

By the time we were lifting our teacups, the pobs would be coming out of the oven, lightly browned on top and gently bubbling underneath. An added touch of heaven would come at the end of this comfort food ritual, with Mother holding my hand as she read the tea leaves in the bottom of the cup, predicting all the good fortune that might chance my way. Swept by these memories, I was struck by the truth in that old maxim "There's no place like home." Suddenly overwhelmed with the realization that I might never see Mother again, or my sisters, I found myself wishing they were with me, swapping tales of adventures and misadventures in our young lives as I sat waiting for Godot, there on that dreary day in a Chicago railway station.

Another shrill whistle followed by a hoarse cry dragged me back to the moment. All aboard! A porter wheeled my suitcases through the gates toward the train tracks, and upon reaching the platform, lugged one of them to an upper bunk in the sleeping car to which I was assigned. Uncertain of how to handle yet another dilemma, I told him I would need both suitcases on the bed, not knowing what was in which one. My bunk could hardly be called a bed, since it looked barely long enough for me to stretch all of my five-feet-four inches down the length of it. The Mauretania sleeping accommodations had been luxurious by comparison. Privacy seemed practically nonexistent, a mere drawstring curtain blocking my quarters from prying eyes, and I presumed that men must certainly be bunked elsewhere.

I didn't care if I never went to bed once I'd seen the stepladder I would have to climb to reach my boudoir. So I spent the last two hours of daylight in the dining car, watching a confusing stream of fields, sheds, and industrial buildings slip by. I didn't know and didn't want to know the names of all the towns through which we rode, but I did want to know where the houses were hidden, the schools, the parks and fields where my children would romp and play. I wanted to know that my expectations were more than those castles in the air Mother had warned me about. Yet all I could do now was wait and wonder, wonder and wait, for three more days of staring through a window, three more nights of fretting the dark away, trying to piece together from what I had already seen of America what would be waiting for me at the end of the line.

I pulled down the shade at the dining car window when it became too dark to see anything more outside, and went hesitantly to the sleeping car, swaying with the moving train, trying to keep my balance as it sped along the tracks, worrying about falling off the bunk bed in my sleep during the night. How could anyone possibly undress and get ready for bed in a Pullman car on a top bunk shared by two suitcases marked V-2? Doing so in the more private quarters of the restroom was out of the question, since a bulky housecoat and slippers were luxuries I couldn't afford to pack at the expense of leaving behind my precious books and other treasures. I was probably too modest, considering the circumstances, but nothing would have induced me to walk down the aisle in a nightgown. I would just sleep in the dress I had on my back. It was the only one I owned, and it could jolly well stay there until I could go out and buy another. I consoled myself with the thought that all the scrimping and saving would soon be over. The war would soon be won, my husband would be sent home, and the promised days of plenty lay just around the corner. I closed the suitcase lid with a bang, and lay back with a throbbing headache, dreading the next couple of days it would take the train to get as far west as Missoula, Montana.

Lulled by the rhythmic sound of wheels on steel . . . tananda landa . . . tananda landa . . . tananda landa, my mind became prisoner to memories of those promises made in Saint Mary's Church of England in Penketh, the old stone church where centuries-old headstones stood over the graves of long-gone members, whose names were eulogized in stone. After the wedding, most of the guests had stood around those gravestones, throwing confetti and handing out good-luck horseshoes as my new husband and I headed toward the iron gates that opened wide for lucky couples entering a new life together. The curious bystanders had already left for a quick one and a game of darts at the pub across the street. A church wasn't a church in England unless there was a pub across the street to quench the thirst, in case the sermon had been too hot for the congregation to handle.

There had been no doubt in my mind that September day that our vows would hold us together through sickness and health, through thick and thin, through hell and high water. Now, alone on the train speeding toward my unknown fate, I had to fight off my tears and force myself to remember those vows I'd taken at St. Mary's. Wedding vows were sacred in England back in 1943, so different from the way vows are looked upon today, where the word "united" in a marriage ceremony could very well morph into the word "untied" shortly thereafter, making a mockery out of promises supposedly made in earnest. How on earth can we ever suppose peace treaties will hold a world together when so many individual promises of unity before God can fall so easily apart?

But I digress.

The rest of the train trip to Missoula went along as smoothly as the circumstances would allow, and I met friendly people who made me feel not quite a stranger now. The waiter in the dining car was especially friendly, as if he had himself felt the pain of loneliness in a crowded room. I had not yet realized how far the dollar bill would stretch and provide for me in relation to the value of the pound sterling. Consequently, I had merely guessed at the American's notion of relativity and had given generously. For breakfast, lunch, and dinner, I realize now I must have tipped thirty percent per meal that first day aboard, just to make sure that young man got what he had earned.

On the second day the waiter, who was tall, black, and very handsome, must have realized my dilemma and came back with a tip of his own. With a nice smile, he placed several bills in front of me on the table, leaned down, and whispered, "You don't have to tip me at all, but thank you." I was slightly embarrassed but drew a breath of relief that I most certainly now would have enough dollars left to catch a bus to Polson. I will always remember that young man. If all Americans are anything like him, I was thinking.

As noisy brakes jerked the car to a standstill, it slowly dawned on me that I was only a bus ride and a car hop away from having it all—the chickens, the pot, the cars in their garages, the plenty that would make up for all the nothing. I picked up my bags and stood in the open doorway of the car, blinded by the sun's glare. I looked beyond the platform and out into the big expanse of blue sky and was struck with the newness, the brittleness of this faraway land of the pioneers that was destined to be my home. For how long, only time and a promise would foretell.

I stepped gingerly onto the platform, dragging the suitcases along the ground after me, stooping a little in the process. I slowly reached an exit to the street, with the beleaguered brogues stepping warily after slipping on ice that lurked beneath the snow, and my bare legs flinching from their first lick of twenty-below-zero temperatures. Bare because, after all, one would not possibly wear laddered stockings in this land of plenty, would one?

Snow-covered rooftops shimmered in the glaring sunlight, the wooden structures beneath them looking as though they might cave in from the weight of it all. A flash of red lit up a sign for some kind of beer, and I wondered if people would be playing darts inside. I peered at a disheveled-looking building that reminded me of the wooden huts in England, the only homes that poor people could afford to rent, little more than four walls, with a window and a roof.

The snow against the amazing blue of this big sky country was blinking diamonds in the cold air, and I narrowed my eyes to protect them from its glare. I longed for the fog-shrouded mystery of old brick that I had loved and lived with over there, at home in the Virginia Creeper–covered cottage that had stood for centuries in my hometown—Warrington, Lancashire, England. "War-ringing-the-town" is how some say the name originated, for the place dated back to Cromwell's time and the Wars of the Roses. Here history seemed to be only a generation or so old, for everything looked newly hewn and unseasoned.

Collecting my wits, I flagged a cab—on the right side of the road this time. As I watched my cases being thrown into the boot of the taxi, I wished with all my heart that I were back home, putting their contents back where they belonged. I was far, far away from my roots and I felt like an invasive weed trying to push my way up through newly turned sod, an unwanted intruder in a well-established, if newly planted, garden, something to be plucked up and trodden underfoot. A longing for the security of the home I loved welled up inside, and a loneliness I had never known before enveloped me.

When I asked the cabbie to take me to the bus depot, he gave me a peculiar look and said we were only a block away. I had no idea how long an American block might be, but I certainly knew how cold a Montana winter's day could be, and the taxi driver gladly accepted the few dollars I offered in exchange for his cranking up the heater and driving me around the block several times until the bus arrived. The only thing I learned about my new land on that short trip was that I must call the boot of an American car the trunk, and the bonnett of that same car would become the hood.

It was a small bus belonging to the Intermountain Line. The V-2s were stashed away in the luggage compartment underneath it, and I found a seat and settled in with a sigh of relief that somebody would be waiting for me, to take me home with them. At that point I decided I could make any place my home that had a comfortable bed and a warm blanket. The bus chugged its way around the outskirts of Missoula on that cold, very cold day in February 1945. The cold seemed to be forcing its way up through cracks in the floor and paralyzing my bare legs as the bus took us past snow-covered fields near Arlee, where the driver announced we might see the buffalo roam. I looked, and didn't see them. What I did see took away from me the loneliness, the weariness threatening to overwhelm me—there, at last were the Mission Mountains, their breathless beauty consuming all the senses my weary body possessed. I watched them come and go from my seat near the back of the bus.

By this time we had crossed the border into Flathead Indian Reservation, home of the Salish-Kootenai people. When we stopped at St. Ignatius, there was not enough time to leave the bus and visit the beautiful church at the Indian mission built by the Jesuits, but I promised myself I would go back there one day. We were about to leave the reservation town, when a woman suddenly appeared at the door of the bus, stepped on board, walked to the back, and sat across the aisle from me. Noting her black braids and dark skin, I thought she must be an Indian lady, the first I had seen on this journey. I said Hello, and she said Hi and asked me where I had bagged the pheasant to get such a fine feather for my hat. Beyond that initial exchange, she wasn't very talkative, but I have long since learned that Indian people do not think conversation is always necessary. Her easy silence suited me well enough, since the tongues of the English don't wag at every chance acquaintance either, and I was glad enough to keep window peeking in silence as one tiny way-stop after another passed by.

Ronan, a town I knew to be fairly close to my destination, sported a few more conveniences than some of the smallest settlements, including a grocer's shop, a furniture outlet, and a pool hall. I don't remember passing Pablo, for it didn't even have a post office at the time, but suddenly, as the bus topped a rise in the road, a picture postcard scene of great beauty took my breath away. My husband's description of "the lake" had conjured up only a flat stretch of water large enough to entertain him for an afternoon of fishing, but there, at the bottom of the hill, was Flathead Lake, stretching itself as far as the eye could see from its southern shore to the northern horizon.

The bus crawled and creaked its way along the treacherous route, trying to hopscotch around the icy patches. But I was too busy taking in the mountain peaks at that point to care how long it took for the last mile or two of my trek. A late afternoon glow was blushing their snowy heights with the delicate pink of rainbow trout, the fish that my husband had boasted of reeling in from the waters of the lake. My mind was already imagining the lady's slipper orchids I might find hiding at the foot of those giant firs in the foothills.

As we made the turn toward Polson, the lumber mill at the west end of the town showed no sign of activity. Indeed, the tiny town itself, snuggled up on the southern shore of the lake, seemed to be asleep, though smoke from its chimneys spoke of the warmth of glowing fires inside the homes along its streets—a welcome thought for someone sitting bare-legged on a poorly heated bus as it drove through a winter scene with temperatures colder than I had ever imagined. I wondered if there would be a welcoming fire awaiting me in my new home.

Whatever awaited me at my final destination, I had fallen in love with those Mission Mountains as I rode the highway alongside them to reach this place, my new home, at last. I felt pacified by their presence, like a baby in her mother's arms, and hoped they might bring strength and consolation into my new life, no matter what evolved. And there they still were, steadfast and unmoving, protecting their territory—the sleepy hollow below—and guarding the waters of the Flathead until they too, those magnificent Missions, became lost in the wild blue yonder, as far as the eye could reach.

I came down to earth as the scene spread closer before me, the lake more visible still, with groves of trees sweeping down to the water's edge. But where was the water? There were no waves crashing the rocks, no birds swooping down to bring up a trout in its claws. All that I could take in at that moment was a great expanse of shimmering white! A poem I had learned as a child flashed instantly through my thoughts,

Ice is on the little pond,
Silent is the mill
Only robin braves the cold
All the world is still

I looked again, and just could not believe I had come to live by a lake 27 miles long and 15½ miles across, whose waters were concealed under a mass of solid ice. I was told later that only the bay area at Polson was frozen solid that winter of 1944–1945. Due to the massive volume of the lake and the winds that tend to keep its surface moving, the entire lake only rarely freezes over. Yet at least twice since my arrival in Montana—first during the winter of 1978–1979 and again in the winter of 1987–1988—the entire 191-square-mile surface of this 370-feet-deep lake became immobilized under a layer of ice that was solid enough to withstand fishermen hacking holes through which to fish. Some old-timers insist that in those winters, ice could be seen on some parts of the lake all year long.

Beauty cloaked in ice. This was no place for the faint of heart. As the bus pulled to a stop in front of the drugstore that also served as the Intermountain bus depot, I wondered what kind of home would await me along those vast Icelandic shores.

Chapter 6

The next day is never so good as the day before.

—PUBILIUS SYRUS

There was no brass band waiting to welcome me at Polson's drugstore bus station, just an old battered Ford and a man who might also have seen better days. I presumed he was Uncle Guy, whose wife, Mabel, was the sister of my mother-in-law, Helen Hedrick. I saw him point to the pheasant feather on my hat as a sign of recognition, and with a grin on his face, he walked toward me. It was an awkward moment. How does one greet a person one has never seen before?

Uncertainly, I offered my hand, and he shook it up and down. I was relieved when the moment didn't progress into a hug or a kiss, since such familiarity was never expected at first meeting in the land I had left behind. He seemed a little miffed at my indifference, but my husband had shared very little about his family, and even had he been more forthcoming, my reserved English nature would still have kept me at a distance until I came to know his uncle on my own.

"Want a float? A shake?" Guy Farnham ventured, and being reluctant to ask a foolish question so early on my arrival, I nodded my head to the shake, since that was at least something I'd heard my husband speak of, while the only "float" I had ever known was the milk float of my childhood. I can still see that horse-drawn wooden cart carrying the huge cans of milk around our neighborhood on delivery days, with Mrs. Smith—the farmer's widow—riding along and reaching out her hand as needed to keep the cans steady.

Milk turned out to be the primary ingredient in Uncle Guy's kind of shake, a thick, ice-creamy concoction with a delicious strawberry flavor. I turned up the glass and guzzled down almost half the contents, not even considering that the straws in the container on the counter were there for a purpose—to sip through, like a lady!

"Don't they feed you over there?" Guy said. And I felt not only too full but also too embarrassed by my gluttony to drink the rest of what had to have been the most satisfying sweet of my life. Had I known it was permissible to take it out of the store, I would have asked for a paper cup so that I might have finished the other half later, instead of leaving it reluctantly on the counter.

As we left the bus depot on Main Street and turned onto the highway leading to the east shore, it was almost too dark to size up the kind of houses we passed. Their outlines were huddled along the roadside, nestled between cherry trees, which Guy pointed out might not bring a good crop that year after such a harsh winter. My husband had always been evasive when asked to describe the ranch that belonged to his aunt and uncle, the ranch he and his siblings had moved to, one or two at a time, as their own home environment had become more and more intolerable. "Just look for the house on the hill, overlooking the lake," he'd said, "You'll see the rest when you get there!" Given such scanty information, my imagination could stretch only as far as a few cows and chickens and a cherry orchard—a sour cherry orchard, according to what I'd been told.

He hadn't mentioned at all the perils of winter driving, and I held my breath as the old Ford went sliding off course more than once as it hit patches of ice. Obviously used to such conditions, Uncle Guy managed to keep us on the road as we drove eastward, drawing closer and closer to the towering, snow-covered mountains. They had looked so beautiful in the sunshine, their white peaks etched against the bright blue sky. Now, in the night shadows with only a crescent moon to illuminate their splendor, they became a snapshot in black and white, formidable and unyielding, yet luring me on into their crags and crevices, as if to test the strength of my own endurance, endurance that was slowly ebbing out of my tired, aching body.

Just at the point where Highway 35 turned north and began its run along the eastern shore of the lake, Guy turned abruptly onto a road that led off to the right, a lane so steep that the headlights seemed to be tilted up at an angle as we started up the icy slope. "Hold onto your seat now," Uncle Guy warned. "We've gotta get up this danged hill one way or another." Though seat belts for buggies and wagons had been invented by Volvo way back in 1849, and patented in America in 1885, Henry Ford had obviously not seen fit to equip his automobiles with such devices. Nor was there any sort of grab bar to grasp. So I clung to the door handle, praying that the lurching of the car wouldn't cause me to push in the wrong direction, prompting the door to swing open and drag me outward with its weight.

The Ford was snorting with indignation by this time, seemingly intent on sliding back down the hill in direct defiance of the driver's attempts to make it to the top. But the driver was equally adamant and obviously well accustomed to the struggle required to keep the car moving upward and onward, even under such perilous circumstances. "I may have to back up and make a run at it," he said at one point, and I sat frozen in place, as man and machine, both tempered hard and feisty, engaged in a battle of wills. It ended with our cresting that seemingly insurmountable hill, rounding another sharp curve, and driving along fairly level ground for a few more yards before Uncle Guy braked to a stop outside what looked, in the glare of the headlights, to be a wooden gate wide enough for a truck to enter.

He fumbled around opening the gate for us to drive through, and once inside and the gate closed he drove only a few yards more before honk-ing the horn, drawing to a full stop, and turning off the ignition.

"Well, here we are," he announced.

I climbed out into the cold night air, stepping carefully along the frozen, uneven ground, and helped him lift the V-2s from the trunk. Without another word, he tucked one under each arm, and I followed him to the door. From what I could see of the rough exterior, the house on the hill seemed more like a hut than a home. There was no paint visible on the door—or on the walls in which it was set—just old wood siding as far as I could make out. This must be the back door, I reasoned, since there was no veranda or porch, just the door-stoop, a single step up from the ice and snow.

Even though they must have heard the car horn as we pulled in, no one came to the door to greet us. Guy stepped inside, slid the V-2s across the floor, and turned around to give me a hand across the threshold to meet my new family. My first thought as I stepped through the door was centered not on the people within the single room into which I peered but on the fact that there was but a single room. Where will I sleep, I thought, too weary to really care about the lack of luxury and privacy, but definitely in need of a place to lay my head and sink into slumber.

A bare, unshaded light bulb hung by a cord from the ceiling, and as I took a step further onto the wooden floor, I tensed instinctively, won-dering how those creaky planks could support the massive pot-bellied stove, and the iron sink across from it that seemed big enough to hold a week's washing. A wrinkled face towel hung limply from a metal bar fixed to the wall nearby, and I wondered as I stared at that towel—obviously used by one and all—whether the sore on Guy's face was something I might catch if I ever used that filthy piece of linen. There was just one small window above the sink, and I could imagine how dim the room would be even in daylight hours.

The only decoration giving life to the whitewashed walls was a Coca-

Cola Girl calendar, whose girl of the month seemed to be marking time until she could shed her cuddly, white ermine wrappings and swing into spring unencumbered. A pile of fagots in a cardboard box jutted out from under a piece of patchwork quilt that had been attached to the bottom edge of the sink, most likely to hide the drainpipe that would otherwise have been exposed. The stove, though massive, lacked the rosy glow of my childhood fireplace, and I wondered how many logs would have to be split and loaded into the door of its potbelly to ever warm up such a cold and dismal room.

With hindsight, there is no way to determine whether the stove's inadequacies would have loomed so large under more cheerful circumstances. Certainly the "welcome" I received from my new family did little to take the chill off my bones. There were three of them seated at a round, oilcloth-covered table that took up most of the kitchen. The gray-haired woman I thought must be Mabel, the aunt; the girl, about eighteen with beautiful chestnut hair, would be my husband's youngest sister, Thelma Hedrick. There were, however, no introductions to confirm those assumptions. The lone male I guessed would be Hank, third child and second son of my in-laws, Isaac and Helen Hedrick. I'd been told that Hank, like his two older brothers, was serving in the armed forces, and assumed that he must have been home on leave.

Uncle Guy had already shed his coat and now sat down to join them in what appeared to be a game of cards. I looked around helplessly, waiting in vain for an opening for conversation, then simply said, "Hello."

"So, you're here," Mabel said, not taking her eyes from the card she was choosing from her hand. "Sit down and we'll teach you how to play pinochle."

I clumsily jerked a chair from under the table, sat down, and put my elbows on the oilcloth top, expecting at least a question or two about my journey. Silence on that topic, though a new hand was immediately dealt, with Uncle Guy receiving his share of cards this time. Too dazed to dare to interrupt such serious playing, I used this opportunity to study the players, but there was no conversation for me to analyze, only an occasional explanation from one person or another concerning the rules of the game. I listened and nodded politely as I watched them play round after round, deliberately refusing to mention that I had already learned how to play the game—and play it well—while crossing the Atlantic. Small solace that little secret was, for no one appeared to be in the least bit interested in knowing anything at all about my long ocean voyage, my exhausting cross-country train trip, or my bus ride up from Missoula.

For the time being I allowed them the benefit of the doubt, assuming that their isolated living conditions had given them little opportunity for practice in the art of communication. Verbal communication, that is. I had already sensed from Hank the kind of sizing up I'd received to a lesser degree from Uncle Guy, who had at least been a bit subtler about his examination of the makeup of "Ramie's" new wife.

Though I deliberately avoided looking at Hank, lest he take my glances as flirtation, I watched Thelma with considerable interest, noticing at once how pretty she was when viewed in profile, with her long chestnut hair and her striking brown eyes, but noticing, too, how the skin on one side of her otherwise pretty face had drawn up into a permanent tightness that stretched across most of her mouth and teeth, leaving barely enough space for her words to come through. And whatever had caused that facial paralysis had also affected her eye on that same side, so that it drooped a little.

In addition to surveying the occupants of that cold kitchen, I dared to take a quick glance or two at my surroundings, while Mabel flipped the cards three at a time around the table. Those furtive glances revealed a door leading from the kitchen—the kitchen I'd at first thought to be the only room in the small cabin—to a room I rightly assumed must belong to Guy and Mabel. I noted as well another exit from the room, a doorway whose only "door" was a curtain hanging from a cord stretched at the top of the facing. If the space beyond that curtain were to be my room, I could only hope there would be something more than that worn curtain to shield me from prying eyes.

After a lot of quibbling about the nature of melds and other intricacies of the game, the evening finally moved to an end with a whoop and a holler from Guy as he smugly said, "I'll shoot the moon," a bid that requires the player to take every trick in the deck without giving the others a chance to get the bid and play to win the pot, which consisted of a pile of wooden matchsticks. He played out his hand, winning every trick in the deck, and with a look across the table to see how Mabel was taking it, he swooped up the pile of matches with a flourish.

"That's it!" said Mabel, her highly competitive spirit dashed by her husband's good fortune. And with that she stood up and stretched, then headed for the curtain-covered doorway, looking back and motioning for me to follow. "This is where you'll be sleeping."

Pulling the curtain aside, she led me into what looked more like sitting quarters. The floor boards in that room were covered with what the English called lino (and Americans called linoleum).

There had been no dingy lino in our cottage back home, though our kitchen floor had been covered in red, square tiles that Mother would scrub whether they needed it or not. The kitchen floor also featured hooked rugs of various sizes, which Mother had made from cut-up rags purchased from the man who peddled his wares past our house, calling, "Rags . . . rags for sale! Any rags today?" And maybe if you didn't need to buy any rags, he would offer to take any you had to give away. The poor fellow always looked as though he needed more than rags. We used to call him the ragged man. Sometimes he would knock on the front door if we weren't outside watching for him, and Mother would take a cup of tea out to his cart once in a while.

I can't remember the intricacies of hooking those home-spun floor coverings Mother tried to teach me to make, but they were colorful and cozy throw rugs that she placed in strategic spots, some to keep the kitchen tiles clean, one positioned in front of the fire for when the children had walked home in the pouring rain. On those rainy days, Mother would remove the fireguard that was always there for our protection from spitting cinders. "Just for now, mind you," she would tell us. And at that we would take off our outer clothing, our shoes, and our socks, and sit on that soft, thick rug by the roaring fire, feet outstretched as close to the fire as we dared, all of us waiting to see if Mother might treat us and bring in a tray of the crumpets she sometimes bought at the grocer's across the street.

Holey Scones, I used to call them because Mother called most quick breads scones. These were about the size of a saucer and were kind of leathery to touch, but had holes across the surface into which you could pour treacle—if you liked treacle, which I did not—or you could spoon butter and jam, or Tate and Lyle's Golden Syrup, which I dearly loved. The crumpets would need to be heated first, however, by staking each one on the end of a foot-long, two-tined fork and holding the crumpet next to the hot coals until it was nicely toasted. Mother would allow us "only one apiece now—for it's nearly teatime."

The other floors in our cottage, those in the parlor and the three bedrooms upstairs, were carpeted, but Mother's rag rugs were used there too, protecting areas by the beds and doors, the spots that had to stand more traffic. The only rug of any sort that I remember seeing in the house that was my new home was a mat made of raffia, or straw, that had been placed by the door to hold dirty shoes that would otherwise drag snow or mud, or droppings from the barn, into the house.

As tired as I was on that cold, February night of my arrival at Mabel's house, curiosity led me to look with great interest at the room where I would be sleeping. On one wall a 9- x-11-inch wooden frame held a print of a howling sheepdog standing guard over a strayed lamb who was lost in the snow. It was a tender, warm scene in spite of its cold, winter setting. I'll move that picture closer to the window, I was thinking, my mind already piecing together a survival plan that might ease the pain of separation from familiar things. I could take heart from the print as I looked through those dingy panes and out onto the dismal farmyard, feeling lost as the lamb in the everlasting snow. It was years later before I learned that this had been my husband's favorite painting as a child—that's why he had somehow managed to bring it with him to Guy and Mabel's house.

To my surprise, there was an upright piano along one wall of this "sitting room," and I noticed sheet music there, suggesting that someone in this family had some musical talent. The wooden piano stool, I noticed, could be raised and lowered as one twirled around on the seat. A horsehair sofa and wooden rocking chair were the only other pieces of living room furniture I could see in that part of the room.

In the far corner was a rusty iron bedstead with a patchwork quilt thrown over an obviously bumpy mattress, judging from the humps I could see rising up under the quilt. As I went over to take a closer look, to see what kind of foundation held up the bed, Mabel remarked, "You'll be having to share the bed with Thelma," then passed out through the curtain, adding words that seemed almost courteous: "I'm going to bed myself now. Goodnight."

As my new roommate shyly undressed and slipped into her nightgown, I sat on the side of the bed in a state of inertia, pinching myself, hoping and praying I was in the middle of a nightmare, and would wake up in our old familiar kitchen.

Though Thelma seemed to slip easily into sleep, I fretted most of the night away, stretched out on top of the quilt that covered that lumpy mattress, trying to hide my sobs as I cried for my husband, my knight in shining armor, and wished with all my heart that his furlough had been granted first so that he could have come home alone to the house on the hill while I, with my emigration papers tied up—forever—in a tight, red knot of indecision, could have been at home in my mother's cozy cottage, thousands of miles away from this inhospitable place. Finally I must have grown cold enough and tired enough to slide under the heavy quilt, still wearing the clothes I had on my back, and I soon gave in to my need for Shakespeare's "sleep that knits up the raveled sleeve of care."

Morning sunlight glanced off the snow and into the uncurtained window of my room. Thelma had already slipped out of bed, and since I heard others up and about, I too arose, filled with trepidation and many unanswered questions. I tried to smooth the wrinkles in my dress, but by then they had become pleats that refused to move. At that point I no longer cared what I looked like, for I didn't even know who I was anymore.

I sat there on the cold piano stool, procrastinating, not wanting to face the day, my first day in the land of the Rockies of which my father had sung. Still not wanting to move, I left the stool to pull on my shoes I had shoved under the bed, flinching at their coldness.

Suddenly Thelma walked into the room, and I was struck again by her beauty—and by the paralysis that marred that beauty. Of course, I dared not ask what had happened to her, and that unspoken question would go unanswered until we became better acquainted and she felt sufficiently at ease with me to explain to me that she, too, had an ear that troubled her. Hers had, in time, become so infected as to require surgery, but because the infection had been neglected for so many years, the surgeon had not only been unable to save her hearing, but had also unintentionally scraped her facial nerves during the operation. I felt so sorry for her, knowing that her features were altered forever and she would have to go through life like that. But selfishly, her story made me terribly frightened for myself, afraid that my own long-neglected ear condition might someday cause me to suffer a similar fate.

Such confidences, however, would not come about until much later. For now we were awkward and shy with one another. So much so that when she asked me how I had slept that first night in her aunt's home, my eyes must have betrayed my discomfort at having to sleep with her, for she said, "Thank your lucky stars you have a bed. When my brothers all lived here, they had to sleep in the hayloft in the barn after they'd milked the cows at night."

Her comment gave new meaning to one of my husband's stories about sleeping in a hayloft at one time. He'd made it sound like a Boy Scout excursion rather than an indignity and inconvenience forced upon him by unfortunate circumstances in his life, circumstances about which he was characteristically tight-lipped. Having now experienced Montana's winter weather firsthand, I shivered to think of him out there in the barn behind this very house in below-zero weather. Surely they must have had more than hay to keep them warm. Or maybe having the cows sleeping below them made the barn a little warmer than it would otherwise have been. Then came another selfish thought: God help these people if they expect me to get even that close to a cow. Fortunately, that never did happen since Guy had already guessed how I would feel about such matters and had given Mabel notice that having me milk would be as useless as setting a milk bucket under a bull—a judgment he later repeated to anyone who asked how I was adjusting to life in Montana.

"You'd have to be tough or crazy to venture out in Montana weather with those bare legs," was Mabel's greeting as I finally ventured into the kitchen on my first morning in the house on the hill. "Here, you can wear a pair of Guy's long johns to cover them up, and I'll bet his old overalls might fit you well enough."

Her words, no doubt meant to be kind enough, left me feeling like an underprivileged foundling out of one of Dickens' novels. How long would I be able to swallow the homesickness that was creeping up again, closing my throat off in such a tight knot that I could barely draw a breath and hardly dared speak a word, lest I break into tears. Did my husband expect me to like it here? Did he expect me to settle down and spend the rest of my life in such living quarters as these? Had he himself been happy growing up here?

Though I would never know all there was to know about the reasons he and his siblings were farmed out to various relatives, rather than growing up together in the home their parents once shared, I knew enough even then to realize that he had no choice when it came to living with Mabel and Guy. And now it seemed I had no choice, either. I had no money and no way to get back home, my father's promise to come and get me and take me home having been nullified by his cruel, sudden death. And where, besides home, could I go to wait out this stupid war? Waves of despair and regret were shooting through my mind and piercing my psyche with far more potential deadliness to the spirit than any shrapnel rounds my husband might encounter in this never-ending war.

Yet in the spirit of my mother—the woman who always managed to get on with things, no matter how dire the circumstances—I mumbled my thanks and took the clothing Mabel offered. But first things first. I placed the long johns and overalls over a chair back, glanced around the kitchen, and asked, "Can you tell me where the loo is located?"

Mabel's amused chuckle should have been fair warning that she'd likely been waiting all morning for this question. Without a word she led me to the door, opened it, and pointed in the direction of the barn. There, a hundred or so feet beyond the house, out in the muck and snow, stood a slant-roofed structure with a half moon smiling on its door. Desperate to escape Mabel's knowing stare, I grabbed my coat, which someone had put on a hook on the back of the door, and jumped down from the door-stoop, bare-armed. Slipping and sliding along the well-worn path, I struggled to get into the coat, furious at myself for having given Mabel such an opening for ridicule, and furious that my husband had not prepared me for this rather major indignity. He should have known I'd assume that every house in the United States would be equipped with indoor plumbing!

With my coat finally on, I stopped for a moment, closed my eyes, and took in a huge breath of cold, cold air, determined to steady myself for what-ever lay ahead. When I opened my eyes, I looked beyond the shabby little outhouse to the magnificent Mission Mountains, their snow-covered peaks sparkling in the morning sunlight. All that awesome beauty, right there in front of me in this very backyard! Looking around, I saw a section of ice that must have been broken open by the ax leaning on a chopping block close by. A hole large enough for a bucket was just beginning to freeze over again, but the water below seemed to be running freely underneath the surface of the snow. Was this the spring my husband had spoken of, the one that originated somewhere in those mountains and ran down to the back of the house? Apparently this was where the family got its drinking water. At least the water hole was above the barn and not too close to the outhouse. If the spring's water ran on downhill, would there be another spot closer to the barn where the ice was chopped so that the cows could drink?

On my return from the outhouse, I looked with new interest at the barn, thinking of young Ramie Hedrick and his brothers sleeping there. As large as the house, it had a second story where the hay was stored. As I later learned, the hay was taken into the structure through a large door in the peak of the roof. A ladder inside led up to a square hole through which I supposed the Hedrick boys must have climbed each night on their way to bed—and through which they would also have tossed down hay to the animals below. On this cold, crisp morning, the cows were lowing for a milking, and a dozen or so cats were slinking into the barn where they had made their home. I supposed a squirt of milk might be directed their way while the milking was taking place.

As I left the barn, I looked beyond the house and down the hill. There, just as my husband had described it, lay Flathead Lake, with the sleepy town of Polson snuggled up against its southwestern shore. And there were the cherry orchards, rising up along the eastern route around the lake. The trees were dormant now, marking time till the advent of spring, when their pink and white blossoms would burst forth with the promise of buckets and baskets of the finest cherries you could imagine, cherries that would be in great demand once they were put on display at the fruit stands all along Highway 53.

The sun's rays were blinking off the surface of the lake, and I assumed that crust of ice must be many inches—even feet—deep in order to support the kind of winter fishing of which Guy had boasted during the previous night's drive around the lower edge of the lake. He had said he would walk far out from the shore across that covering of ice and saw a hole through its surface, a hole large enough to allow him to "drop a line into the water below and pull out a trout!" This was a far cry from what my husband had told me about his own summertime fishing experiences, but I guessed from his stories that if spring ever came, I would see many boats bobbing about on those ice-shrouded waters.

But in this frozen moment, the lake was mine and mine alone. Not a single car moved along the road below, though a flock of small birds rose up from one of the cherry trees, then settled down in another. The rest of the world stood still. "Beauty is truth, truth beauty. That is all there is to know on earth, and all ye need to know," wrote Keats, speaking of and to the porcelain lady in his "Ode on a Grecian Urn." At that moment in my life, I knew those words held the wisdom of Solomon, for I felt at peace with the natural world, if not with myself and my fellow human beings.

"You better get on in here before you freeze to death!"

Mabel's warning cut through the calm of that moment and made me suddenly aware that my legs and feet had grown numb, my cheeks were frigid, and my hands were stiff and cold, even though I'd kept them jammed in the pockets of my camel's hair coat. Fortunately, the pot-bellied stove that had put off so little heat the night before had been stoked up to an almost cozy roar, and someone had thoughtfully moved the chair with the long johns and overalls close enough to the stove to mean they were toasty warm for me to slide into.

That "someone" might have been Guy. I wasn't yet ready to assume that Mabel was capable of such kindness, but Guy seemed determined to go out of his way to make me feel welcome. Later that very day, he kept his promise to take me ice fishing, an experience I will never forget. Unwilling to give in to my fears, I went sliding warily along the ice behind my guide, terrified by thoughts of what would happen if the surface began to crack.

We must have been a hundred or more feet out from the shore before Guy finally came to a halt and started to work with axe and chisel, making a round hole big enough for a fish to come flipping through—if and when I snagged one on the worm-covered hook he instructed me to drop into the water. It took me a lot of dip-ins to come up with one small flipper, but between Guy's fine catch and my one fish, we brought home enough fish to feed the family that night.

Having made it through my first day without any major catastrophes, and given the fact that I'd fished the frozen lake and made at least a small contribution toward the evening meal, I felt a bit more confident as I prepared for bed. This time I slid under the covers right away and hugged my side of the double bed, keeping my distance from Thelma, even though I knew from sharing a bed with my sisters—and with my husband—that there is something to be said for the warmth afforded by sleeping close to another. Besides, I was warmed, in a sense, by the realization that I had not shown fear or distress in front of Mabel. That thought alone made me almost able to believe my mother's standard reassurance—'twill be alright come morning, Love.

One day at a time, I began to accustom myself to the winter routine of the house on the hill. Mabel apparently noticed my increasing sense of security, for only a week or so after my arrival she announced that it was time for me to be presented to the neighbors, and ordered Guy to get the buckboard ready. I was hesitant to ride on something that so closely resembled a milk float, but Guy said not to worry about there being no seats. "This old mare knows where all the ruts are, and I promise you won't get shook up overly much," he said.

I thought I might as well muck in and show some enthusiasm about the excursion. I pulled on my camel's hair coat and my green hat, climbed aboard, and off we jogged to visit the closest neighbor, whose house was situated up the hill from the Farnhams. Somewhere along the way Guy bluntly informed me that my husband "hated enjuns." Puzzled, but afraid to ask yet another foolish question, I assumed he must have been trying to explain why we were traveling behind a horse rather than inside a motorcar. When I didn't respond to his comment, he went on to say I would be seeing one of those "enjuns" myself in a minute, and I realized he was talking about the neighbors we were about to visit.

"She's married to a white," he rambled on. "His old man'll never forgive him for that! But it looks like she's there to stay—and they've got five little enjuns to boot."

I could see the house from a distance, for there were no fences keeping it out of bounds to anyone who wished to enter. It was a two-storied house with many windows, the kind of house that didn't need a welcome mat at the door, and I wondered if the white man's father had ever visited his son and grandchildren there. It was painted dove gray with darker gray trim, and I sensed an aura of open arms and a pot of tea and crumpets by a roaring fire. The light shining through those windows seemed to be spreading warmth to all the world, reaching out over the acreage as far as I could see. The rosy glow of that light took in the wooded hills in the distance, reaching right up to those omnipotent mountains that seemed almost to be smiling down on the house and its occupants.

Despite the chill of the day, children with happy faces were hollering and chasing one another around and around the house. A couple of dogs were chasing after the children, and one or two chickens were strutting and pecking their way beside a small structure that must have been their home. Another building, also dove gray with darker gray trim, stood close by the house. Though large enough to be a barn, it looked more like an office building, given the number of doors and windows that ran along its sides. And like the house, this barn-like building had a slate roof. A family sedan was parked on one side of the house itself, and close to the other building was a red, open-bed truck, loaded with large steel milk cans.

A strikingly beautiful woman came to the door. Her name was Geraldine and her hair was black as my mother's hair, her eyes almost as beautiful as my mother's eyes. I had thought that all Indian women wore their hair in braids, like those worn by the woman on the bus, but Geraldine's hair hung down around her shoulders, as free as the wind that played in the branches of the cherry trees. Her husband had light blonde hair, and his eyes were the most piercing blue I had ever seen. Later, as our friendship grew, Gerry confided that she had longed for a blue-eyed boy with every pregnancy. I saw the way that Geraldine and her husband looked at one another as they talked. I heard the way they spoke to one another, calling each other by their first names—something my husband and I had never done even in our courting days. A look of anxiety crossed Gerry's face. "Where's Glenny?" she asked. "Ray, could you check on him for me?" Ray? Yes, Ray, for the man who rose at once to do her bidding had the same given name as my husband. Without hesitation, Ray Fulkerson walked to the kitchen door and stepped out into the yard, returning in moments to say their youngest was still romping about with the others, but he'd call them all in if Gerry thought it best. Such a gentleman, this Ray, so naturally attuned to his wife's every wish, yet totally unaware that his behavior was being so closely scrutinized by the new neighbor from down the hill. His actions toward Gerry and hers toward him were obviously as natural and unpretentious as could be, and the beauty of their relationship made a mockery of the scathing comments Guy had made on our way to their home. Guy had pulled his chair close and leaned his elbows on the table, as if he wanted to be part of the conversation, yet I can't remember his saying a single word for the rest of our visit.

Silent or not, surely he must have been able to sense, as I did, that the warmth filling the Fulkerson's kitchen came not only from the space heater at one end of the large kitchen. That warmth was in Geraldine's happy smile, in her husband's hearty handshake, and in the sense of family that was undoubtedly there among five children and their parents. I spent a happy hour drinking Gerry's java and enjoying her freshly made apple pie, topped with my first taste of homemade ice cream, a doubly delicious treat since it was made from cream from their own dairy cows. This informal gathering in Gerry's kitchen turned out to be the first of many such occasions during that first year in America.

Those times spent at the Fulkersons' were precious, for life on the hill could be lonely for a person used to being surrounded by friends and family. I did occasionally go with Mabel and Guy to pinochle and pie get-togethers with other neighbors, but the talking there was generally focused on the game we were playing. And though there must have been social gatherings of various types down in Polson, those of us living in the east shore community were too far distant from the heart of town to be involved in such events. We didn't even attend church, for Mabel and Guy seemed to have no interest whatsoever in religion, though the fervor with which she played and sang old hymns—on the rare occasions when she found time to sit down at the piano—suggested there had been a time when she attended protestant services of some sort in some place other than here. But that time had long since passed, and even had I been inclined to go to church myself, I'd have had no way to get to Polson without having Guy crank up the old Ford and drive me there.

Besides, there was hardly time for socializing of any kind—even at church—since most of the women of the east side community tended to be confined to their kitchens and gardens seven days a week. They spent their summers growing the vegetables that fed their families, and after each harvest—as well as after each hunting season, when their men folk brought in fresh game—they cooked, bottled, tinned, and binned every edible thing that came to hand, including rhubarb, green tomato mincemeat, rabbit, deer, antelope, head cheese, and bear meat. And I, of course, was expected to do my share of gardening, cooking, and putting food by. Nothing could induce me to kill the chickens, but I was persuaded to help cook and can them. In addition to her various tomato concoctions, the shelves of Mabel's cellar—the dugout storage room beneath the house that allowed foods to be stored underground at a constant temperature throughout the year—were stocked with jars of sweet and sour cherries, plus jars of venison, pheasant, and a few birds of a different feather, all properly sealed and dated, but many put up so long ago that they had likely fermented and should have been thrown away. The previous year's crop of carrots and potatoes were stacked in boxes on the dirt floor of the cellar, which she entered through a trapdoor in the kitchen. I wondered how long their lifespan would be.

Though I sometimes resented the constant hard work, I was grateful to be where I was for the time being, until my husband came home. I grew to appreciate the time and effort Mabel had expended over the years to make a home for her nieces and nephews. I saw how she had worked without rest to ensure there would be plenty to eat for her family year-round. And I appreciated her willingness to share the fruits of her labor—and the wealth of her knowledge about domestic matters—with a virtual stranger, even if that stranger was her nephew's wife.

Ultimately I came to see that this first, tough course in Home Economics in Rural America was very beneficial to me. For in addition to learning the basic skills of country living, I learned enough about the economic advantages of raising one's own food that I resolved to do my own canning—if and when I ever owned a home with a garden—so that I, too, could feed my family during the harsh winter months when all my garden would grow was snow.

Chapter 7

Everybody's talking about people breaking into houses,
but there are more people in the world
who want to break out of houses.
—THORNTON WILDER

*I*don't remember exactly when the rift with the relatives began. I think it might have been the moment I told Mabel I thought I might be pregnant, since I had not menstruated since a month before leaving England. As I shared my joyful news that late February morning, there was no way to hide the tears that arose as I thought of how my beloved father, who had never had a son of his own, would have loved to show off this grandson—if indeed this was a boy and not a girl I was carrying. There was no way of knowing until the child's arrival, of course, for back in 1945, parents could never have imagined a time when science would make it possible for them to see inside the womb to learn in advance the sex of their child. And what if this baby turned out to be a girl, a sweet, adorable princess upon whom my mother would lavish her attentions? That thought also brought tears to my eyes, for there was no way my widowed mother would sail across an ocean and find her own way to this faraway place just to welcome a grandchild.

And so the tears came as I shared my news with Mabel, tears prompted by apprehension for the well being of my unborn baby, and by the fact that I felt utterly helpless and alone, with not one soul to turn to in this great expanse of snow and ice.

"What's all the crying about?" she demanded in her usual, no-nonsense manner. When I whispered back that I was scared of having the baby, that I was homesick and wanted my mother, she snorted, "Well, you can go back home to Mama any time you can afford the trip."

Not one word of reassurance. Not one word of comfort. No hint of pride at becoming a great aunt. There were no congratulations—rather she showed more disgust than pleasure at my news.

Actually, I had good reason to be fearful. Awash with memories I had no inclination to share with Mabel, I dried my tears—only to have them flow again as she blurted out, "I don't know why that husband of yours married a foreigner anyway when he could have married a nice little girl from around here."

And with that, she turned her back, pushed her way through the curtain of my doorway, and headed into the kitchen. Then she paused and really put the cat among the pigeons by mumbling just loud enough so that I could hear her through that thin veil of privacy, "God knows, the kid might not even be his!"

More hurt than angry, I gathered my courage, and with as much dignity as I could muster, jumped from the bed, and strode out after Mabel. Grabbing her arm, I turned her around and forced her to look me in the eye. The words came out, deliberate and cold as the ice on the frozen ditch, as I told her that the date of conception and the expected arrival date of her nephew's child left no room whatsoever for her to speculate on any shipboard romance or unexpected layover somewhere between New York City and the place I was standing, right there!

She shook off my grip and barged over to the stove, giving me no indication whatsoever that she'd heard and accepted my words. I retreated to my room, shaken as much by my boldness as by her slanderous onslaught. But despite my courageous outburst, I realized that she would likely hold onto her doubts until the baby's arrival—and I could only pray that the birth would be exactly on schedule. Many months of waiting stretched out before me, and from that moment of Mabel's outburst, there was wariness on both our parts. If I had been lonely before, at least I had not felt like a deceptive spouse who had been unfaithful to the man who was risking his life for his country "over there."

I spent many silent hours on the creaking bed, blinded by bright sun on everlasting snow as I looked out the window at the mountains that had once seemed so reassuring but now seemed to be penning me in. The weeks immediately after my confrontation with Mabel were spent wishing I were somewhere, anywhere, on the other side of that fortress. My father's words were ringing in my ears as I suffered through my self pity: I'll come and get you, Love. . . . I'll come and get you, Love. . . . I'll come and get you and bring you home."

Why did you have to die, Father? You didn't have to die so soon. But your death was more my fault than yours for not checking out your doctor's diagnosis after he had referred you to the sanatorium for treatment of tuberculosis. Had I not been so wrapped up in my wedding plans, had I lived up to your trust in me, you would have been home with Emily and your girls in a warm, loving place to help you bear the pain of the lung cancer that eventually took you from us.

But why did you have to die so soon? You knew I would be needing you, just as surely as you knew my husband would turn people away from me. You knew I would never go crying home to Mother, a child expecting a child. You knew that having her daughter so blatantly disregard her marriage vows would have completely destroyed Em's dignity.

And besides, what would the neighbors think?

Despondent over the strained relationships that would surely follow my outburst with Mabel, I lay there night after night in that cold and inhospitable room thinking of Gertrude Stein's words, "A rose is a rose is a rose is a rose." Things are as they are and must be accepted as such. How could I ever argue with a writer so full of wisdom? Yet I knew that there was no comfort in those words if that rose were as lifeless as the flowers on my mother's kitchen wallpaper. There can be no comfort unless we are able to breathe in the living essence of that rose and touch its velvet to our cheek. We need to see the deep scarlet of its petals before their beauty fades away. And in that frozen wasteland, all I could see was snow!

I longed for the warmth of a loving embrace, for permission to cry for no apparent reason, and for strength to laugh at myself through the tears. All I had, all that I could depend upon at that moment, was me—and a pregnancy of which my husband had not yet heard. So, why was I lying there, my mind fitfully wasting time looking for someone, something, to make things right come morning? Come morning, I'd just have to make things right myself.

I rose early, dressed, and made a beeline for my coat hanging on the back door hook. Mumbling some excuse to Mabel about skipping breakfast and taking a walk, then rushed out of the house so quickly I hoped she'd think I was suffering from morning sickness. That would give her something to gloat over. But instead of walking down the well-trod path to the out-house, I headed up the road toward Gerry's house. From that one visit in her cozy kitchen, I knew her love for her own little ones and knew that she would be delighted to hear my news.

She welcomed me with open arms, almost as if she'd been expecting me for breakfast. The children, though still shy in my presence, smiled when I spoke to them and seemed glad enough to have a guest to share their eggs and ham. Her husband, just in from milking, welcomed me also, and by the time everyone else had scattered, I'd helped with the dishes, and Gerry and I had sat down for a second cup of coffee, I was bursting to tell her about the baby.

Her response was all that I could have wished, and she assured me that my husband would be as happy as she was over the news. I should call him as soon as possible, for knowing he had a child on the way would make him all the more eager to come home. My walk back to the house down the hill was a happy one. I could and I would get through this just fine—with help from my new friend.

That evening at supper, I announced that I wanted to phone England and give my husband the news about the baby. Uncle Guy agreed to drive me into town the next morning and introduce me to the lady who operated the Polson switchboard. She graciously invited me to stay overnight at her home, while she attempted to reach my husband's air base in England. Not many personal calls got through during the war, she warned me, so I was not to get my hopes up. Sometime the next day she finally got a connection and handed the phone to me.

I said, "Hello," and the moment I heard the garbled response of a male voice, I blurted out my news, uncertain that the man on the other end of the line had heard and understood me. I could not even be sure I was really speaking to my husband, since the connection had not improved by the time our three minutes were up. Thankfully, communication was truly communication back then, and operators were live people and not robotic voices, instructing you to push a series of numbers on a hand-set until you were so frustrated you gave up trying. This real, live operator was kind enough to give us a few more minutes—perhaps because she'd heard my message and sensed its importance, even if Ray had not. This second time, I was able to get a better connection.

Once again I said, "Hello," and then repeated my news, asking him to speak up as loudly as he could because of my deafness. I had trouble listening and talking between my sobs, and had no notion of his feelings about this child-to-be. I could catch only a word here and there, and any emotion his voice might have conveyed was lost in the crackles and squeals on the line. Then we were cut off again, this time with no hope of reconnection.

That call to my husband did nothing to bolster my self-confidence concerning how to handle my problems with the relatives. Nor did it give me any reason to be optimistic about our future as a family, a couple with a newborn baby to care for. I felt as though I had been swept up in an avalanche and sent careening down the mountainside to end up lodged in one of those frozen cherry trees. Mother and her remonstrances were haunting me as never before: You've made your bed—now you'll have to lie in it, won't you! It was your decision to leave your country and your family, so don't come crying to me. It's nobody's fault but your own, so stop feeling sorry for yourself and get on with it!

In a sense, she was right. If I could not count on my husband or my family for reassurance and a sense of direction, I would have to count on myself. A few days after the confrontation with Mabel, I got up without awakening Thelma, put on my best dress and those sturdy leather shoes I'd worn on my voyage to America, and slipped and slid my way down to the main road below, determined to stand by the roadway until the school bus rounded the bend. In response to my wave, the bus pulled to a stop, the door opened, and the driver gave me a quizzical smile but nodded me inside for the ride into town in the company of a busload of screaming youngsters. I got off at the drugstore where I'd had my first shake, bought a newspaper, circled an ad for a legal secretary in the help-wanted column, and went straight to the attorney's office. There, I was interviewed on the spot, hired immediately, and told to report to work the following day. My new employer, I learned, was not only an attorney but also the state senator from our district. He was truly one of the most considerate men I've ever worked for, and when he found out I'd ridden the school bus into town and had no other transportation, he offered to adjust my hours to fit the bus schedule. I could cut my lunch break to half an hour, and as long as I got my work done, he'd pay me as if I were on the job until 5:00.

When I returned home, elated, Mabel turned my good news into bad, making it perfectly clear that no nephew of hers would approve of his wife's gallivanting around town every day and working for some high fallutin' senator. She and Guy were supposed to be taking care of me until my husband returned. How could I even think of doing such a thing as going off to work! I can't imagine how much more angry they'd have been had I let them see just how happy I was at the prospect of going off to work every day, and breaking loose from the leash of restrictions they tried to impose—plus escaping the unctuous insincerity toward myself and my unborn child.

Each morning thereafter, as I stood at the bottom of the hill, waiting for the school bus to come chugging along, I'd look up, taking in the grandeur of my mountains, so close it seemed as if I could reach out my hand and touch them. As I looked up at those strong and silent peaks, I managed to take from them a bit of their grit and stability to see me through yet another day, a bit of their endurance to help me bear the pain of loneliness. And as I studied those silent sentinels untouched by the world below, I saw in their seemingly inaccessible heights the possibility of other heights that I myself might one day hope to attain.

My reverie was often interrupted by the bus honking its arrival. On other days a whiff of skunk cabbage might float up from across the road and bring me down to earth again. But nothing could dispel my feeling of freedom in being able to leave that house and go to a world of my own each day.

I was so happily involved in my work that I was caught completely by surprise when I was invited out one evening and greeted by fourteen lovely, energetic young ladies. Having heard that the English bride of a local American airman had arrived in their town, they'd decided to give a party for that unknown immigrant—namely me! I was amazed and delighted to find myself being welcomed into a beautifully appointed home in Polson that evening, for this was my first social event since arriving in Montana, except for the pinochle outings with Mabel and Guy, and my occasional visits with the Fulkersons.

I received a warm welcome from the two hostesses, one of whom turned out to be Gerry Fulkerson herself! Everyone present was apparently well acquainted with my dear neighbor and seemed to have the highest regard for her, all of which helped me to feel at home. I was asked many questions, but they were warm, personal, eager-to-know-me questions that were not in the least inquisitorial, or nosey parker as Mother used to say. Indeed, the questions from this gathering of Montana women opened up my heart to them and to their country, restoring my longing to become a part of this land of the free.

One comment did set me wondering, however. After one of the women mentioned that this surprise party was a shower, I puzzled all the way through the delicious hors d'oeuvres, the canapés, and the petit fours we nibbled on while sipping something bubbly. It wasn't until the tables were cleared and everyone was sitting comfortably around the room with smiles of eager anticipation that it dawned on me that the word "shower," as used on this occasion, had nothing to do with water. I was to be showered with the beautifully wrapped boxes the two hostesses were dragging across the carpet in a huge basket.

Oh my, if all these gifts were truly for me, what on earth had I done to deserve them? Such a thing had never been the custom in England, at least not as far as I knew. I'd received wedding gifts from some of my friends, but I'd never had—or been to—a shower before. I felt somewhat self-conscious about taking so much time to open each package, but habits of thrift were a part of my being, and I began by trying my best to preserve the beautiful ribbons and wrappings for future use. Then excitement took over, and my good sense of preservation was soon gone with the wind. Mother would have been shocked at the pile of tatters and shreds lying beside the lovely array of thoughtful gifts from the wonderful women surrounding me.

Gerry and the others had planned this night so carefully, telling the guests this was to be a combined wedding and baby shower. I was overwhelmed as I passed around one gift after another for all to see how fortunate I was. Everything was a treasure for me to cherish—pieces of china, hand-made crocheted doilies, kitchenware—everything I would need to set up a home, if my husband ever came home. I would have loved for Mother to be there, yet I couldn't help but wonder whether she might have spoiled the magic of the evening with a look that raised the question of whether or not I deserved all these presents—especially the items for the baby!

Indeed, up until that night, I myself had shoved the fact of pending motherhood to the outposts of my mind, and in that state of self-denial, I'd deemed pregnancy to be just one more burden that had been thrust upon me unfairly. I had certainly not planned on having a baby this soon, and I simply could not let myself think of being responsible for providing for and tending a newborn, perhaps without its father by my side. And yet as I opened up the first of the baby gifts from these women who knew how to open up a mother's heart, there lay an adorable pair of crocheted, white baby booties.

"I didn't know whether to make them pink for a girl, or blue for a boy," a voice came from across the room. "So I made them white!"

I struggled to hold back the tears as the wellspring of mother love came flowing up and through me. For the very first time, I allowed myself to imagine my baby, my very own child, kicking up his heels in these tiny white booties as he lay, smiling, in his cozy crib. There was a beautiful quilt, too, and a rattle, and a number of commonsense presents like towels and diapers, which I referred to as nappies, drawing a ripple of laughter from my new circle of friends.

One can't be expected to remember, over a span of sixty years, every minute detail of even so wonderful an event as my first shower, but I still have a lovely china cake plate and matching server in my china cabinet, as reminders of that marvelous evening. And if they hadn't been lost in transit during one of the many moves over those sixty-plus years, I would still be using the eight lovely antique wooden lap trays received at the shower—trays upon which I proudly served tea and crumpets to special guests over the years.

I went home that night more hopeful than I'd been since I arrived in America. Even the house on the hill seemed a little brighter and less foreboding in light of the evening's festivities. I walked into the house with a lighter step, knowing, yes, yes, Mother, 'twill be alright come morning!

My spirits were also lifted by the promise of spring in the air. The blanket of snow was shrinking away from the trunks of the cherry trees in the orchard, and melting snow watered the grass that seemed to be sprouting everywhere at once, including the hillsides leading up to the Missions—that forbidding, yet enticing, fortress guarding the lake below.

As much as I would have loved to walk up into those foothills, exploring the nooks and crevices hidden by the expanse of Douglas fir and lonely pine, I had never been at ease in high places, and could not imagine venturing out onto even the lowest of the foothills leading up to those snowy peaks. On the other hand, there were times when my longing for freedom and escape tempted me to throw caution to the wind and climb up, up, up into the very heart of those mountains.

My chance came on a warm, sunny day when Mabel seemed to be in a jollier mood than usual, perhaps cheered by the welcome spring weather after such a long, hard winter. Despite my differences with this crusty, irritable woman, my attitude toward her had softened somewhat after I realized that she was obliged to give herself a daily shot in the arm, or leg—or someplace else that didn't already look like a worn-out pin cushion—in order to keep her diabetes at bay. Such a daily ritual was enough to make anyone crotchety! I would also feel sorry for her when I caught her looking with longing at my plate of cake at the pinochle parties.

As a child, I too had a very sweet tooth and longed for chocolate, especially the tiny bottles of chocolate liqueurs Auntie Lil would keep in a huge apothecary jar out of reach on a top shelf in her cigarette, newspaper and sweet shop on Liverpool Road. I would hold out my hand to show her how many coppers I had and ask, "How much are they today, Auntie Lily?" She would count out the pennies one by one, placing them on the counter, then take off the big, round, glass-ball stopper from the apothecary jar, while I watched her hand, with deliberate intent, picking out just one of those delicious treats for which I yearned.

"Sorry, Irene, that's just not enough money for any of them, and I've told you time and again that liqueurs are not for little children." So saying, she would unwrap the foil from the sweet, pop it into her mouth, and reach under the counter to bring out the penny gob-stoppers. "There! You see, you get four of these for your money."

Yes, I had come to empathize with Mabel—at least concerning her love of forbidden sweets—and on this particular spring morning, I realized she was issuing an invitation of sorts. I looked up to see her staring into space, her eyes tightened up as if to see things more clearly. "It's such a nice day, dear, why don't you ask Hank to take you up the hill for a walk? Do you good. You could do some posy picking. Should be some yellow bells up there by now. Me and Guy are going to take it easy today since it's Sunday." I must have hesitated, stunned as I was by her cheerfulness, for she urged, "Go on now and get your coat, and I'll run out to the barn and ask Hank if he'll go with you. I know he'd enjoy your company."

I wasn't altogether certain that I would enjoy Hank's company, and I should have had better sense than to go anywhere with him unaccompanied, considering the way his eyes tended to undress me anytime he thought no one else was watching. But I put on my coat, thinking of the yellow bells I'd heard my husband describe. Besides, anything sounded better than spending yet another dreary Sunday hanging around with Mabel and Guy. Hank must have shared my feelings, for he appeared almost instantaneously to act as my escort on this unexpected excursion into the trees at the base of the mountains.

Not much conversation passed between us as we started up the hill, and it soon became evident that the flowers I'd hoped to see had not yet come up, despite Mabel's prediction. I was somewhat surprised to find hidden beyond the evergreens the bare branches of deciduous trees, and guessed from the stark white of their trunks that spring would bring forth the quaking leaves of the graceful aspen about which I'd heard so much. But spring was still a long way off, and once we had gained elevation, a wind came up, the warmth of the spring day disappeared, and I found myself shivering and ready to turn around and head back to the relative warmth of the house on the hill. Yet I was determined not to be the one to turn back first.

However, my resolve weakened as the path grew steeper, for the rocks and grass were slippery and wet. My fear of heights came back to haunt me, but I trudged along, telling myself I had no choice but to complete Mabel's assignment—even though by then I'd begun to realize that this man with whom I was climbing, my husband's older brother, was intentionally bumping up against me at every opportunity, deliberately, boldly pressing his shoulder against mine. And he was becoming more and more brazen in his actions the higher we climbed.

It took us a long time to reach the tree line, and once we arrived, there was obviously nothing more to see but tree trunks and increasingly deep layers of snow. Finally I announced, "I'm going back down. I'm tired, I'm cold, and I shouldn't have attempted this trip in the first place."

"You're scared!" he retorted.

"Of what?" I wanted to know.

"Of me!" he said with derision. "Mabel let on you'd enjoy an outing with me, or else I wouldn't be making this fool's errand on a Sunday to bring you all the way up here for nothing!"

He stood there jeering at me, the big gap between his front teeth turning him into an animal ready to devour me. I turned, ready to run, but stopped in my tracks. With any hint of speed down that steep hill to the house, I would for sure, in Mother's words, be a goner! Being ever so careful of every step, I timidly started down the slope, knowing full well that my slow pace would be an invitation for Hank to come clomping after. I was terrified. The trees seemed to be closing in on me. My shoelaces, and I along with them, were coming undone.

"You're shaking," he said, inches away, then pulled me close against his chest in a gesture that chilled me still further.

Furious, I shoved him away but slipped and fell onto the damp grass, pine needles, and snow. As I attempted to regain my footing, he snarled, "You wouldn't be thinking of telling my little brother about all this, would you?" Before I could answer he stooped and reached for something in the grass and needles in which I lay. Quick as could be, he deposited whatever he'd picked up onto the back of my hand. "Here! Maybe this will help remind you to keep your mouth shut."

I looked at the tiny black thing crawling toward my wrist. I had seen one of those tiny insects before, when Thelma placed one on my pillow just for fun, the night after Mabel had described to me in great detail how the creatures burrow into your skin and, if not removed, can cause Rocky Mountain Spotted Fever. Not long thereafter, I'd had the unpleasant experience of finding one so tightly attached to my leg that Mabel had to apply the hot tip of a burned match to its hindquarters to get it to let go and back out from under my skin. She'd then dropped the blood-filled little thing on the hot stovetop and watched him shrivel up in agony, all the while cackling to herself. From that point on, the whole family knew how I feared and hated ticks, and never missed a chance to tease me about my cowardice, especially in front of the neighbors.

And now one of the dreadful creatures was about to disappear under my coat sleeve. Gathering my courage I picked the thing off my arm and threw it at him.

"There's plenty more where that one came from," Hank said, pointing at the grass and pine needles from which I was attempting to rise. I looked down to see a swarm of ticks milling around me, apparently just emerging from winter's grip. No longer fretting about how I could possibly manage to get safely down the steep and slippery hillside, I scrambled to my feet and started running pell-mell down the path, my fear of what lay behind dispelling any thought of what might lie ahead.

Hank didn't move, just squatted there on the hillside, watching my headlong flight, honking out his laughter like a hyena in heat.

Thelma was waiting for me at the door. "What on earth was going on up there!" she exclaimed.

It was then that I saw Guy through the open door of his bedroom, standing near the window, his telescope trained on the slope I had just descended. He and Mabel had been watching my every move! Tears of anger and embarrassment rose up as I pushed aside the curtain that led to my makeshift room. As I fell across the bed, desperate to hide my sobs, I could hear Mabel saying to Guy—loud enough to be sure I would hear: "I'll sure have a thing or two to tell Ramie about that little hussy!"

After that incident I made it a point to avoid being in Hank's presence, except at family meals when there was no escaping his cocky gaze. And I made sure to claim the side of the bed that was pushed up against the wall, leaving Thelma on the vulnerable outer edge, which was too close for comfort to the thin curtain that provided the only barrier between our room and the "living quarters," where Hank slept on the sofa.

As tension in the house on the hill increased, I was more thankful than ever for my home away from home, Senator Wallace's office. That welcome refuge was located on the second floor of an old building used by other businessmen and city and county officials. I met some of them in the course of my duties and chatted with them when time allowed.

The senator himself was amiable, easy to please, and a man of good conscience, who represented his clients with integrity and concern for their well-being. My business college courses stood me in good stead, but even though I held certificates for taking down dictation at 120 words per minute in Pitman's shorthand, I had to keep my wits about me, since the senator used legal phraseology with great speed and facility. He was a kind man, however, and whenever he would notice my hesitancy at a certain point, he would wait for me to catch up with him.

I loved to sit at his huge, polished wooden desk, waiting for him to dictate a brief or a letter. There were comfortable chairs placed around a long, elegant conference table on the window side of the wood-paneled room. The opposite wall held bookcases fashioned from the same beautiful wood, with glass doors protecting an extensive array of law books. In the center of the wall of books was a space where the door to my office was located. The floors in Senator Wallace's section of the building were all carpeted, presenting a far different aspect from the floors to which I'd grown accustomed in the house on the hill.

My office, which also served as a waiting room, was furnished with several high-backed chairs, a small table, filing cabinets, and a larger desk that held a manual typewriter, my appointment book, a dial telephone, and a dictionary of legal terms. I bought a print of the Mission Range and hung it on the wall.

Office work in 1945 was a far cry from office work today. The electric typewriter was a thing of the future, and pushing a heavy carriage back to its starting place after every line was definitely manual labor! The only way to copy documents back in those days was to insert carbon paper between each of the two or more pages rolled into the typewriter, and if an error was made, there were all those carbon copies to be amended without smudging. This was generally done by lifting each sheet in turn, for if you took the layered sheets out of the machine during or after the erasing chore, it was virtually impossible to arrange them in exactly the manner in which they'd been put together in the first place.

The telephone in that office was merely a means of conversing, one-on-one, with a live person on the other end of the connection. No answering machines. No call waiting. No caller I.D.

By May the cherry blossoms were in full bloom, hundreds and hundreds of acres of them all along the eastern shore of the lake. Each morning as I walked down the hill to the bend in the road, I was greeted by a panorama of flowering trees up and down the highway, and they welcomed me back in the afternoon, the scent of their blossoms borne on the breeze as I climbed the hill to a house that wasn't a home. Despite the dismal aura that surrounded the place on the hill I held tight to the success I had achieved on the job and my acceptance by people with whom I came in contact, so that I was regaining some of my old English pluck, and week by week I dared to make more and more decisions on my own. The Fulkersons, my dear friends up the road, kept in close touch with me, for which I was grateful. I'm sure my mother would not have been pleased by my shirking my duties at the homestead, where Mabel could surely have used my help at scrubbing the floors or washing the cream separator, but the coming of spring seemed to increase my daring, and often as not I went straight from work up to the Fulkersons for afternoon visits with Gerry.

Though I could sense the relatives' disapproval of my keeping company with the 'enjuns, I chose to ignore their scowls and snide remarks—at least until things came to a head. My afternoon visits with Gerry always took place in her kitchen, except for the evening we'd spent together at the shower back in February, and up until that summer I had never before socialized with the Fulkersons at public affairs. But when Gerry and her husband asked if I would like to go along with them to a dinner at the country club, I was delighted and said I would love to go.

I didn't ask Mabel and Guy's permission, but simply told Mabel I was going to the country club with my friends. Her only comment was "Oh," but her lips were pursed into a circle, her chin was drawn down, and her eyebrows were raised all the way into her hairline as she said it.

I remember the country club affair as being pleasant enough, and though there was a dance band playing after the meal, I don't remember dancing with anyone. I do remember, though, that as the three of us walked out onto the deck, a group of people on the grass below called up to us and beckoned my friends to come down and join them.

They turned out to be acquaintances of Gerry, and I was pleased that she asked me to go along. There were six or seven of them, all American Indians, a couple of them relatives from Gerry's side of the family. As we joined in the circle they had made, it soon became apparent that they were passing around a bottle, with each person lifting it high in some sort of toast. I had no idea what was in the bottle, but when it reached my spot in the circle, I lifted it high, took a quick sip, and passed it on. It would have been discourteous to refuse to participate in a toast, even though it was from a shared bottle, and even though I had no idea who or what we were toasting. This was a far cry from the toast that was made in honor of Our Eve the night of her triumph at the Lever Brothers drama festival, but Gerry was my friend and I was honored to be part of this gathering on the grass below the balcony of Polson's country club.

It was nearly midnight by the time the Fulkersons dropped me off at the house on the hill. The door was bolted shut, all the lights were out, and I was suddenly back in Sankey Bridges, an adventuresome teenager locked out by her own parents for staying out until two in the morning. But my father was not inside to quietly let me in, and it was Guy who grudgingly opened the door when he thought it might come down at my banging. "About time!" he grumbled. "You'd better get off to bed. We'll talk about this tomorrow."

I woke to the cock's crow, threw the absolute necessities into the one bag I thought I would be able to carry, stepped out onto the grass, and left that place behind me. No point in staying around to "talk" when I hadn't yet had a single real conversation with anyone in that house since I arrived there. I closed the gate behind me and trudged past the house and on up past the orchard, dragging the battered V-2 along the ground, leaving behind the only place that stood for home in this land so far away from home.

I hurried as fast as I could, half dragging, half carrying the suitcase, intent on getting enough space between myself and the house on the hill to be sure there was no chance they might catch up with me. And yet with every step came the nagging thought, "What would my husband have to say about this sorry mess?"

I was picking my way through a horde of grasshoppers, feeling their crusty bodies strike my bare arms and legs, when Geraldine saw me from her kitchen window and rushed out to welcome me with open arms. It must have been very early in the morning, for Gerry was an early riser, yet she was still in her housecoat and slippers, and had just put on the coffee to brew when she caught sight of me. She knew I would never have come so early and with no warning if there was not something wrong, though she simply put her arm around me and led me up to her house with never a question of why, or how, or what had happened. And I knew that she knew I had come to stay—even though I arrived empty-handed, having abandoned the suitcase way back down the road when it became too heavy to carry.

In that house, high, high up the hill and far from the relatives' house below, I shared quarters not only with Gerry and her husband but also with two teens—a girl and a boy, both strikingly handsome—from Geraldine's earlier marriage to an Indian of the Flathead tribe, plus three youngsters, ages ten, eight, and three, from her present marriage. Though large in comparison to the house I'd shared with Mabel and Guy and their nieces and nephews, the Fulkerson's home had only two bedrooms. Although I was deeply embarrassed by the idea of sharing the "master" bedroom—which was, at the time, their living room—with Gerry and her husband, we all politely ignored any mention whatsoever of that potentially awkward circumstance.

There was really no other alternative, since the narrow staircase to the children's bedrooms on the second floor was a little too steep for me to climb. The ventricular imbalance due to my injured ear often brought on dizzy spells, and I would never put my unborn child in danger by risking a fall. I never remember seeing those upstairs rooms, but I do remember Gerry telling me her girls were excited about redecorating the room they shared.

It was by no means a fancy house, but it was a home. The big, cheery kitchen, painted white, featured large cupboards that stretched from countertop to ceiling. Having already tasted Gerry's cherry pie, I knew she was a good cook, so I wasn't surprised to find her cupboards stocked with plenty of cookware. Perhaps it was because of the work being done on the upper floor that the parents' big double bed was down in the living room. But it, too, was such a large room that even with the bed in place, there was plenty of space for a settee and comfortable chairs and the wood space heater.

And there was indoor plumbing with a toilet in the small bathroom.

I enjoyed many happy hours looking for wildflowers with Gerry and her children. She said the early bloomers, like the dogtooth violets, were gone, but we saw honeysuckle twining through the hedges, and a patch of woody nightshade here and there. From my childhood study of plants, I knew that the berries of the nightshade were poisonous and told her to warn the children, if she hadn't already. On one of our walks later on, I pointed to a tall, white flower alongside a hedge, which she called the Indian moccasin flower. Obviously a member of the orchid species, it featured a beautiful cluster of stems filled with blossoms that actually looked like moccasins.

Gerry not only shared my love of flowers and other beauties of nature but she also had a keen sense of humor, and I loved her for taking the gloom away. She bought me my first pair of nylon stockings, and I will never forget the sense of luxury they brought, the feel of that spun gossamer as I slid my foot into the top of the stocking and down the length of the leg, gingerly feeling my way, nails retracted like cat claws until my foot finally came to rest in that sheer elegance.

When I asked whether she'd bought a pair for herself, she gave me a sheepish grin and said, "I have a natural tan, so I don't have to wear them when the weather is warm."

One day when she had just shampooed and was leisurely combing out her lovely black hair, I watched with delight, ever so glad that rather than plaiting it into a long braid like most of the Flathead women do, she was simply setting it free to catch and keep forever bright in my mind's eye all the colorful beauty still locked up in my mother's hair.

Gerry's home had the comfy coziness of a middle-class English home, without the frills. It was economically equipped to provide the necessities with a little bit of luxury thrown in, yet no "showing off," though they could have afforded to do so, considering their dairy farm income. "No need to show off," she said. "A happy family is my most precious possession."

I was accepted as a member of that loving, caring family, a welcome guest in my kind of home, the rose-covered cottage of my dreams, the kind of house that should have been waiting for me amid the cherry orchards along the lakeshore.

Chapter 8

*True friendship consists
not in the multitude of friends,
but in their worth and value.*
—BEN JONSON

Once school ended for the summer, I knew I would be without transportation to work, so I arranged in advance to catch daily rides with a fellow courthouse employee who passed the school bus stop every day and agreed to pick me up there—provided I could manage to walk down the hill each morning and back up it each afternoon. I knew she was concerned about whether I could manage such a hike over the later months of my pregnancy, but I assured her the exercise would be good for me.

Her concern set me to thinking. Moving farther up the mountainside to Gerry's had made for a much longer walk to and from the highway, but perhaps I could find a shortcut. I did a bit of exploring and found a shorter route that led me along a narrow cow path through the weeds. The new route steered me a bit farther from the homestead, and I was so thankful to avoid contact with the relatives that I endured the shortcut's one major unpleasantry.

The dead cow belonged to Guy, I know, because Mabel was always nagging him to get rid of it, which he promised to do one of these day, but never did, and to see that rotting, foul-smelling carcass lying across my path as I walked to the highway in the morning and back again in the afternoon I had to resist the growing temptation to take out my frustrations by kicking that disgusting carcass, for the helplessness of that poor animal's plight heightened my longing to escape, and my growing realization that everything was not likely to be all right come morning.

Fearful that I couldn't keep a stiff upper lip much longer, I would gladly have gone anywhere, taking up with the first person who might say, I've come to rescue you. I even went so far as to speculate on possibilities. Father had died, and I couldn't depend on Mother. I thought of the English girl I had befriended on the *Mauretania,* but appealing to her for help seemed a crass thing to do, even if I had had an address for her. I thought of writing to one of the Americans with whom I had crossed the Atlantic, perhaps the young man who had come to my rescue when the steward interrupted our conversation to hand me a note. The captain, it seemed, wanted to see me in his cabin, but before I could rip open the envelope, my American friend said, "Thank you, but she'll take a rain-check on that!"

Later when I opened the note in private, I saw that the captain had wanted to meet me because he had known my mother and wanted to send her word that I was okay. Perhaps this invitation had been innocent enough after all, for Mother seemed to have known quite a few seamen. I remember one of them in particular. His name was Tommy and he used to visit us when we were children. He had a seamstress make sailor suits for each of my sisters, and he once brought me a beautiful shawl from Spain. I loved my shawl almost as much as I loved Tommy for buying me such a lovely thing.

Looking back, I wonder about Tommy's attachment to Mother and her four daughters. Could he have been an old beau? There are so many mysteries still unsolved. Mother had always told us Grandfather Knight was a sea captain, but when I sent away for a copy of her marriage certificate, I found her father listed as a stoker. But would a stoker have been able to afford the fine house and furnishings my Granny Knight enjoyed?

I recently uncovered something else from reading and rereading that marriage certificate Mother had never shown her daughters, something I wish I'd known when I was pregnant with Haydn and praying he would come in October, as expected, to squelch all of Mabel's speculations. The date Mother and Father were married was February 19, 1918. Eva, our oldest sister, was born on May 11, 1918. Mother had been six months pregnant at the time she married! Mother, whose moral judgment I had always respected and feared, had once had her own reasons to call on her English pluck and get on with life. Surely Eva was my Father's child, but I cannot imagine why my parents would have waited so long to marry. Had they been swept away by passion and love, then separated, perhaps by my father's obligations during the first World War? Suddenly my mother's strictness concerning our relationships with boys—and especially with the American soldiers who might or might not be honorable enough to stand by a pregnant girlfriend—made perfect sense. Considering the anguish and embarrassment she must have known while carrying her first born, she must have been determined that no daughter of hers would suffer that same fate.

But there was still that bothersome question: Was Eva really my father's child or had that gentle, loving man accepted my mother's situation and married her, knowing their first child would be his in name only? With both my mother and father long dead by the time I began this memoir and obtained their marriage certificate, there is no way of knowing the answer to these questions. But would I have dared to ask them anyway? Probably not. So I suppose it's just as well I didn't have those troublesome unknowns to worry about during my first, difficult year in Montana.

Though the war supposedly came to an end on June 6, 1945, I heard not a word from my husband as to when he would be coming home. In fact, he had not written for some time by that date—at least he had not written to me, though he may well have been in contact with Guy and Mabel. Fortunately, working in a busy office and spending the rest of my hours in the loving company of my newfound family kept me too occupied to dwell upon the uncertainties of my life: my husband's return and our relationship thereafter, the dreaded pain of childbirth, and the looming responsibilities of motherhood.

June brought not only the end of the war but also the opportunity for a temporary escape from my worries. Senator Wallace had given me a week's vacation, and since Gerry had been planning to go to Portland, Oregon, to visit her father, she asked if I would like to go with her. Of course I said yes, excited by the thought of spending a few days in a place where the grass actually was greener on the other side—the other side of the Rockies, that is.

In anticipation of our trip, Gerry had sent one of the children down to Guy and Mabel's for my other V-2 suitcase, but Mabel had refused to surrender it. I felt like a strand of my embroidery floss being pushed through the eye of a needle, with somebody waiting to tie a big, tight knot on the end of that thread to be sure there was no way to slip back through the eye to freedom. But it seemed there was hope of breaking free after all. The day before I left for Oregon, as my friend's car pulled up to let me out at the bend of the road, there was Guy, standing beside his parked car, with my other suitcase on the ground beside him. I thanked my driver, not wanting to involve her in any way, got out of the car, and walked toward Guy, wondering whether I'd be expected to carry this suitcase up the hill as I had the first one.

But to my surprise, he said, "Get in!" So I did.

Not another word passed between us, and he let me out of the car a hundred yards or so from Gerry's house, set the suitcase on the road, swung the car in the opposite direction, and took off. One of the teens came hurrying out to greet me and help carry the bag to the house, and I spent the evening going through clothes I had not seen since leaving Guy and Mabel's weeks ago. Sure enough, I was able to put together a few of my old items from that suitcase and a couple of dresses I had bought with my wages, so I went to bed that night knowing I'd soon be Portland-bound.

For my first excursion beyond the fortress of the Mission Mountains, I boarded a bus that wasn't exactly a covered wagon, though I had the feeling of a pioneer heading west. The bus was much more comfortable than the English buses back home, but it was crowded, making the journey somewhat grueling for a woman nearly six months pregnant. I stood in the aisle and was jostled about until a kindly gentleman offered me his seat. But Gerry's good company and her promise that we'd watch the Rose Parade when we arrived in Portland helped the time pass pleasantly enough. We visited Gerry's father, who lived alone, and I was swept by memories of my own dear father as I shared in the happiness of two people reunited after many years.

Gerry kept her promise, and in the City of Roses we watched the Rose Parade. As I stood on the sidewalk, the perfume of those beautiful flowers came floating down, carrying me back to Wood Lane, where the wild roses grew along the path to my secret garden. There was only beauty in those memories during that trip to Portland, for my mind had long since buried what I would not again remember for another fifty years. Also, having Gerry by my side meant the scent of the roses did not make me as lonesome for home as I might otherwise have been. Shaking off the nostalgia, I focused on the throngs watching the parade, hoping that one day I might feel as much at home as they did in this new country, hoping I might one day become as one with them.

There was one more surprise in store for me—a sail across the waters of Puget Sound to visit Port Angeles, where Gerry's sister-in-law and family lived. Having been landlocked for so long, I found myself delighted with the salt air and the roll of the waves. Grateful to have been a part of this trip filled with joyous reunions and the beauty of roses and the sea, I returned to my job at the law office with a little more hope for the future.

Meantime, there was plenty of diversion down in Polson, for summer tourists were arriving to enjoy Flathead Lake, though not in the numbers Montanans see today. And by late July it was cherry-picking time. First came the sweet cherries, such as the Bing variety, and all along the shore, families and hired hands worked to strip the luscious, dark red berries from the branches of those trees. Those cherries most perfectly matched in size and shape were packed into gift boxes and mailed to addresses around the country. Growers also sent crates of fruit to grocers across the region, and many families sold cherries from their orchards at stands they had erected along the highway. Traffic on the road along the eastern shore increased, as visitors and locals alike sought to find the sweetest, most delectable fruit available.

My husband had told me that the trees in his uncle's orchard bore only the sour cherries used in pies. These trees bore their fruit a short time later than those producing sweet, edible cherries, and Mabel's roadside stand was not nearly as profitable as those of many of her neighbors. Though this was the busiest time of year for her—they did their own picking, slim as their profits were—I didn't volunteer to return to the house on the hill to help Mabel pick. I had always thought of Mother whenever I saw someone climbing a stepladder—remembering her fall the day I broke my glasses long ago. She had lost her balance while climbing a ladder and was lying on the grass when I found her there, unconscious, her eyes closed. So you can understand why nothing would induce me to climb a ladder during a pregnancy, and no one could blame me for not doing so.

I worked on at Senator Wallace's office for the rest of the summer, grateful for the income, since I had no idea what Ray planned to do to support us when he returned to Montana. I was also grateful for the company of those who came into the office, and looked forward in particular to those days when a local judge with a keen sense of humor would stop by to talk. A good friend of Senator Wallace, the judge owned a big hunting lodge somewhere in the mountains, and knowing my husband would need a job when he came home, he asked whether the two of us might like to become managers of this place. I was delighted by the prospect of a home in the mountains, but I had my doubts that Ray would be open to any suggestion that came from my contacts with colleagues of Senator Wallace. From remarks he'd made in his few letters home, I sensed he was somewhat jealous of my working relationship with the senator.

The days passed quickly, with afternoons spent helping Gerry put up vegetables and fruits for the winter, and days spent in the office in Polson. Though my husband had no knowledge—and seemingly little interest—in the way his unborn child was kicking against my ever-expanding belly, Gerry took pleasure in that knowledge, telling me which of her own had been the most active in the womb and which ones had been quite content to float about with minimal movement. It was Gerry and not my husband who marked off the months, the weeks, and finally the days with me, so that by the time the cherry leaves were turning rust brown and the aspens were gold against the evergreens.

I worked right up to the day before delivery, though in those final weeks I was lumbering down the hill to catch my ride, and the climb back up every afternoon left me breathless. On one unforgettable afternoon— October 10, to be precise—I stepped out of my friend's car and waved my thanks, as usual. But when I turned and started up that long, steep path, I doubted I would ever reach my destination. Something was different. I felt as if a stone was lodged between my legs, making each step more difficult that the last. As I arrived at her door, Gerry took one look at my flushed face and told me to go and lie down. That "stone," she said, was a sign the baby was settling into birth position. Her husband was attending a meeting out of town, but she would figure out a plan of action while I got some rest.

I was soon feeling somewhat better and joined Gerry in the kitchen. Her oldest son, Bob, was taking care of the milking that afternoon, assisted by his teenage sister, Jeannie. We were sitting at the table, waiting for the two of them to finish the chores and come in for dinner, when pain shot through my entire being and I felt a surge of something warm. "Your water's broken," Gerry said. "But the baby still might not come for hours."

Though her words were reassuring, I began to fret, knowing that the timing was not at all convenient for my host family. With Gerry's husband away, the family sedan was gone too, and I knew Gerry had never before left her children alone, especially at night. But with my pains coming closer and closer, what else could she do? She decided that Bob and Jeannie could put the little ones to bed and watch over them until she returned, trusting that there would be no emergency the two teens couldn't handle. And with no other vehicle on hand, she revved up the milk truck and we headed for the highway, leaving the children behind us.

I held my breath—with my hands holding up my belly—as we hit rut after rut along the narrow wagon path. Once we were on the highway, the ride was a bit smoother and I tried to relax, but I must admit I was relieved to see in the distance the lights of the "Hotel Dieu," which Gerry explained was French for "Hospital of God." Founded and largely staffed by French Canadian sisters from Kingston, Ontario, the place was certainly a welcome sight on that dark and frightening night. But while my journey had come to an end, my anxieties had not, for I suddenly realized I would be left alone to face yet another major event in my lifetime. Holding back my tears, I fought the urge to beg Gerry to stay with me, understanding all too well where her priorities lay. I kept a stiff upper lip as she said a quick "goodbye" at the hospital doors and climbed back into the cab of her milk truck to hurry back home to her children.

Within a few minutes, I was checked into my assigned room, waiting to face alone what turned out to be an ordeal but could—and should—have been a beautiful experience. Not long after the only nurse on duty set out on her nightly rounds, the pain began to increase. In all my young life, I had never experienced anything approaching this, yet I stifled the impulse to scream and cry in such silent surroundings as a hospital. I gritted my teeth in agony as the pains came and went with increasing regularity and intensity—until there were no more moments of respite. I had not the slightest idea of how the baby should be born, and was so delirious with pain that I ended up hanging over the side of the bed with my head on the floor and legs in the air, and remained in that ungainly position until the nurse finally came back to check on me.

"Dear God!" she said, as she struggled to pull me back up, and lay me down. As I felt my wrists being strapped to the head of the bed, I looked up and noticed the letters T.L.C. printed on a card and wondered at the irony of the meaning.

An Indian summer sun was blinking through the blinds of my hospital room the following morning, October 11, 1945, when they presented my son to me. He was snuggled in a blanket with only his red and wrinkled face apparent, crying fiercely. Even though I didn't know the first thing about caring for that angry little baby in my arms, this was the most beautiful moment of my life thus far. As I looked down on this tiny being, my spirits soared, almost as if we'd been bathed in the light of God's own love, my son and I, partners in His scheme of things. I felt at peace and closer to God's own truth than ever before. I vowed, as I hugged him close, that I would pass on to him the truth that I was learning in that beautiful moment of intimacy—that one must face the challenges life presents, learn to endure and conquer one's fears, in order to truly understand and appreciate what truth and beauty were all about. Until that moment, my baby's arrival had been an unexpected and almost unwanted event, one that I had brought upon myself without intention, and one for which I had been held responsible from the moment of conception. Yet from the moment of his birth, I realized that there had been purpose in his arrival at this particular point in my life, for from that moment onward, his life would be a joy and comfort to me.

I named him Haydn, after my father, and gave him my husband's middle name, Robert. Some people believe in naming their offspring after a mother or father, but I chose one of the three given names belonging to his grandfather—my own dear father, Harold Henry Haydn Hope. Father and his siblings had grown up in a music-loving family, where all of the boys—Pierce, Reginald, Beresford, and my father—were honored with middle names of famous composers, thanks to their father, who was himself a composer, though one of lesser renown. I had heard from my earliest days that my own father would have given that name to me, had I not been born a girl. And even as I bestowed the name Haydn on this tiny, wrinkled son of mine, I could already sense that he deserved that name and was destined to become the kind of grandson Father would have loved and admired, had he not passed away before coming to his promised land, America.

Though Haydn's own father was not there to welcome him into the world, his Uncle Foster was home on furlough from the Armed Forces and came to the hospital to see his new nephew and myself. It touched me deeply that he should have done so. Though Foster was my husband's brother, he had spent most of his childhood living with a family who had lost their only son in a boating accident. He had thus been spared the harshness of life on the hill with Mabel and Guy. Perhaps that was why he had earned the nickname "Hap," for having a happy disposition. The only member of the family who visited us during our long stay at Hotel Dieu, Hap arrived with his perpetual smile and a dozen red roses.

In those days, childbirth was viewed as a strength-sapping event that required confining the new mother to bed for a week or so. Mercifully, the Catholic sisters in the Hotel Dieu swept in and out of my room with the grace of angels, helping me to endure those long, lonely bedridden days until I was dismissed with my baby, relieved to know that I would be eagerly welcomed back by Geraldine and her family, rather than having to face the humility of running home to Mabel, or the impossible task of finding other living quarters.

The Fulkersons all fussed over the baby, and the girls begged to help me care for him, as I'm sure they'd helped care for their little brother, Glenny—eager to assist with every chore but the diapers. I would let even the youngest one sit and hold Haydn, but I stayed close, for fear they might drop him. I didn't trust the heater to stay warm enough through the night, so I piled on the baby blankets just to be sure he was snug and secure. I didn't trust that I would hear him if he cried, so I turned my good ear to face him through the night. I was embarrassed that there wasn't enough privacy when

I nursed him through the day. And I didn't trust my ability to keep this baby alive and healthy. I wanted my mother. And I needed a husband.

Finally I received a telegram saying my husband had landed in New York and would be in Montana "within a few days." With no word of exactly how soon he might arrive, we were quite surprised when he appeared virtually without warning at Gerry's kitchen door. It was late at night, and I couldn't help but wonder how long he had spent with Guy and Mabel before making his way to the Fulkerson's. A few hours? Overnight? Several days? All he would say was, "Just a while," and he offered not one word about whatever conversations had gone on during his time in the house on the hill.

Though he looked at Haydn with interest, I immediately sensed his resentment toward this little intruder and wondered what had been whispered to him by the relatives. Could he actually think that his son was someone else's child, as Mabel had hinted? There was no sense in confusing the issue further by asking him straight out. He might have taken my question as a confession of guilt, and any attempt to defend myself would have been humiliating and probably futile.

Whatever he thought about the baby, my husband didn't spend enough time around the house to get to know his son or to get reacquainted with the wife he hadn't seen in over eight months. To his credit, his absences were purposeful. He went out looking for a job and a place to live. And when he was "at home," conversations flowed any way but easy. Suddenly I had to face the fact that there were now two "Rays" in Gerry's household, and I seemed to be addressing only her Ray and not mine. The practice of not calling my husband by his given name had arisen on the very day I married my Montana man—and it had grown like a prickly pear cactus between us after the honeymoon, when he had started calling me "Candy." I loathed the idea of being thought of as a piece of chocolate or a gob-stopper, but he kept it up, regardless of my feelings. As time wore on, his given name meant nothing to me, so I would address him as "Love," the catchall substitution used in Lancashire when a given name is an unknown, but the person in question is in need of some sort of recognition. Even then I sensed that talking to someone without a name was like standing on the sidewalk conversing with a total stranger. But there the problem lay, inexplicable but enduring, another little black cloud blotting out any hope that all would be right come morning.

In recent years, a psychotherapist friend of mine has explained that the inability to call another person by name constitutes a denial of emotional identification with that person—certainly a bad sign in a relationship, especially a marriage. Could that inability to form an emotional attachment to my husband have been a result of that long-buried incident in my hidden garden? Has everything in my life been a matter of cause and effect?

During the times he was at home, my husband managed to mask his feelings so completely that I found the situation quite confusing. At least he managed to hold at bay his racial prejudice against our hostess, with attempts of congeniality at mealtimes. Those were the best times for me, especially when the children were all gathered around the table as a family, and were asking lots of questions about my husband's time overseas. Geraldine would cook a beef roast, or do something wonderful with ground beef. She served trout or salmon whenever her husband and oldest son had been out fishing, and there were always lots of potato salads and canned vegetables from the garden. My husband actually praised Gerry for her homemade bread and heavenly cakes and pies. He also made it a point to help Ray with the farm chores, and I was relieved about this, since Gerry had always refused to accept money for my room and board. I had no idea what my husband planned to do about compensating them for our keep if we stayed there much longer.

Two families living together is never the best situation, and I was longing to move into a place of our own. Sleeping in the same room with another couple and a crying baby might have been the perfect solution for planned parenthood, but it was not the most accommodating circumstance for a hus-

170

band expecting his due after a long absence, and a baby accustomed to being cuddled, fed, and changed in the middle of the night. Having our nightly conjugal ritual carried out in the presence of others was more than my reserved nature could stand, and I longed for the privacy of any spare room. Any room at any price—other than the one in the house on the lower hill.

The joy I'd felt living there with Gerry and her family was being swallowed up in the darkness cast by my husband's long shadow. I was beginning to feel caged, with wings unwilling—or unable—to fly, wanting to get away from them all, to flee the house and the situation, just the baby and me, but my fears convinced me there was simply no way out. With no money of my own, confidence in my abilities was fast slipping away, and a sense of shame crept in. How could I allow us to continue in such tenuous and less-than-ideal circumstances until the festering tensions threatened to explode?

In desperation, I dared to mention the judge's offer of life in his hunting lodge in return for our watching over the place, but my husband dismissed that suggestion without even allowing me to describe the picturesque setting of our possible abode. At another point, I suggested we might do better to put a down payment on a house somewhere along the lake, maybe someplace around Finley Point. I had heard of a small place being offered for sale by folks who'd grown tired of Montana's hard winters and were looking for a young couple who would care for their home as well as they had. There were even a few cherry trees. Couldn't we at least find out what they were asking?

"So they can laugh in our faces when we tell them you have nothing for a down payment—and that I don't even have a job?"

Though there was nothing further said about buying a house, at least my husband realized as well as I did the untenable nature of our situation there at the Fulkersons, and the urgency of the need for him to find at least a rented home of our own. I'd wait through the day, anxious for his return with good news. Then late in the afternoon, as we heard his old Ford Coupe straining to make its way up the hill, Gerry and I would exchange nervous glances, fearful that yet again he'd come in wearing the downtrodden look that meant no one needed—or dared—to ask how his search had gone.

Admittedly, his task was not an easy one. Until he found steady work, we could hardly afford more than a simple room that would see us through to our next housing. And it was hunting season, with lodgings filled to capacity. Finally he reported that he had found a one-room motel cabin on the west shore of the lake, but we'd have to wait several more days for the place to be vacated by the hunters who'd been staying there. Despite Gerry's patience and graciousness, I'm sure the mattress in the other corner of the room creaked with relief as I told her we had finally found a place to stay.

I began gathering up our belongings, and on the appointed day, we loaded everything into the old Ford Coupe, promised to keep in touch, and drove down the hill toward the highway as the Fulkerson children waved a teary goodbye.

And still not a word from the relatives.

Part 3

Chapter 9

A retentive memory may be a good thing, but the
ability to forget is the true token of greatness.

—ELBERT HUBBARD

The one-room motel cabin on the west shore provided one bed, one ancient, decrepit wood stove, and one sink for washing dishes, dirty linens, dirty diapers, the baby, and ourselves. Every evening, the minute the dishes were done and the sink was empty, we would toss a coin to determine who might take a sponge bath before the fire in the cook stove burned down and the hot water turned cold. My husband worked faithfully to gather and chop enough wood to see us through each day, but there was no wood to be wasted in building up the fire just for the sake of heating bath water.

There was no indoor toilet, and though I had managed to live without that convenience during my months at the house on the lower hill, doing without indoor plumbing with a baby to care for was another matter altogether. Back in those days, diapers, nappies—whatever name they went by—were absolutely indispensable cloth items that needed toilet flushing as mother held her nose with one hand, while holding onto a corner of the soiled, smelly garment with the other, in order to prevent that reusable diaper from slipping away and disappearing down the toilet drain. Once the contents of the soiled nappy had been flushed away, then came the second round of cleansing, using hot, soapy water and a corrugated scrubbing board. For the final sanitizing steps—according to instructions set forth by Dr. Benjamin Spock in the book Ray had purchased for me shortly after his homecoming—the diapers had to be boiled for half an hour or so, then rinsed and hung outdoors to dry, where they would be further purified by sun and breeze, though not, of course, made as fluffy and soft as a dryer would have made them.

This labor-intensive regimen had worked well at Gerry's house, but one thing that escapes my memory concerning our time at the motel on the west shore is how I ever managed to get Haydn's diapers clean enough in the first place for them to be scrubbed on a washboard, then boiled in a big old copper canner, and rinsed in cold water in that sink. What I do remember all too well are the difficulties I encountered in attempting to hang them out to dry, for they froze as soon as I snapped out the wrinkles and pegged them onto the clothesline at the back of the cabin. I felt as if my spirit was freezing along with those nappies.

In this land of the free, I felt freedom slipping through my ice-cold fingers, and my mind was becoming petrified by the thought of the almost impossible odds against there ever being anything more promising than this to look forward to. I tried to hold to Mother's reassurances that you'll be right as rain come morning, but her words seemed a mockery. In this frigid land I now called home, I knew that morning would only bring more snow, more diapers freezing on the line, and more pangs of longing for the olden days over there. Even in the hardest of times, we had the warmth of family togetherness as we battled for survival and advancement in that tiny cottage on Gatewarth Street.

While my father's homecoming each day had been something I looked forward to, my husband's absence was more welcome than his presence, for with every passing day his unsuccessful search for employment made him more and more moody and belligerent. I honored my wedding vows, preparing his meals, keeping the place swept up and wiped down, and diligently keeping up the pretense of receiving pleasure from the rough practice of his lovemaking. For my part, I was afraid to think any further than today, and my life in that miserable motel room became more and more centered on my baby. Though during those first few weeks after his birth, I feared I would never be able to care for him properly, I can see now that I had, from the beginning, the natural ability and boundless love that were the major keys to success in mothering an infant, and reading Dr. Spock's manual had given me much more confidence in my new role.

I found it reassuring to read that my basic instincts concerning the care of a newborn were basically those of the famed physician—except in one crucial regard. Dr. Spock had written that babies need only be fed every six hours, but my instincts told me otherwise. My husband, who had read the book as carefully as I had, and who was becoming more and more controlling and less and less inclined to hear my views concerning the whys and wherefores of our deteriorating relationship, thought he also had the right to dictate the mothering of our newborn son. And with little else to occupy his hours, he was there, always there, to make sure I followed Dr. Spock's ridiculous feeding schedule.

Against my will, I would sit there with the baby screaming in hunger. I held my tongue, not daring to defy my husband's orders and face his wrath, until the prescribed six-hour nursing curfew ended and my tiny six-pound Haydn could be fed again. One night when my husband awoke to find me sitting in the rocker, nursing the baby before the clock struck twelve, he forcibly snatched him from my arms and put him on the bed, then ran back to sit on me until the little one cried himself to sleep. I suffered through it all, stupefied and horrified that I was being denied my right to be a mother, yet too caught up in my vows to be a good wife to fight for my baby's rights as well as my own.

The only opportunities I had to make up for all the cuddling and nourishment my baby was being denied were the days my husband went to look for work or went out on the lake to fish. Those were the happy days, when I would hold my son for hours, nurse him at will, and sing him lullabies, letting the rest of the world do what it might. There was no point in continuing to wish that my father were still alive and ready to come and rescue me. Better to try to find comfort in Mother's sensible words, "You'll feel better when you get to school now." After all, I had gone through hard times before, and I would learn to cope, just as Mother had.

She coped, yet she never ceased to complain about the hardships she endured for our sakes. She would grumble often and long about the shortage of money and the empty coal scuttle, with a blast of self pity thrown in for good measure, a reminder that she had never taken a single vacation during our growing-up years. Little impact the saga of her sacrifices carried for a hungry child who yearned for chips with fish, and a few "afters" like trifle and vanilla wafers once in a while.

Doing without food was one thing. Doing without understanding was quite another. Mother's constant grousing about my bothersome behavior made an even emptier hole inside on that long-ago day when my soul stopped singing, and she never even noticed. But that painful time was far too well buried to alter the rosy glow that suffused the memories of my childhood, which haunted me during those miserable months in the motel cabin. Nostalgia was constantly dragging me back to the home I'd left behind, and I took my infant son along with me.

Whenever we were alone, even if only for a few precious hours, I would bring forth my albums and memorabilia, holding up pictures and pieces of paper for my son to see, sharing my past with him as though he might understand me better than his father did, and so might actually care about the things that had sustained me in my childhood. I read aloud the citations printed on certificates of merit I'd earned and prizes won for conscientious study, telling him there would be bigger and better things for him if he could only learn to believe in himself. Though he was no doubt cooing and smiling in response to having my undivided attention, he seemed to be watching intently, taking in my every word.

A bit of lost pride came back as I fingered the parchment pages from Price's Business College, which recorded my completion of their program in a matter of six months of night classes, taken after working all day in a department store. But my wounded ego begged for more, and I continued to leaf through and describe the bits and pieces from my past, even after my voice had lulled the baby to sleep and I had placed him in his crib, making sure the blankets were snuggled up around him. I always ceased the minute my husband came through the door, of course, for he would never have understood or approved of his wife's talking to herself. But the memories persisted even as I put away the pages and the albums for another day.

My nostalgia was not limited to thoughts of my academic successes, for trapped as I was, with no means of earning income, I thought back to my first job—and my first paycheck. Earned at the department store where I clerked, that paycheck wasn't very big. I was earning approximately ten shillings a week, all of which went into Mother's outstretched hand every Friday. It was expected in those days in Lancashire that upon leaving school and finding employment, English children should begin to repay their parents for the cost of their upbringing. It wasn't exactly a law laid down by the government, but Mother thought it should have been, and she adhered to the concept, handing back to me only the one shilling and sixpence she expected to cover the cost of my clothes, toiletries, picture shows, tram fare, and whatever else might be on my wish list.

Here I was, supposedly an adult with rights to her own money, yet financial independence was still not mine. Though there had been no indication that I would be expected to pay for my lodging at Mabel and Guy's while Ray was overseas, once I went into Polson and got a job with Senator Wallace, Mabel—like my mother before her—met me at the door on payday, hand outstretched for the $20 a month she called "egg money." My pride made me glad enough to pay for my hated lodging, but when Gerry and her husband refused to take a penny for my room and board, I began sending small, but regular, payments back home to England. Old habits die hard, and I still felt morally obliged to continue to be a good English daughter and repay my widowed mother for the cost of my upbringing. The rest of my paycheck went toward clothes—the senator's secretary was expected to be dressed to meet the public—and, in time, hospital expenses for Haydn's birth and various other expenses pertaining to his care.

Though my paycheck was modest and my expenses consistent, if not large, I had also managed to build up a savings account, knowing I'd not be able to work after the baby's birth, and not knowing for sure just when my husband would be home to take his place as family breadwinner. Whatever relief I felt upon his return was short-lived, for within hours he had demanded to know how much money I had in the bank, and soon thereafter drove into town to add his signature to my accounts, making it clear that he would now manage "our" money, since we'd have to depend on what I'd saved to support us until he found work.

I shouldn't have been surprised by this turn of events, for my earnings, not his, had supported us during our years together in England. It was my paycheck that covered our rent and our groceries, and I do not know to this day exactly what my husband earned at the airbase. As with all other matters, he considered it his business and his alone, and he kept his counsel, leaving me to assume he might well not be earning any money at all, since this was a war and he was quite likely expected to serve his country without financial recompense.

Now that he was without income, the money for the bleak little cabin at the motel on the west shore came from my carefully saved earnings, as did the money spent on groceries, gas and upkeep for the car, and the few items of clothing we felt we could not do without. With no office to go to and no one to visit—my husband said we weren't going to be there long enough to meet the neighbors or form any friendships—I had no need for new dresses or shoes for myself. But as Haydn began to outgrow the outfits from the shower and those I'd bought in anticipation of his arrival, I longed to be able to purchase clothes worthy of my baby. And knowing I could not afford to do so set me thinking back on those days before the privations of war reduced us all to rags, days when a young working girl could save her money and manage to fulfill a few of her dreams.

On a snowy morning when my husband set out to visit his relatives, I hastened to get the one-room living quarters as squeaky clean as the old linoleum and battered furniture would allow them to be, then settled into my own world, knowing I had all the time in the world to rock and play with the baby without interruption. On this particular day, as I dressed him in a well-worn outfit, I promised myself there would come a time when he would have fine new clothes to wear, clothes he could pick out for himself, though he might have to wait until he was old enough to earn his own money and spend it as he chose.

As he drifted off to sleep, content with my promises, my mind drifted back to the time I saved up for over a year to buy a dressy outfit for a special occasion. I loved pretty things and dreamed of looking as beautiful as Greer Garson's *Mrs. Miniver,* with her namesake rose in hand, or as elegant as Paulette Goddard, the hem of her lovely long gown held out in a graceful arc as she swept down the winding staircase in Auntie Mame. I selected every item of that long-awaited ensemble very carefully so Mother would not be displeased by my choices. The dress was a forget-me-not blue, long sleeved crêpe de Chine, fitted to the waist and with a pleated skirt reaching down to the fashionable length, mid-calf. It had a rounded neckline, serviceable double-stitched seams which I knew Mother would love, shoulder pads, and a narrow, blue leather belt which I could fasten around my twenty-six-inch waist if I breathed in. A matching bolero jacket topped off the outfit. I wanted to show off my ensemble by wearing it to work the next day but mother said, "Absolutely not."

I loved that outfit. It was all mine! Chosen by me and paid for by money I had earned on my own. From that moment I decided I would continue to save my money and gradually add to my wardrobe, until there were no more hand-me-downs made over from Mother's cast-offs!

Though that first special dress was an exception, for the most part I never liked any kind of clothing that was gaudy and conspicuous. In fact everything else in my wardrobe was black, including black, lacy gloves with a purse to match, and a straw hat that Mother always considered a little too saucy with its large, droopy brim and moiré ribbon trim. At that time—and to a certain extent even today—high-heeled shoes certified a woman's coming of age. Mine were black and sophisticated, soft leather, with crossover straps embracing my high instep. I practiced walking round the kitchen on my first pair of high-heeled shoes before Mother would allow me to wear them outside. They were very lovely, and I learned to walk in them in no time at all.

At fourteen, being able to earn enough money to buy clothes for myself helped to make up for all the unfair things that had happened to my education. Our Eve was still at school taking Latin and French, chemistry, botany, and all the other fascinating courses I'd always dreamed of taking, while it looked as though I would be dragging myself off to work every morning for the rest of my days, having been deprived of a scholarship that could have enriched my life immeasurably. Losing those scholarships had long-range, as well as immediate, ramifications. As the eldest daughter, Eve would seemingly have been first in line to begin repaying our parents for her upbringing. Yet given her status as a scholarship student, Our Eve had no worries whatsoever about contributing income to the family. All that was required of her was to go to school, study, and have everything else she wanted served to her with a silver spoon—tasty lunches, handsome school uniforms, hockey stick and uniform, books, books, and more books, for which my parents were required to pay not a single penny.

Then along came the war, altering all our lives, making even the thought of buying a new dress or hat seem ridiculous, and overturning our world in unforeseen ways. My world, in particular, for had it not been for the war, I would not have been standing ankle-deep in snow out behind a run-down motel, struggling to unpeg a line of frozen nappies. With not a penny in my pocket, the only hope in my heart was the distant memory of my father, singing and dreaming of springtime in the Rockies. Yet it was becoming more and more evident that his dream of a good life in America had turned out to be my nightmare.

Meantime, within the bounds of that vow I'd made at St. Mary's, my husband, myself, and the baby were surviving early winter days by the lake, living on my savings and eating what staples we could afford, plus the fish my husband caught while rowing the waters of the Flathead. Those fish became an essential part of our meager diets, and over the weeks and months, I learned a variety of ways to cook them, though I well remember how bewildered I was when faced with the challenge of preparing the bounty from his first trip out on the lake.

The very idea of being back on the water had lifted his spirits, and when the motel proprietor agreed to lend him his rowboat in exchange for a few fish for himself, my husband was almost ecstatic. He stayed out there a long time that first day, and I had begun to worry that the boat had leaked and he'd been lost in those icy waters by the time the little boat came into sight. I watched as he tied it up at the shore, picked up a huge fish, and almost ran into the cabin, plopping the monster into the sink. "There," he said with a triumphant grin, "clean 'er up. . . . I'm going back out!" And with that he was gone, leaving me to decide what to do with his catch. Tail still flapping as it lay on its side in the sink, that fish fixed me with a one-eyed stare, as if daring me to touch it, so I gave it a little grace time in which to die properly as I tried to figure out what I should do with it.

I looked through the cookbook my husband had said I could use— the T.M. 10-412 War Department Technical Manual, Army Recipes, published by the War Department, on August 15, 1944, and used during his supervision of a mess hall, whose cooks were preparing dishes to serve hundreds, sometimes thousands, of hungry men.

The first problem I had was to identify the kind of fish that lay there with its mouth sagging open as though begging for pardon. I flipped through the pages detailing awesome amounts of ingredients, finding recipes for salmon, haddock, halibut, and mackerel—but not a single one for trout, which I finally had decided this fish must be, since it resembled my prize catch the day I fished through the ice with Guy. So I settled on a recipe for creamed codfish. There was comfort in that decision, for cod was a familiar sounding name—there were thousands of them caught daily off the eastern coast of England, and some of them must surely have found their way into our house and onto my mother's table at one time or another.

During the coal strikes, when we had so little money, we could hardly afford even fish. But during the war years, fish was plentiful and coupon-free. If Father fancied a piece of cod for supper, he certainly didn't go out and catch it himself. Instead, Mother would have to rise very early in the morning and queue up at the fish market for an hour or more, awaiting her turn at the counter, where the fishmonger would slap the piece of cod on a square of the Manchester Guardian. "There y'ar, Love," she would say, folding the fish into a neat package for Mother's market basket, "and there's plenty more where that cum from."

Apparently there were plenty more trout where my husband had caught the one that stared up at me from its resting place in the sink, and my attention returned to the army-issue cookbook at hand. Ah, yes. "Creamed Codfish." The first ingredient called for in that recipe was "Codfish, skinned and salted, 16 pounds." The second ingredient: "Toast, 100 slices." Discouraged by the thought of figuring out how to whittle down a recipe designed to feed one hundred airmen into one that would serve the two of us, I was even more defeated by the realization that I had no idea how to go about skinning a fish. Knowing better than to risk doing the wrong thing with a fish that had been handed over to me with such pride, I left that trout where it lay and went to feed the baby, hoping my husband would come home in a mellow mood with a few more fish, and feel magnanimous enough to do his own skinning and gutting. He even cooked his catch that evening, basking in the glow of my compliments concerning his skills as a chef as well as an angler. The lesson was not lost on me: If a successful day of fishing could lift my husband's gloom and allow us a few moments of relative happiness, I would encourage him to fish as often as he could—and I would learn how to clean and cook whatever he caught from that day forward.

Fishing did help to dispel the gloom, but as the days grew shorter and the nights grew longer and colder, my husband's restlessness became more and more apparent. Angry outbursts over even the slightest irritation or annoyance became the rule rather than the exception, and it became increasingly evident that there would be no hope of finding employment until winter loosed its grip and spring thaw brought more demands for lumber, more traffic on the roadways, and more opportunities for work. I can't even recall whether or not I was aware of the passing of Thanksgiving, though I had earlier looked forward to my first celebration of that uniquely American holiday. I'm certain we gave no thought to turkey, and were glad enough to have fish, which were harder and harder to come by as winter began to hold us in its grip.

I waited out the future one day at a time, nerves on edge, until one particularly dismal morning when my husband received a letter from an old air corps buddy who was going to school on the GI Bill. Why couldn't he do the same? He had already completed one year at Montana State College before his enlistment in the U.S. Air Corps in 1941. In only three more, he could have a degree that would pay for itself in increased earnings. Knowing as little as I did about the GI Bill, I couldn't imagine how two people who could barely afford to pay their modest rent and put food on the table could possibly afford to pay for tuition and textbooks. But since there was no point in arguing with him once he settled on an idea, I joined him in writing to the college and the army for more information. Up until then, neither of us had realized the implications of the bill President Roosevelt had signed into law some two weeks after D-Day, back in June of 1944. After all, the war did not end for another sixteen months. If I heard about the bill at all in England, I can't remember thinking it had anything to do with our future. But now that the letter from his air corps friend had alerted us to the opportunities that bill offered, I dared to think that there might, after all, be an escape from our dead-end existence.

By the time we had received confirmation from the college that my husband was eligible for full tuition and a living allowance for his family, I had begun to look forward to a new adventure, a new town, better housing. I even dared hope that maybe, just maybe, our move to a college town meant that I would be able to take a few courses to further my own education—not that I mentioned that hope to my husband, knowing it was his own schooling and not mine that he was planning for.

There was lots of planning to be done, for I was convinced that the old car could not possibly make it all the way to Bozeman. Traveling over snow-packed and icy roads through Montana's mountains, with temperatures that could fall well below zero, was perilous even with the best of cars, and as fearful as I was to take a stand on most things, I made it clear that I would not risk our baby's life by traveling through blizzards. Not until Christmastime did my husband finally agree to draw enough from our savings account to buy a used Ford Coupe that was in considerably better condition than our present car. And shortly thereafter, we were on our way!

Along the foothills of the Mission Mountains, battling snow storms and slipping and sliding on icy roads across two mountain passes, we made our way ever south and east, stopping only to fill up the thirsty gas tank and scrape ice and snow off the windows and headlights. On and on my husband drove, as I nursed a hungry baby and changed his diapers, and passed out the sandwiches and cookies I'd made for the trip, along with water from a jug and cold coffee from a battered thermos.

On and on we traveled, seemingly forever, until suddenly we were driving into Bozeman, the home of Montana State College. Having survived the long journey, we were about to begin the obstacle course of higher education, with the goal of my husband's obtaining a B.S. in Dairy and Food Manufacturing, the course of study he'd begun there before he set off to help "keep the world safe for democracy."

Though the GI Bill had also promised housing for veterans and their families, the housing that Montana State had erected for that purpose had filled up during the fall semester. The dormitories were also full, and with single students and families competing for lodging, apartments were hard to find in the middle of a school year. Without even realizing how lucky he was, my husband managed to find an unfurnished apartment over the Bon Ton Bakery on Main Street the very day we arrived—Christmas Eve. The smells wafting up from below reminded me of aromas from the bake shops back home, and weary as I was, this seemed like a fortunate find for us. The barren room would look better with furniture, and though I had noticed a few cockroaches scampering away the moment we opened the door, I reasoned I could kill those invaders and make the place our own.

Without even taking time to carry our belongings up the narrow flight of stairs, we dashed over to the furniture store across the street and bought a pull-out couch that would serve us for sleeping and sitting. Though the owner pointed out an inexpensive little kitchen table and even offered to sell it with only two chairs—we could buy the other two later— my husband refused to purchase anything more, insisting that we wouldn't be living over there that long, and the next place might be furnished. Accustomed by now to making do with what we had, I created a bed for Haydn by placing a blanket in a kitchen drawer, and I draped a cloth over a discarded wooden box left behind by other tenants to form a makeshift table. Deciding there was no point in going to the grocery store, I served up a supper of sandwiches that were leftover from our trip.

But I was determined to do a little special shopping on my own. After all, it was the day before Christmas, 1945, my first Christmas in the United States, and for the sake of our baby, if not for ourselves, I was determined to celebrate in the way I always had at home. I dared to brave the snow-covered streets with only the few dollars in my pocket, confident that I would be able to buy at least a few presents for the three of us—to celebrate new beginnings in our new home. Back in the apartment, I went about the grisly business of killing cockroaches, served our sandwiches, tucked in the baby, then set out the presents—wrapped only in the paper bags from the shop, but brightened by the Christmas seals I'd bought at half price just as the storekeeper was closing up for the afternoon.

My Christmas breakfast surprise consisted of day-old pastries purchased from the bakery below, but I was the one who was surprised, for to my horror, the cockroaches I had killed had been replaced by their swarming cousins, one of which I found under the waxed paper that held our breakfast fare. These hideous creatures—which I'm told are among the most resilient insects of all time—had obviously become almost genetically programmed to inhabit the apartment we had rented. Day after day, night after night, they persisted in popping up from below, where the bakery staff had shooed them away from the donuts, and I was having nightmares knowing that once the lights were out each night, they were bound to be crawling around at will in the baby's makeshift bed.

Though my husband scoffed at my worries, saying that cockroaches didn't bite and the baby mustn't mind them or else he'd be crying all night, he himself was growing increasingly cranky because we were still eating our meals served on the surface of the wooden box. He had homework to do as well, and he often stayed at the college library rather than come home and put his books and papers down on that hated box.

Sensing this was the ideal time to talk about the mortgage breaks for which veterans were qualified under the GI Bill, I did a little research and as he walked in after school one afternoon, I posed the question I'd dared not ask since he'd vetoed my idea of buying a house on Finley Point. "How about buying a house, as long as the down payment didn't totally deplete our savings? With the $92 monthly allowance from the GI Bill, we could probably make ends meet and still manage a house payment."

To my surprise, he seemed open to the idea. "If you don't go looking for something fancy, you can go buy a newspaper and we can see what's for sale," he said. "No guarantee I'm going to buy one, but you can do the looking." I put the baby in the pram he had reluctantly bought for Haydn a week or so earlier and pushed him along the snow-covered sidewalks. I headed for the office of the realtor who'd driven me around town that very morning, while my husband was at school. He had showed me several lovely homes, some of them within walking distance of downtown and the college.

I'd insisted he tell me the price of each one, and time after time I looked with longing at a house but refused to go inside and look at any of them—until he pulled to a stop in front of a tiny house across the street from a park on Eighth Avenue, adjacent to Irving School and right next to Cooper Park. This time the price seemed within our means, so I dared step inside. The owner was a grandmotherly sort, and I knew she had made her house a home. It had an aura about it that reminded me of my own home. I was so excited by my find that I took the steps two at a time and burst into the apartment with my good news—only to be met with my husband's negative response. "No, we can't afford to dish out all of our savings! We'll just have to look for something to rent that we can afford."

That proved to be easier said than done. The influx of servicemen returning home and going to school on the GI Bill had seemingly filled up every empty living space in the whole town of Bozeman. But we finally found a basement bedroom-sitting room with kitchen and shower in the home of a gracious lady named Bartholemew at 819 South Third. It was sparsely furnished—with a kitchen table and chairs and a real bed—but we brought over our heavy pull-out couch and splurged on a crib for the baby. I was happy to be free from the cockroaches, but with the coming of spring, I found that a basement apartment attracted its own special creeping things.

My husband walked home for lunch as often as he could, and one day I'd made up a batch of biscuits for a special treat. As he picked one from the plate, he shrieked in indignation: "What are you trying to do—kill me!!" I jumped to attention and rushed over to the table in a panic. He pushed the plate up to my face for me to take a look at the swarm of tiny ants creeping around his freshly buttered biscuit. So much for my beautiful biscuits of which I had been so proud, the biscuits I was so sure he would love so much he'd possibly offer a word or two of praise. He stormed out of the house and said he was going back to school where he could find something clean to eat.

Later, as I was putting the dishes away, I opened a drawer and found the rolling pin covered with a thick crust of the creatures. I scraped them off and scrubbed the rolling pin clean of any trace of dough or shortening, and reported the incident upon my husband's return. His response? "What do you expect? You can't even wash the dishes clean!"

While I prided myself on keeping a spotless kitchen, cleaning our clothing during our time in Mrs. Bartholemew's basement was another matter. We had only a very small kitchen sink, and a shower with no tub, and I found myself missing the comparative luxury of being able to do the laundry in the old claw-foot bathtub in the apartment over the Bon Ton. Not that I recognized the value of that old tub while I was bending over it, scrubbing diapers. At the time I was haunted by thoughts of how horrified my mother would be to see that I had apparently forgotten all she taught me about the proper way to put out a wash.

Monday was always wash day back at the cottage on Gatewarth Street, and Mother rose well ahead of the rest of us to put the kettle on for a good 'ot cuppa tay to start the day off right. While the tea was steeping, she would go out to the shed in the backyard and throw a bucket of cold water (ours was a cold-water cottage) into the cast-iron boiler clad in concrete that served as a wash pot. Then she'd toss a shovel of coal chunks into the firebox under the washpot, add a few sticks of wood and kindling, and hook up the hose that ran from the kitchen sink to the shed in order to fill the wash pot with water as the fire began to roar. It took quite a while for her to fill the line of dollying tubs with the correct amount of water for rinsing the clothes, but Mother never seemed to mind the wait. She had her routine well established and would take her cup of tea and the cozy-covered pot out to the shed, where she would sit and sip until the dollying tubs were filled and the water in the boiler was hot enough so that the pieces of strong soap she'd added had melted and made a foam. Only then was the pot ready to receive, boil, and sanitize the whites, which included linens and towels, items that were always white in those days.

Getting the dirt out of the rest of the clothes entailed using a large, hard scrubbing brush and a pail of the hot, soapy water dipped out of the boiler. It would take until late afternoon before all the boiling and scrubbing was finished and it was time to move on to the next step. That consisted of putting a load of the colored wash, one color at a time, into one of the cold water dollying tubs. Then Mother would root out the dolly peg from underneath the scrubbing table.

It isn't difficult to imagine what a dolly peg looked like in the long ago. Similar to a milkmaid's wooden stool, it consisted of a flat, round, twelve-inch-diameter circle of sturdy wood, from which extended three sturdy pegs with rounded bottoms on the underside, slightly sprawled outward to facilitate good movement of the clothes through the water as they were forced out and around the circular tub. The broomstick-type pole, screwed in on the top side of the wooden, three-legged circle, extended high enough for Mother to grasp the wooden handle, a rounded crosspiece secured horizontally across the pole. Cupping her palms upward she would grasp each end of the handle, place the dolly peg inside the tub of clothes, and gyrate the contraption gently till much of the soap was dollied out of the clean wash.

As if the clothes hadn't suffered enough already, they were run through the wringer to squeeze out the last vestige of strong-smelling soap, then transferred to the second cold water tub to go through the same punitive action all over again. Many of the items in Emily's weekly wash needed starch, like father's collars—which were supposed to stay stiff but didn't—along with the tablecloths and serviettes, or napkins, the doilies, and our petticoats. Nothing—not even starch—came ready-made then, and I always volunteered to supervise that part of the process, measuring the powder and the water to just the right consistency. Of course I loved to do the dollying too, though I was not allowed that honor until I'd grown tall enough to manage the peg.

If the weather cooperated, Mother would then hang everything out on the lines in the top garden to dry, but come rain, fog, or a blustery nor'wester, come hell or high water, Monday was washing day and she was prepared for anything. My father had devised a contraption for drying clothes made from two wooden laths hanging parallel from the ceiling about eight inches apart and both attached to a pulley which Mother could manipulate to lower the racks, fill them with damp clothes, and raise them back up again. I loved the job of tugging that pulley rope and raising the rack almost all the way to the ceiling, then securing it so that the clothes could dry in the warm air wafting up from the fire in the hearth.

While the bathtub at the Bon Ton had been a poor substitute for all the steps in my mother's wash-day ritual, the lack of a tub—and the dampness of the basement at Mrs. Bartholemew's—left me with no choice but to take most of our clothes to a laundry. I managed to wash the baby's diapers in the tiny sink, and did my best to hand wash most of my own clothes, but my husband's shirts I sent to the laundry.

I did not have long to worry about such matters, for within months of starting classes at Montana State, my husband appeared at the basement apartment door and rolled in a huge oaken barrel. "Pack everything up," he ordered. "I've decided to rejoin the Air Corps." Apparently his idea of getting a college education had evaporated as quickly as it had appeared, though I could see why he would want to leave the classroom for an environment in which all he needed to do was follow orders and receive a paycheck. I only learned after his death, when I was putting the estate in order and came across his withdrawal papers from Montana State, that his stated reason for dropping all his classes and leaving college so abruptly was not lack of nerve, as I'd always assumed, but an unspecified "problem with his nerves."

Chapter 10

Nothing is got without pain but dirt and long fingernails.
—ENGLISH PROVERB

I don't know where the courage came from, but upon hearing of my husband's re-enlistment plans, I told him that I would not go with him unless we drove to Oklahoma City, where he could possibly re-enlist at the same air base where my sister and the American airman she married had been stationed for a year or so. While my own journey on the *Mauretania* had been made under wartime conditions, Our Eve had sailed across the ocean on the *Queen Mary* after the war. And while my husband's tour of duty had ended when the war ended, her husband had risen to the rank of major and been sent to his new assignment at Tinker Air Force Base near Oklahoma City, where Eve had joined him. They had a lovely home and, by all reports, life at Tinker Air Force Base might be an attractive possibility for us, too. Ray reluctantly agreed to drive to Oklahoma and check out the situation, primarily because Our Eve's husband was one of his wartime buddies, and he felt obliged to go and see him.

Miraculously, the old Ford made the trip and we arrived safely at Eva's home, which was located in an Oklahoma City suburb called Midwest City.

Her home seemed to lack nothing for comfort and coziness, and I could easily see that her journey to America had ended in a happy reunion with a warm and loving husband, who cared about her desires as well as his own, and who treated her with great respect. Once again, Our Eve seemed to have had all the good fortune, yet strangely enough I can't remember being jealous of her situation, perhaps because it was absolutely lovely to be in the company of my sister and her easy-going husband. She insisted we stay with them until Ray got situated, and in anticipation of our agreeing to her plan, there was a railed crib waiting for Haydn to take a nap. She was equally interested in my comfort and well-being, for the first thing she said to me was, "Your hair's a mess! I'm going to take you to the beauty shop at the base tomorrow." And oh what a treat that was—massage, shampoo, manicure, pedicure—the whole day was a cure-all for a spirit depressed for so long.

We talked the hours away, with Haydn playing at our feet. I was hoping against hope that Ray would end up being stationed right there at Tinker Field, but it was not to be. In truth, I don't know whether he even tried to enlist at Tinker, for by that time he had become fairly consistent in doing the opposite of anything I asked, and I think he sensed how much stronger, happier, and more confident I was in the presence of my older sister.

Be that as it may, he came in one afternoon with orders to report to the air base in Roswell, New Mexico. In preparation for his work there, he was to report first to a base in Tacoma for weeks of training. Once again I was to travel ahead without him, this time with the added burden of finding someplace for us to live until he joined us and we could locate a real home. This time I was not so lonely, for I traveled with my son, who was now approaching his first birthday, beginning to put his words together, and growing into a little person whose presence took up the empty space in my life.

Looking back, I treasure the memories of the time I spent with my son on that railway trip to Roswell, and the time we had to ourselves after I found lodgings in a private home. Our kindly landlady was a widow who seemed to enjoy our company and found pleasure in cooking for us. She was also very engaging, and I remember her telling me she loved New Mexico because the sky was not so high and it seemed you could reach up and touch the stars.

Frankly, as the time approached for my husband's training to end, I fretted about how this kindly woman might react to his presence, but she gave him a warm welcome and he treated her with respect for the relatively short time we lived there. He wasn't at home much in the daytime, for he began his duties at the base almost immediately, settling into his new position of purchasing supplies—nuts and bolts and such. Or at least I think that was what he was doing. Characteristically, he told me as little about his work as he told me about his life before I met him, and I knew enough by then not to push for details.

In fact, I was so determined that this move would signal a new beginning for our little family that I did my best to keep things peaceful and harmonious. In general, my spirits were higher than they had been since my husband's return from England, perhaps, in part, because Roswell was a pleasant place to live. We found a furnished home to rent with an option to buy—a step I feared he would never take—and, wonder of wonders, after we had lived there for several months, we took the risk, and for a small down payment, bought that lovely house.

At last we had a home of our own! It was white stucco with a red tiled roof, and was carpeted, with three bedrooms and lovely furnishings. Situated along the bank of a dry creek bed, there were pansies that grew along the low stone wall surrounding the garden, and a latticed fence that was decked with yellow roses climbing to reach the sun. In February I had learned to love the mountains and the big sky of Montana, but here you could see the earth meet the sky as far as the eye could see, and my landlady there in Roswell had been right: I was so close to the stars I felt I could reach up my hand and turn on their lights.

I took pleasure in keeping house and learning to cook, and keeping in touch with my sister now and then. We were both very homesick and wanted to go back to England to see Mother, Joyce, and Our Little Dot, and we talked about it so often that it became a plan of its own choosing. Within a week Our Eve just decided to come over and stay to look after Haydn, while I found a job to earn enough money so we could both make our dream come true. Leaving Haydn in someone else's care in order to go to work would be a major step, for I had tried this once before. From the moment he arrived in Roswell, my husband had resumed his old pattern of taking total charge of our finances, giving me only what I needed to have in order to buy what he approved of purchasing. He definitely did not approve of my buying the baby food available in the PX, for though I insisted that those little jars had been carefully formulated to meet our son's nutritional needs, he refused to allow me to buy a single jar on the grounds that he had been healthy enough as a kid and he had grown up hale and hearty without baby food!

Having earned my own money for so many years, I chafed at this arrangement. For one thing, I felt that if I had a job, I could help us pay off the mortgage on the house. And I'd have enough to spend a few dollars on things I cared about having. For almost a year I looked forward to the time when Haydn would be old enough to accept staying with a sitter for at least a few hours—just long enough for me to check out job prospects. I was sure that once he got used to being with someone else, he would surely be content to spend a few hours every day in a nursery while I worked part time. In this belief, I had asked a neighborhood woman to keep him while I went out job hunting. On the appointed morning, I tucked Haydn into the stroller and walked the short distance to the sitter's house. He seemed fine until I lifted him out of the stroller and into the arms of the stranger. I kissed him goodbye, turned abruptly away, and hurried down the sidewalk as fast as I could in order to shut out his cries of betrayal. I got only as far as the end of the block before turning around and running all the way back to the house—where he was still crying. I mumbled a quick apology to the startled sitter and we were on our way back home.

So now here I was again, thinking of leaving him with someone else. But I knew my sister, who had no children of her own as yet, would enjoy caring for Haydn, and I never doubted for a minute that he would be content in her love for him and would feel doubly secure, since he'd be in his own familiar environment. Eve and I had decided that the most sensible plan was for me to seek employment that I would have the option of continuing when we returned from our visit overseas. Almost immediately I found an office job at Hinkel's Department Store, happy that I could produce college credits and employment evaluations to satisfy my employer's need for confirmation that I was up to the tasks assigned to me.

On my way to and from my secretarial desk at Hinkel's Department Store, I took note of the salesgirls who worked the various departments. Most of them were young, but none were as young as I had been during my cashiering days in England.

Unlike today's salesgirls who tally up a customer's purchases with the help of a scanner and computerized cash register, the girls on the floor when I was employed by Broadbent and Turner's Department store in Warrington, wrote down each item on a billing slip presented the total owed to the customer, and accepted payment for the purchase. Then the money and the sales slip were placed in a contraption somewhat like a small bowling ball, which unscrewed into two halves.

Once the ball was screwed together again, it was pulleyed up to the cubby hole at the top of a flight of stairs, where I spent all day from 9:00 A.M. until closing time, looking out over the floor below and waiting for the sales slips and money sent up by the clerks. My duties were to take out the contents of the little ball, double check the amount charged for the merchandise, check the accuracy of the amount enclosed, enter the specifics in my cash book, then place the receipt, plus any change required, in one half of the little ball, screw the two halves back together, and send the carrier back down to the waiting clerk. The most difficult part of the job was holding my breath till the ball reached the counter below and the clerk handed over the receipt, fearful as I was of having made a mistake in my calculations, in which case I could always count on a reprimand from the salesgirl, whose loud voice would travel across the store to further embarrass me. I was fourteen years old at the time.

With years of experience behind me, I felt at ease working at Hinkel's there in Roswell. The work was relatively easy, especially compared to the work I'd done for Senator Wallace. And best of all, I went home every night to a happy baby. For once, things seemed to be going well. My husband seemed content with his job on the base, Eve was pleasant and helpful company to have around, the baby was obviously thriving, and in addition to the money I was saving toward our trip, I had enough extra cash to get along without having to pester my husband for every penny I needed or wanted. The situation seemed almost too good to be true. And it *was,* for we had no sooner gotten our routine established when Eva's husband was transferred to Ohio. Naturally, Eva had to return to Oklahoma at once to pack up their things, help sell the house, and then help find a new one in Ohio.

We split what money we had saved, Our Eve went on to Ohio, and I quit the job and put my travel dreams on hold. Eve and I weren't the only ones disappointed by this turn of events. Mother and Our Ike were writing often to see what was holding up our plans to go home and see them, and I grew increasingly restless.

Even though I'd been delighted by how early the yellow roses had begun climbing to the top of the trellis, my first taste of New Mexico's hot summer weather was rather hard to bear, especially having just survived a Montana winter so cold that the sub-zero temperatures at Flathead Lake had frozen over the bay at Polson. Going from one extreme to the other was taking its toll. As the temperature rose, so did the winds, and the sands of Roswell whipped up into storms dense enough to blacken the sky and scorch the already parched earth. The doldrums set in, and I longed for rain, something I'd missed ever since leaving England, and something this arid countryside was surely in need of. Then came a thunderstorm that

taught me to be careful what I wished for. The realtor who had negotiated
the purchase of our home had neglected to tell us the full truth about the
creek bed that ran through our property. We had asked if it had ever been
a flowing stream, and he'd shaken his head as a "No." What he hadn't bothered to tell us was that the bone-dry creek bed occasionally filled with water
and had been known to overflow its banks.

We found that out for ourselves when a flash flood came roaring down
and a wall of water traveling at great speed filled up that narrow, empty
channel, sending water over our lawn, sweeping through our garage apartment, and on out into the alley and surrounding streets. Fortunately Hadyn
and I had been indoors, for the waters came without warning. We were
lucky, too, that our house was too high off the ground to suffer any damage,
but the garage apartment was flooded with mud and muck and took a lot
of cleaning up.

Knowing how disappointed I'd been when my trip to England had been
canceled, my husband promised to find some way to send me home for a visit.
His way led to the garage apartment, which consisted of one bedroom-sitting
room, a small kitchen, and a toilet and shower. Even so, he decided that if
we would move into the apartment as soon as we'd cleaned it up, we could
begin renting out our house for some extra cash, which he would let me
spend on a trip home. He kept his word, and in September 1947, Haydn
and I flew to England.

As we stepped off the plane at Heathrow Airport in London, I
greeted my mother, and she said, "Ooh, you've got a southern accent!"
Then she picked up Haydn and gave him a hug, saying he was a nice little boy. She loved him on the spot. Though I regretted that Our Eve had
not been able to make this long-awaited trip with us, Haydn and I enjoyed
a lovely reunion with family and friends. We celebrated his birthday with
a cake and presents, and he enjoyed being doted over by his grandmother
and aunts. Joyce—Our Ike—had married a Royal Air Force man and was
working for the Americans at Burtonwood. We laughed about the time

Father had asked her where her young man was stationed, and she'd answered, "Midoshea." Father had replied, "There's no such place, Love." Then he'd thought for a minute and started to smile. "You must mean mid-ocean!" Joyce never forgot funny moments like that.

Doris, who had married a year or so after I left for Montana, was living away from home. She made it a point to come over and visit as often as she could, however, eager as she was to share news about her marriage—and to hear news about my life in America. In fact, everyone seemed to be enthralled by my descriptions of life in the snow-clad Rockies, my report of the stifling heat of New Mexico, and my dramatic account of the flash flood that had ripped through our idyllic world. Of course, I reported only the happy parts of my new life across the Atlantic, seeing no need to burden my mother, especially, with the more somber aspects of living with a husband I despaired of ever really knowing.

Mother had already been making plans to fly back with me for a visit to America. In fact, she'd already obtained her passport and visa for the trip. I managed to book a reservation for her on the flight Haydn and I were scheduled to take. By the time of our departure, Mother and I had already settled into our old roles, and I realized that she was positioned to take charge of me, my new pregnancy, and my two-year-old son—and stood ready to take on the whole of the U.S. of A. if necessary. Though my feelings were mixed, I felt secure in her presence, and I've always been glad that I welcomed her into our home. My husband always respected Emily, and I was thankful there were no unpleasant scenes during her visit. Her "third eye," however, put two and two together, and Joyce confided to me that Emily knew "something was up."

In addition to visits from Our Eve and my mother, two things happened there in New Mexico's Land of Enchantment that remain among my fondest memories. Our daughter, Hope Anne, was born on April 28, 1948, and she, along with her brother, filled my life with something akin to contentment. Mother stayed on with us for a couple of months after the baby's arrival, and I appreciated everything she did to help. Hope was a beautiful baby, and her father lavished her with attention. She glowed with a zest for life and had a ready smile that was apparent in every snapshot taken of her in childhood.

The only other major New Mexico event happened in November, on one of the happiest days of my life. I had studied all the materials I'd been given and felt I knew everything I needed to know on the morning I arrived at the courthouse building in Roswell, County of Chavez, ready to go through the formalities of becoming a citizen of this country. My witnesses had already been closeted with the examiner for some time when I was finally called to stand before the Fifth Judicial District Judge. I was excited, yet as nervous as a long-tailed cat in a room full of rocking chairs. My anxiety must have been visible to his honor, but the interrogation went smoothly enough, and I was sure that I had it made. Then the judge smiled and said in his quiet voice, "Just a couple of personal questions now that shouldn't take long."

The questions seemed inconsequential enough. He asked how long I had known one of my witnesses, the frequency with which I'd seen him over the past two years, and whether there had been any periods of time in which I had not seen him. I answered his questions as honestly as I could and stood waiting for the judge's approval. A dream was about to come true. I was exhilarated! I could hear my father's voice singing, "When it's springtime in the Rockies, in the Rockies far away."

So I was rather surprised when the judge, with a quizzical look, asked yet another question: "Have you not traveled abroad in the last three years?"

"Yes sir," I answered without hesitation. "I visited England earlier this year."

The judge gave me another quizzical look and, still in his quiet, even voice, remarked, "Then you could not possibly have been abroad and at the same time been here in the U.S.A. seeing your witness as you previously stated, could you?"

I was stunned. How in God's name had I not connected how these two trick questions had seemed to be putting me in two places at one time? And now here was the judge, asking me to go and sit in the waiting area while he talked again to my witness.

Oh no! I was waking from a bad dream. I was in shock. I had lied, in court! What on earth would my witness, who had taken the stand on my account, think of me when the judge questioned the truth of his answer to the question of contacts with me? Very much shaken by my foolish lack of discretion, I answered the summons to return to the courtroom where, in a very serious voice that made me feel like a chastened schoolgirl, the judge lectured me on the importance of true statement of fact.

But all's well that ends well, and I left that ceremony waving the flag of my new country.

In due course, I received my Certificate of Naturalization, stating that I had "complied with the applicable provisions of . . . naturalization laws and was entitled to be . . . a citizen of the United States of America." I look today at my serious countenance pictured on this slip of paper, my treasured certificate of citizenship and ask myself: Have I earned the right to be called an American citizen? I can only truly say I have tried, and I have many witnesses who would gladly vouch for that fact.

Until very recently, I had pushed back in my mind another event during my years in Roswell, an event that hinged on my negative reaction to my husband's stated intention of making a life-time career of service in what was now officially the United States Air Force. I could not imagine that his doing so would benefit any of us, and there was another aspect of his decision that made me even more reluctant to go along with his plans. He had put in a request for officer's training, saying that if I agreed to it, he would be sent wherever that training might occur—but it would not be feasible to take his family with him. And no, he couldn't say exactly how long he would be away from us.

Perhaps someone stronger than I would have jumped at the chance of having her husband promoted to officer status, but there were a number of reasons—or maybe excuses—that made me wary of this plan. First and foremost was the fear that he might not make the grade, considering he had spent less than one semester in school at Bozeman before changing his mind about any more schooling. And what if he didn't make it through OCS? He had already shown how ready he was to blame someone else for his shortcomings, and I did not relish the thought of him lashing out in anger at Haydn and me, as he had begun to do during those last weeks before he withdrew from his college courses.

The worst of my worries was that I might not make the grade myself. I was terrified by the thought of being left alone for a repetition of 1945, especially now that I had the responsibilities of motherhood to consider. If he would only take us with him, I said, perhaps we could manage. But he announced that if he had to drag his family along with him, then he'd rather not go at all. I felt like hell for a long time after that scene. Logically, I know that I made the only decision I could have made, given my fears and the uncertainties concerning his proposal. Even so, the memory of my dashing his hopes of succeeding in this venture leaves a pain in my heart. I cannot help but wonder whether things might have been better for us all around if I hadn't let him down before he'd had the chance to get up and grow.

Another excitement during our stay in Roswell was the supposed sightings of UFOs, those Unidentified Flying Objects that seemed to signal the coming of aliens from outer space. With my own sights centered on a husband, a lively toddler, and a newborn, those visitors from outer space were the least of my worries, though in the down times I wished I could gather my children in my arms, step aboard one of those glowing ships, and leave the world behind me forever.

Haydn was three-and-a-half and Hope was just a toddler when my husband decided to quit the Air Force and go back home again! And by "home" he meant back to Montana, to live with his Aunt Mabel and Uncle Guy until we could find a place of our own. A family trait he had adopted was to just pick up and go somewhere, invitation or permission taken for granted, including permission from his wife, who was obviously reluctant to go back to the house she still hated and live among relatives who would be even more reluctant to have her there now that she was bringing along two young children.

The long, hot trip from New Mexico to Montana was an ordeal. There were four of us crammed inside a two-seater, meaning I had one child on my lap and the other one balanced on the ledge above the back seat in a laundry basket. In this age of child restraints and seat belts for one and all, I look back on our precarious seating arrangements and marvel that we survived three long and tortured days crammed into that old jalopy, at the mercy of the moods and demands of its miserably morose driver.

Though saving pennies was of paramount importance to my husband, the few he saved by not stopping for gas when we should have resulted in his making not one but several long walks back to petrol stations, leaving a wife and two crying children stranded on the roadside, making do with a pack of gum until he returned. Under such circumstances I found it difficult to hold my tongue each time we passed up yet another petrol station, with my husband behaving as if he were trying to wean that poor old car of its need for fuel—and show his total control of our lives in the process.

He had slept but little during the journey, and as we moved into more mountainous territory, the trip became a hazardous undertaking. At one point the car went off the road and down a steep embankment, coming to a standstill in the middle of a meadow, miraculously right side up. I will never understand how Hope managed to land in my lap on top of Haydn, instead of flying through the window on that perpendicular plunge. Having survived that terrifying side trip, we managed to get back on the highway with the kind assistance of the people in the car behind us, who stopped to give us a hand. My husband's grudging gratitude turned to resentment when a highway patrolman stopped us a bit down the road and questioned us about the accident, which our Good Samaritans had rightly reported.

No charges were filed, however, and we were soon on our way—until my husband would hear a suspicious rattle or knock and insist on pulling into a service station to open the hood and spend an hour or so joshing and joking with the mechanic, then trying to turn a trick, beggar-man style, in hopes that the mechanic would take pity on him and knock a few dollars off his bill. Embarrassed as I was by such behavior, I was glad enough to distance myself from my husband's dealings, though I did not enjoy walking up and down the dusty street with two little ones in tow until he blew the horn to let us know it was time to be on the road again.

The only place we stopped overnight to sleep in comfortable beds, take a hot shower, and do the washing, was a little tourist court someplace in Wyoming. Otherwise I felt like a vagabond, sleeping in the car with Haydn on my lap and eating sandwiches on the go after picking up a loaf of bread and something to put between the slices. Though the old car had seemed almost as eager as I to postpone our return to that cold, dark house on the hill overlooking Flathead Lake, by the time we rounded the bend on the lake's sudden shore, and I caught my first glimpse of the Mission Mountains, I was glad to be home. In the midst of such beauty, I could not help but find momentary peace.

The relatives made a fuss over the children while trying to ignore me completely, and that suited me, even though it was a most uncomfortable feeling. I managed to slip away occasionally to take the children to see Geraldine and her family. I was especially glad to get away when Mabel announced it was time to make the green tomato mincemeat that would be taken to the cellar to sit beside last year's green tomato mincemeat—which sat next to the bear meat, which sat beside the jar of sour cherries, next to the last jar on the shelf whose label was missing. It wasn't clear what the contents were, and the missing label could well have been dated in the year 1900!

I don't know how much the relatives expected in return for lodgings. Ray was tight-lipped about anything related to finances, and I was feeling more and more out of focus in the scheme of things, with no certain future and a husband who hadn't yet grown up but was seemingly quite content to hang around with his relatives forever. I must admit that ever since we had left there at Christmas of 1945, Hank had made great strides in building Mabel a new house, with lots of rooms for stray relatives such as ourselves. The new house even had an indoor bathroom, but since there was still lots to be done before the house was completed—like putting on a front porch with steps all the way down to the road, Hank took full advantage of our presence there, making sure each of us did our part to complete the project.

Since my husband continued to exclude me from his plans for the future—and even from his discussions of those plans—I was happily surprised to hear him announce to Mabel one day, "I've found a place for us to live."

The proposed home was a cabin we were to lease, and I was delighted to learn that it was located on the eastern side of the lake, where the cherry orchards showered blossoms in the breeze. I looked forward to the day when the trees would be lush with fruit, boughs bending under the weight of sweet, luscious cherries, for I knew that I would be able to earn a few dollars by helping with the harvesting, and could count on picking a few baskets for our own use.

We loaded our few belongings and the children, and drove along the shore to Gravel Bay, where the cabin sat on a ledge overlooking that great expanse of water. The cabin had been designed with a view of the lake in mind, and I could look out the picture window to see beyond the rocks and stretch of sand below to where fishing boats bobbed up and down on the calm waters and larger cruise vessels moved along in the distance.

With such beauty to feed my soul, I gratefully settled into our new home, despite the lack of hot water and indoor plumbing and the presence of an old rooster, who chased after me whenever he saw me gathering eggs from the coop that housed his brood of hens—all of which had been thrown in with the cabin for the monthly rent.

I have happy memories of our time on that bit of land, where flowers grew in the garden spot and a huge patch of strawberries begged to be picked for pies, strawberry ice cream, and delicious jam. The children were also happy there, and my spirits rose as I concentrated on being a good wife and mother, baking up exquisite cakes from the new *Better Homes and Gardens Cookbook* I had bought in New Mexico. One after another I turned out my marvelous confections: the Martha Washington cake, the George Washington Cake, the Lord and Lady Baltimore Cakes.

With plenty of eggs on hand and enough money coming in from Ray's job at a nearby lumber mill, I began to feel secure in our new situation. True, we did not have the benefits life in the Air Force could have provided, but neither did we have the worries or the loss of freedom that were an integral part of military life. Indeed, life in that cabin on Gravel Bay would have been idyllic—had it not been for that pesky rooster.

For a long time I thought the rooster definitely had something against me personally, because he didn't bother Ray, who would just ward off the bird with a kick or a brick if he got close to him. But I soon discovered that he had it in for Haydn, too. One day I looked out to see my terrified son running as fast as his legs would carry him, the rooster nipping at his bottom. He arrived panting at the doorway, sinking to the floor, a hen's egg held high above his head in each of his hands. He had dared go inside the coop to check the eggs for me, and the rooster had spotted him raiding the nests. As I shooed the mean old creature away with my broom, Haydn put on a brave face, his lips quivering, "See—I saved the eggs for you, Mom."

Relief from that tyrant of the henhouse came when my husband decided we wouldn't have turkey for dinner that Thanksgiving. Instead, he picked up the chopper from where it hung in the kitchen and started out toward the chicken yard. The cause of all the commotion was about to cause no more. Sure enough, an hour later—after a lot of hooting and hollering— Ray plunked the beheaded bird onto the kitchen counter ready for the plucking. I'm glad that the execution had taken place outside, because I would not have wanted to look that big bird in the eye.

I happily dressed him for cooking, then roasted him in the small electric appliance—just about his size—in which my pies and cakes always cooked to perfection. But that tough old bird still had a few surprises in store. After a few hours, he looked brown enough to be done, but his hide was so tough the testing form bounced right back at me. With dinner scheduled within the hour, I gave him another chance and put him in the stew pot. But he was not about to be stewed, and it soon became clear that we were not going to have him for Thanksgiving dinner after all. I served the rest of the dinner, and we went to bed knowing full well that cocky old bird had gotten the best of us.

Life remained good in that little cabin, for Ray loved working outdoors and seemed to be pleased to be earning a living at the mill. He never was opposed to digging in and doing his share of hard work, and I felt better about our relationship during this time than I had since his return from the war. He was easy with me and with the children, probably because he felt good about his ability to earn a good living and about how happy I seemed in that little cabin. Whenever she could find time to get away, Gerry Fulkerson would come up for a cup of tea and a taste of one of my cakes, and one Sunday afternoon she and her husband loaded up their children and drove up to our cabin for dinner and a real visit.

Once again life seemed too good to be true. And once again fate intervened to change our course. I was hanging out clothes when a truck came driving up the road, much too fast, I thought, for the conditions of that bumpy byway. "Ray's been in an accident," the man cried out. "A big log fell on his leg, and I'm afraid it's broke, real bad. The boss has taken him into Polson." I ran inside to put shoes and coats on the children, then handed both of them into the cab of the truck and climbed in myself. Only then did I realize I was shaking. And not from the cold.

By the time we got to Hotel Dieu, the doctor had already set the mangled leg, which had been broken in two places. Once the cast was in place, we were told, he could go home again, as long as he stayed on crutches until the leg healed.

My husband was not a man who enjoyed being told what he could and could not do. Within days of his return home, he was doing his best to go outside and chop wood for us, certain that I was not capable of doing that chore myself. Pain won out over valor, and as he realized only time could restore his virility, he became more and more despondent. At his lowest ebb, a letter arrived from one of his Air Force buddies who'd decided to go back to school on the GI Bill. Tuition would be free, and this time there might be housing in the married student barracks, which had expanded in the years since we left Montana.

Worried as I was that he was once again setting himself up for failure, I was nonetheless heartened to see his spirits rise as he wrote away to the dean of the School of Agriculture, to ask about returning to his old job in the dairy barns—the job he'd held during the year he spent at the college, before his enlistment in the Air Corps. When the dean wrote back with news that he could not only have his old job but that there would be room for us in student housing, there was no turning back. Ready or not, we were college-bound again.

This time we would go in style, for Ray had stashed away enough money before his accident for a down payment on a brand new Chevrolet. As he returned from Polson in the shiny new vehicle, he called out to me and, driving drove down the steep path to the cabin, said, "You'd better come learn how to drive it while I'm in the mood to teach you. You might need to give me a hand on the road, once we ever get packed up and out of here."

And with that, he slid over to the right and I hopped in on the left, and found myself sitting in the driver's seat of a car for the first time in my life. My husband pointed out the shift to me, explained about the clutch, and warned me not to grind the gears—whatever those might be. Next he explained that the pedal on the right was the one I stepped on to accelerate, while the one in the middle was the brake. The clutch—well, the clutch was another matter altogether.

I was becoming more and more tense, trying to remember how many gears I was supposed to go through and just where those gears were located on the stick that controlled them. I was to press down the pedal on the far left while I moved the gear stick with my right and slowly pressed on the gas pedal. I did my best, but nothing moved except my pounding heart. "It won't budge!" I yelled, daring to take my eyes off my feet and look up at him, as frigid with fear as I'd been on that first night of our honeymoon.

"Well, turn the key, stupid."

But I just sat there, my hands frozen to the wheel, paralyzed by the fear of doing everything wrong and risking the wrath of hell. Right now, all these years later, I am asking myself, "Why on earth didn't you just belt him one long, long ago and fly solo?" And with that thought comes my father's voice, "It's still not too late, Love."

"We can't sit here all day! Turned the damned key, for God's sake!"

And I did, afraid not to follow his orders, afraid of what might happen once I did. "Now, shift into reverse and back up," he barked.

Back up? In those first few seconds or so, looking down and sorting out all those pedals and gadgets, I had not taken note of the fact that the front of the car was about three feet from the edge of the cliff, with the great expanse of shimmering water below and beyond. Fear was searing my mind, a fear compelling enough to have carried me along in senseless panic right over the edge in that shiny new car, my husband's angry yells echoing in my ears.

Suddenly an elbow dug into my ribs, pushing me out of the driver's seat and against the door of the passenger side. A hand reached over to turn a key, and the engine stopped its grinding and purred into action. I pulled up on the door handle and leaped from the car, not hearing a word of what my husband yelled after me, content to let that beautiful blue Chevrolet take care of itself and knowing that had I stayed inside another minute, I'd have thrown up all over the upholstery.

I knew my driving days were over for a long time to come. My husband reached over and pulled the passenger door inward, slamming it shut. Then he whipped the car into reverse and backed halfway up the hill at top speed, so angry he must have forgotten the protruding stones that made the road hazardous even for trucks and the old coupe. My heart sank as I heard the ominous sound of metal striking stone. The car shuddered to a stop, and I turned and ran into the house, not wanting to know just how much damage had been done.

The car was towed into Polson for replacement parts before it was even a day old, and it was all my fault of course. If I hadn't insisted on driving lessons . . . . I stifled my protests and began packing up for yet another move. We had only a few weeks more before college classes began, and I knew there would be more tough lessons ahead—for both of us.

Chapter 11

If youth only knew. If age only could.

—HENRI ESTIENNE

Once again we were on the way to school, the Chevy all bandaged up and raring to go. With the GI Bill offering my husband the opportunity to improve his education and gain an edge in the work force, he looked forward to taking advantage of this route to success, and I was optimistic about the opportunities that might be mine in that college town of Bozeman. But college life for me did not constitute sitting at a desk to soak up all that wonderful knowledge I had longed to acquire, the knowledge that had so greatly enriched the life of Our Eve.

Sadly, by the time we had settled into student housing, my husband heading out to his first class, I was already remembering Father Time's sage advice: "One of these days it's going to be too late, my dear," and I realized that my own aspirations would be put on hold just one more time.

Campus wives at Montana State were expected to stick together as we stood behind our husbands, pushing them on to fulfill their academic goals and dreams. I was able to give my struggling spouse a little help with his English courses, and for a technical writing assignment, we wrote together

"How to Make an Apple Pie," an essay that earned him an A+. German studies were "double Dutch" to him, but I was ready, always there behind him, having studied what the Germans call "High German," with an emphasis on the grammatical rather than the conversational. Even with my ready assistance, he barely passed the test, although I do believe that in the end, he understood the mechanics of that language better than he understood those of his own.

His lack of reading and writing skills had always created a problem for him, though pride had stood in the way of his admitting the problem and seeking help to overcome it. In desperation, there came a day when he asked me to help him read more fluently and gain a wider vocabulary, a chore that I was more than willing to tackle. Together we sat down at the table, and I asked him to begin by reading aloud a paragraph from one of his texts. At the first hint of correction, he threw the book down, stalked out of the room, and refused to continue the project.

My husband's attitude and anger were shared by many—perhaps most—men of that day, many of whom had returned from the war to find women wearing their pants and filling their shoes on the production line or elsewhere. Even after those capable women—the Rosie the Riveters of our time—were summarily fired so that the best man for the job was, again, a man, my husband was certainly not the only male to harbor resentments toward women who sought a higher place in the world. Little wonder, concerning the mores and attitudes handed down through the ages.

Indeed, I consider the advances and accomplishments of the "fairer" sex nothing short of miraculous in view of the advice women, as well as men, have received from time immemorial. Consider the words of that ancient philosopher, Epictetus, the learned Stoic who said with his foot in his mouth, "Women from fourteen years upward are called madam by men. Wherefore, when they see that the only advantage they have is to be marriageable, they begin to make themselves smart and set their hopes on this. We must take pains, then, to make them understand that they are really honored for nothing but a modest and decorous life."

Such a gentle hint, and truly Stoic, but what a smashing blow to a woman's dream of achieving anything else! Was this the Stoics' interpretation of a woman's role in life, or the suggestion that this modest and decorous image was one which women fashioned for themselves, so by heck they had best learn to live with it? Fortunately, somewhere across the centuries, remarks such as those by Epictetus got our dander up, and we have, at last, put aside the dustpan and the broom, and shoved the dirt under the rug to make a place for ourselves in a once male-dominated society.

The students' wives formed a club called ONO (Our Night Out), and I made friends there in the small Quonset where we met once a month. We shared confidences, and just as in the war years in England, when difficult circumstances brought people closer to one another, so difficulties brought us all closer there, in Bozeman, Montana, where GI wives made do or did without, living under relatively primitive conditions in the age of electricity and gas. We cooked on coal stoves and warmed our apartments by means of a big, pot-bellied stove that either left the apartment cold or worked too well, endangering the occupants.

We student wives stuck together, relying on the strength gained at our monthly gatherings to help us take ourselves lightly through the rugged course called College Housing. We all looked out for one another, and I remember one occasion when we were house-sitting the apartment below at the request of the family who lived there. As they departed one cold, cold morning, they told us they had stoked up the heater sufficiently to last the day, and since it was essential to keep up the heat in order to prevent the plumbing from freezing, we assured them we would tend the stove from then until they returned after spring break.

As we were sitting down to lunch later that day, I smelled smoke, and we all made a dash for the downstairs apartment. Had we not been home, I believe the whole block of housing might have gone up in smoke. Apparently, in their haste to tidy up the place before their departure, someone in the family had left a straw broom leaning up against that hot stove. The straw had gone up in flames, sending sparks and burning particles to the bare wooden floor, which had flared up just as quickly. We called the fire department, but luckily were able to contain the fire before they arrived. Another near-miss occurred was when a neighbor foolishly used lighter fluid to spark up the dying embers of the coal cook stove. The resulting fire ate up part of the floor before it was extinguished.

At last we were allowed to move into a two-bedroom, ground level unit at the far end of the complex. I was delighted, for we would not only have more room and be spared the bother of climbing the stairs with children and grocery bags, but since we would have only one adjoining wall, the noise of shouting children, quarrelling couples, and blaring music would be somewhat diminished. Upon the completion of our move, I breathed a sigh of relief—until I discovered that the coal bin that provided fuel for the entire row of housing was located at our end of the street. I cringed each time I heard the squeaking of hinges that meant the heavy lid on that ten-foot-long bin was being lifted by a neighbor who needed to shovel out a load of coal. The sound of that cover slamming shut again would knock the pictures off my wall.

After the rent and doctor's bills were paid, there wasn't much of the $92 GI Bill allotment left for other essentials, like clothes and food. I bought sensible shoes, as Mother had done at Eddie Perrin's. Other student wives, who were equally strapped for money, were happy enough to have a few extra dollars in exchange for hand-me-down dresses, shirts, and trousers the little ones needed, and since I very rarely went out, except to shop or visit with friends who were on equally tight budgets, I made do with the clothing I had accumulated over the years. My husband's school and work clothes were carefully washed and pressed, and I was thankful to own an electric iron that spared me the kind of labor my mother had gone through every Tuesday, for Tuesday had been ironing day as surely as Monday had been washing day.

Every time I think of Miss Snoddy, my domestic science teacher at Evelyn Street Girls' School, I get goose bumps. She lived quite close to us, so I would often hear about her private life. She loved to cook, but I can hardly stand to think of the things she would sell from her home kitchen to supplement her earnings as a teacher! The only dish I liked was her "Savvery Ducks," meat concoctions that are boiled down, something similar to what Americans call meatballs. Savvery was the sloppy Lancashire dialect for the word "savory," which is actually an aromatic European mint. Why she called them "ducks," I'll never know, but I imagined it was because they were always swimming in a bowlful of sumptuous gravy. Mother didn't buy those very often.

Perhaps she was only kidding, but Mother once told me what Miss Snoddy put into those big, black and purple conglomerations she called "black puddings." The pouch that held the ingredients was fashioned from a piece of the animal's stomach, and the gory contents consisted of chopped up innards, probably from the same poor old cow. She could have used snigs and snails and puppy dogs' tails for all I cared. Even though Father would eat them just because Emily bought them, I would rather go hungry.

I suppose that memory made me sufficiently sympathetic to my children's refusal to eat leftovers to cause me to resort to a little creativity. Instead of putting out whatever scraps of meat and dibs and dabs of vegetables I had saved from our last family meal, I'd doll up those nutritious leavings by wrapping them in a bit of pastry browned to perfection, or whipping them into a Yorkshire pudding mixture, and giving them fancy names.

I borrowed some recipes—and some fancy names—from *The Art of Home Cooking,* my mother's forty-eight-year-old cookbook. Published by the Stork Margarine Cookery Service, that old book was filled with names like "Shepherd's Pie," "Bubble and Squeak," and "Toad-in-the-Hole," a long-time favorite rendered infamous by my memory of the incident in my secret garden. I remembered all those names and the way those dishes looked and tasted, even though the pages on which the most memorable ones appeared contained neither butter stain nor a fingerprint. Mother never thought she needed any help from a book in cooking them.

Like Mother, I didn't always follow the recipes precisely, but I enjoyed getting an idea from what I read and then concocting a dish that roughly approximated the one I'd read about. The *Better Homes and Gardens Cookbook* became my standby for simple fare, as well as company cooking. And much later, when the wonderful world of television came into our home, I watched Julia Child carve up a hunk of venison, and from that point onward I couldn't get enough of her.

Life went on during those years at the college in Bozeman, and my husband worked hard at his studies, hard enough that I began to believe that he would, indeed, be earning a degree, even if he wasn't getting an education. Meanwhile, Haydn and Hope were happy enough there in the housing complex, and I threw myself into activities that revolved around their lives. I became a Cub Scout den mother, a Blue Bird leader, room mother at school, and mother to all the kids in the housing complex, bandaging scraped knees, drying tears, and putting babies to sleep, in a neighborhood more closely knit than any other I would live in for the rest of my life.

Yes, I was caught up in the duties of motherhood and in the life of a student wife, but in that relatively intimate setting, I had the opportunity to observe the great difference between how other student husbands treated their wives and how my husband treated me. Just as I'd seen the vast difference in the two husbands named "Ray" when we were living with the Fulkersons, so now I could not help but see that my situation appeared to be vastly different from the situation of my friends in the ONO club. I say "appeared" because there is really no way for me to know how many of those women did as I did and kept up a good front. I know that no matter how discouraged I became, or how defeated I felt, I did my best to act the role of happy housewife, an act that took far more courage than any role I'd played on the stage back in my younger years. I was determined that no one should know my true situation, for I could not have stood to have them pity me.

During those difficult years—and despite our limited finances—Ray resumed the fraternity alliance he'd begun during his first year at the college, prior to his enlistment. He and his buddies at Alpha Gamma Rho enjoyed themselves immensely, and I was in no position to deny him a little fun after all his hard work at the college. Still, it galled me to think that he could have been home with the children—or earning extra money by working at the dairy lab. Was I expecting too much of him? Perhaps. But I resented his choosing to spend time and money at the frat house, when we rarely went out for dinner—or any meal, for that matter—except on the evening my friend Cassie invited us to join in a celebration of her husband's graduation by dining at a fine cafe on Bozeman Hill. That was a memorable night for me—and I still have the cafe's recipe for blue cheese dressing!

After two long years of schooling—including summer sessions—my own husband completed requirements for his Bachelor of Science degree in Agriculture in August of 1952, though he had to wait until the following spring to don his cap and gown and stride across the stage to accept his diploma. He wasn't the only one to "graduate" on that June day, for I, along with the other wives whose husbands were receiving their degrees, was awarded a Ph.T.—(Putting Hubby Through) degree. That certificate still hangs on my study wall, signed by the college president, Dr. Roland Renne, and by Governor Nutter. I often look at it and think of the giant steps for womankind that have been taken since those days.

Back in 1953, I had not yet taken any giant steps myself, though I was looking forward to a better life now that my husband had a degree that should ensure a steady, secure income and a nice home. I was ready for a change, ready to be free of the constant worries about money, and when my husband offered not a word as to his plans for the future, I dared to bring up the question myself. He answered without hesitation—as if I should have known all along what he would be doing next. Dr. Nelson, dean of the graduate school, had persuaded Ray to continue his schooling and pursue a master's degree—just as his brother Ted had done before him. Ted Hedrick had, indeed, gone through Dr. Nelson's graduate program before going on to earn his doctorate at Iowa State University, and then becoming a professor at Michigan State University. However the two brothers were so different in terms of early attitudes toward learning, interest in studies during their teen years, and performance as undergraduates at the college, that I found myself questioning the wisdom of Dr. Nelson's assumptions that my husband should be put in the position of trying to equal his brother's achievements.

I could understand that longing, in a sense, for hadn't I spent all those years regretting my loss of the educational opportunities Our Eve had enjoyed? With my husband's completion of his undergraduate degree, I had dared to look forward to the possibility of applying to take a few classes myself, now that Hope was entering kindergarten and I would have time to pursue that long-deferred dream. But once again I would be the support force, standing in the wings and cheering on the chosen one.

And once again, as I had been when I'd learned there could not be two scholarships awarded to children from the same family, I was overwhelmed by the feeling that "it just wasn't fair." Life has since taught me to hark back once more to the words of that old Stoic, Epictetus: "Ask not that events should happen as you will, but let your will be that events should happen as they do, and you shall have peace."

Though those words might also have been intended especially for women, I had no other recourse but to follow that advice. Yet trying to be at peace with my circumstances did nothing to quench my thirst for learning. So I volunteered to record textbooks for blind college students, thereby gaining knowledge in literature, history, philosophy, psychology, German, and whatever other subject a seeing-impaired student might be taking.

I also took another brave step and decided to type theses and dissertations for graduate students on my Royal portable typewriter at home. Hard work that was, too, since I had to type duplicates, error-free copies, for manuscripts that were sometimes over a hundred pages long. Many, like Dr. Roemhild's dissertation, "The Metamorphosis of the Grasshopper," were filled with technical data. Though my means might have been a bit unorthodox, I had ended up with a fairly well-rounded education, while contributing a modest amount toward Ray's graduate work. My earnings added up very slowly at a mere ninety cents an hour, with no time wasted from the moment the children went off to school until the minute they returned . . . plus the hours I put in after they were fast asleep. Best of all, I was learning to have faith again in myself and in my ability to cope.

With hindsight, perhaps I underestimated my husband's ability to deal with the challenge of graduate school, for once he began his concentrated courses in agriculture—a field in which he'd always had great interest—he applied himself to his studies with new energy and determination, even as he continued to work long hours instructing lab students in the college dairy. And he managed to complete his coursework within the usual two years, receiving his M.S. in Dairy Manufacturing in June of 1954. His master's degree was cause for great celebration, and I felt proud to have played a role in his accomplishment. Though he never would admit I had helped in that tremendous undertaking, in my heart I always knew he could never have done it alone.

While the completion of my husband's degree would normally have brought an end to our eligibility for student housing, his teaching at the university allowed us to stay on there until he was able to save enough money to allow us to afford a home of our own. Knowing that time would come within a year or so, I was able to settle in and enjoy my time with neighbors in student housing, even daring at one point to take out the precious tablecloth I had made back home and pass it around for my closest student-wife friends to autograph. Embroidering on those signatures was a joy, for as I worked on each name, I was filled with appreciation for that person's support during all those years of putting our hubbies through school.

I was happy for other reasons, too. Our third child was on the way, and Ray seemed so relieved to be finally done with his studies and earning a good living for the family that he didn't seem to mind the news that there'd soon be another mouth to feed. Indeed, he seemed genuinely pleased by the news. The older children, now nine and seven, were delighted to welcome a little brother that June of 1955, and my husband seemed almost as pleased as they were to have this tiny wonder in our lives. There was one rather touch-and-go moment, however, for proud as he was of his new son, he did not get his way in the matter of naming him. For some reason I felt brave enough to tell him this boy was mine—and I had promised Haydn he could be the one to name him. How could I disappoint our oldest son, especially since he already had the name picked out—Daniel, after Daniel Shively, his best friend since kindergarten and the son of Bozeman's superintendent of schools.

Once again I was required to stay in the hospital for a number of days after delivery, but this time my husband came to visit, bringing flowers and regaling me with stories of how much the kids loved his cooking, and how the house shone like a new coin. He had even been putting up Hope's hair in curlers every single night, he reported with pride—though her hair was naturally curly, brown with a chestnut glow. Proud as he was of his achievements as caretaker, I held my peace and reminded myself to be thankful he had taken such an interest in the children. Perhaps his new status as bread-winner, and his freedom from the pressures of school, meant our lives would finally be on the right track, provided we could finally have a home of our own.

We could buy something within our means, I argued. Then if his work took him elsewhere, we could sell the place for a profit, just as we'd sold our home in Roswell. And it made no sense to throw away rent money when we could afford to buy. Assured by the dean that he could continue his work at the college, my husband agreed that I should look for a place for us. I stifled my instinct to lash out at him for having refused to even consider buying a house on Finley Point back in 1949, after our return from Roswell.

I never ceased to be amazed how the days of our lives can be tempted back for second helpings, especially lured in by the smell of home-baked bread, crusty and golden, and piping hot from the oven. The day, the year, the moments breeze back to me on a ribbon in the hand of a ten-year-old boy. My goodness that ten-year old boy will turn sixty in October and I still picture him as my little boy.

I remember I had been feeling somewhat delicate that day and had decided not to bake. He came racing home from school with his friends to an empty breadbox and hollered, "Mom, you've just got to make bread today. It's the Fair tomorrow and I know your bread will WIN A RIBBON." "Who? Me?" I said. No way! Not in competition with all those farmers' wives, and besides, it's an all day process.

He harped a bit longer and looked so crestfallen I felt I wasn't measuring up to his expectations of a mother who loved to bake bread, so, making a few quick calculations for the mixing, the three risings, the molding and baking, if I started now it should be coming out of the oven around 2:00 A.M. if the baby went to sleep when he should.

The bread was perfect, the morning air had a nip to it, and I was bathing the baby when my husband, who had taken the bread to the fair earlier, called to say it needed a recipe in order to compete, so I read it over the phone with my finger crossed that he could interpret baking language well enough to make sense to the judges. My daughter listened on the radio for the judges' decision, and my ten-year-old just sat there, down at the fair, mesmerizing the judges into a one and only decision. When they presented him with a white ribbon for my bread, he romped around the fairgrounds waving it in everybody's face, hollering, "My mom's bread won this! My mom's bread!"

That competition was impetus for one of my earliest attempts at publication, and the letter I wrote to a Montana farm paper appeared under the heading "What's In a Loaf of Bread." Seeing my words in print meant more to me than having my bread declared a winner at the winter fair. Characteristically—for I was still intent on portraying our family as ideal—I was careful to give everyone but little Dan a part in the winter fair drama.

And there was truth enough in my closing lines: "What's in a loaf of bread? The usual ingredients, but I'll always treasure that extra something which made my recipe a prize winner—a dash of encouragement, a sprinkling of togetherness, and a whole heartful of faith from a small boy who was sure no other bread could possibly taste better than his mom's."

There was a sense of togetherness in that venture. We seemed, at last, to be making our way toward the kind of peace and stability I had always longed for. My husband had continued his work as a lab instructor at the college and, though there were days when he complained of boredom, by and large he seemed to be content. But within months of that triumphant day at the winter fair, he came home with news that Dean Nelson had persuaded him to take a year's leave to begin doctoral studies at the University of Wisconsin. I was to start looking at once for a renter for the house, since we'd be leaving for Madison in late summer.

Once again there was no discussion as to what I thought of this plan, and I would have had plenty to say indeed, for I had strong doubts about the wisdom of this decision. For one thing, earning a Ph.D. would require mastering at least one foreign language, and my husband had already sworn he would never take another German class. I also doubted he had sufficient reading and writing skills to earn a doctoral degree. But what use would there have been in trying to stop him? He was obviously bound and determined to emulate his big brother through yet another educational endeavor.

The dean had assured him that he would be able to complete his course work in a single year, and then write his dissertation upon returning to his work at the college in Bozeman. While it was true that Ted had achieved his Ph.D. in record time, it was also true that Ted had been unencumbered by a wife and three children, and studying had always been his passion. Mabel, who had taken him in when he was barely five, had boasted that he'd been so bright that he'd read the dictionary from A to Z during his first years of school. At the time I'd wondered how a cursory look at a book filled with words in any language could possibly be a boon toward putting those words together in a meaningful way, so as to demonstrate excellence in their usage and impart knowledge therein to others. Yet over the years I've come to see that Ted's early fascination with words must have been of some benefit, considering his distinguished career.

Though my husband had seldom picked up a dictionary, let alone read one from cover to cover, Dean Nelson's faith in his abilities knew no bounds. His offer of a year's leave of absence from teaching to study for the doctorate carried with it a half-year's salary. Generous as this was for the times, I knew how hard it would be to make that money stretch far enough to cover tuition and books, as well as our housing and food, plus clothing for three growing children. Haydn was entering junior high, Hope would be starting fifth grade, and Dan was still a toddler. We had been happy in the house on West Lamme, and I was reluctant to uproot the family and go chasing after a dream I feared would turn into a nightmare of failure and frustration.

Even so, I felt I had no choice but to follow my husband's instructions. We rented out our home in Bozeman to a family with seven children, and I left the television set behind for the renters—a disheartening move for Haydn and Hope. We also left all our furniture, and the cellar shelves laden with the strawberry jam I'd made from the garden's gleanings at the east shore cabin on Flathead Lake.

Details of the long haul to Madison escape my mind after fifty years, so the trip must have been mercifully uneventful. We had been unable to obtain student housing before our arrival, but fortunately we were able to find an affordable third-floor apartment consisting of a small kitchen and two bedrooms. After the low humidity and cool evenings of Bozeman, Madison's humid summertime weather was hard to endure. But my husband, who spent most of his time in the relative cool of the university labs and classrooms, would give his usual reply when I asked whether we might try to find a used air conditioner or a fan, anything to provide relief from the stifling heat: "Oh, quit your complaining. It's not that bad in here."

Fortunately the apartment was close enough to Vilas Park to provide free entertainment, and the children and I spent many lakeside hours there. The zoo at the park was a favorite destination, and when they tired of merely looking at the animals, they could look forward to elephant rides on designated days. After being out in the open air, we would walk home together in the sweltering heat, dreading to enter the stairwell and sense the rising temperatures as we climbed to the third floor. My whole body dripped perspiration as I cooked up something that resembled Mother's cottage pie, and I found some comfort in the familiarity of food that took me home again.

I was totally surprised when my husband came home one afternoon and announced, with a smile at his children, "I've found a house." My first thought was I hope we can afford the rent. My second: It can't be much of a house if we can afford the rent! Located on a street leading from the capitol building, the house was within walking distance of the children's school. It wasn't very big, but there was an all-purpose living room, and a narrow, rickety staircase that led to a loft with do-it-yourself sleeping space for the family.

While the move to ground-level lodgings and a freestanding home of our own should have been enough to lift my spirits, I found myself spiraling into depression. A stay-at-home mom by choice as well as necessity, I was becoming restless, missing my friends in Bozeman, and longing to have discretionary funds with which to purchase some of the niceties I'd grown accustomed to in the house on West Lamme. I could go out and find a job, I would tell myself, at the same time realizing the impossibility of earning enough to pay for a baby-sitter and have anything left over.

I had become so depressed during this latest venture into the good life that I would wake up in the mornings, my muscles tightened and clenched against what the coming day would bring. I had actually become afraid to face yet another day, in spite of having a nice back lawn and a porch upon which to swing while Dan was taking a nap. I was more afraid still of walking to the grocery store a couple of blocks away to buy a loaf of bread and actually do what mother had done—ask the grocer for day-old bread, since it was a little cheaper than freshly baked.

Being thrown back into circumstances so reminiscent of traumatic incidents in my childhood brought on a series of nightmares from those long ago days.

I am standing at the butcher's counter down on the green, a girl of less than four years, clutching my mother's hand so tightly she shakes it off roughly and says, "You stand still now, till I've paid the man for the meat." Then I am backing away from the counter and wandering out of the shop with its sawdust floor and bloody meat droppings all around the butcher's block. Then I am on the street, standing by the lamppost, afraid to cross. Suddenly Mother appears, grabbing my shoulder and whirling me around to face her, then slapping my hand and shaking me hard, right there on the street, where everyone is watching and listening. "You naughty girl," she is yelling at me, "some old man could of picked you up and dragged you off and you'd never ever see me again!" All around me people are looking at me and nodding their approval of my mother's reprimand. One old lady comes clogging over, hands on hips, to poke her nose into the affair, saying loudly enough for all to hear, "She deserves a good 'idin' she does! I'd get the strap to 'er if I was you!"

That dream was a recurrent one during our stay in Madison, bringing with it the fear of being lost all over again. And there were other dreams that went back to the war years, dreams in which I was always running with my sisters from one hiding place to another, with soldiers in black helmets chasing after us as we tried desperately to outwit them, and fighter planes buzzing around so low they touched the ground. Yet another nightmare would come riding back on many nights and in varying forms.

My passport and visa are nowhere to be found, and I am searching in a panic, trying to find them, afraid I have missed the return trip to England. Every step I take, walking from somewhere—possibly Montana—back to New York to catch the ship, I can only hope the captain, my mother's old friend, will remember me after all those years since 1945 and let me back on board, sans passport and visa. I am slipping and sliding and falling on ice-covered, empty streets, wandering into parts unknown, into places where no one can help me. And then I am standing on a long white runway, watching the huge, familiar vessel sail out of sight without me.

I always woke up at that point, fearful of going anywhere, including the corner grocery store.

Thoughts of childhood and of Mother were recurring in daylight hours as well as in my dreams. I would see her before my eyes, taking a determined step toward the fireplace, the stove, or the laundry basket. And I would think of what she must have been saying to herself during times that had been even harder than my own situation: Em, you must set your mind to this problem. You can't let your fears lead you astray, so that thinking rationally becomes an impossibility! You must keep your mind occupied, every minute of every day, concentrating on doing the things you can accomplish just for that one day. Get to work right now on what is important. You have enough work to keep you busy from dawn to set o' the sun. Enough work to smother your worries and allow you to forget yourself and your problems. And quit feeling sorry for yourself!

So, on a bright Wisconsin day, swinging away the time there on my back porch, I began to notice for the first time that a beautiful, brilliant red cardinal was perched in a tree toward the back of the lawn. There were cabbage butterflies fluttering around my flowers, flowers I could have plucked and painted had I felt so inclined. Yet I sat in idleness. Another day, perhaps, I told myself.

What a waste of your life and your talent, I could hear Mother protesting, and her presence became very real—and rather threatening—during the days I prayed for the courage to ride out this rocky road to a Ph.D. I felt would never come. Then as if a veil had lifted from my mind, I realized that if I could not go out to work, I could earn money right there at home. Once before, I had immersed myself in a project that took me out of the doldrums and into the wonderful world of word weaving. And so I began to think about a hobby my Bozeman friend Carol and I had briefly taken up, having decided to channel our passion for words into more satisfying creative endeavors than decorating cakes and making Christmas tree ornaments, and the myriad other voluntary tasks and services for which our children so eagerly volunteered us, hands held high, voices rising, Yes, yes! My mother is very good at that! Carol had actually won first prize in a national contest, and I had won several lesser prizes that allowed me to make a small contribution to our daily living expenses.

Now that I had even more time on my hands, why not once again contribute to our earnings by entering contests that promised prizes for writing twenty-five-word slogans, coining names for new products, or writing verses in praise of appliances and packaged foods. My husband was skeptical about this plan from the first, so he was pleasantly surprised when my entry in a national competition won third prize, beating out over a million or so entries from around the country. My accomplishment: naming the new Betty Crocker Kitchens the Knack in the Box Kitchens. I was very happy with my much-needed prize of a brand-new Frigidaire washer and dryer, and Hope Anne was delighted with the Toni doll that came on Christmas Eve from another reputable company as a prize for praising their product.

During that difficult year, the children were a blessing to me, helping me through a time of deep depression as it became more and more obvious that the doctorate was slipping out of reach with every examination. Frustrated by his failures, my husband once again took out his anger on his family. All of us tried to read his moods and humor him; even little Dan seemed to understand when to stay out of his father's way. Hope made every effort to help me with household duties and the care of her little brother, and Haydn, who had just turned thirteen, found a newspaper delivery route. Rising at 5:00 A.M. every day of the week, he lugged a heavy load of papers around his city route. He saved every dime he earned—and surprised us with a TV set to replace the one we'd left behind in Bozeman.

The best that can be said of our year in Madison is that we pulled together and managed to survive the year's leave of absence. The Ph.D. had turned out to be nothing more than a pipe dream, and I knew my husband would never again consider going back to school. We would go back to Bozeman and pick up where we had left off—but with a stopover in Minnesota.

My right ear had always been sensitive and often caused me a lot of pain. But during the year in Madison, the pain became so excruciating I went to an ear specialist, who insisted I undergo surgery at the Mayo Clinic in Rochester, Minnesota. Dr. Halberg, a specialist on the staff at Mayo, had recently perfected and successfully performed a new surgical technique that involved taking a portion of skin from behind the ear and fashioning a tiny patch to serve as a new eardrum, replacing the damaged one. This surgery, known as a tympanoplasty, would be performed with the aid of a microscope.

We traveled from Madison to Rochester, where I met Dr. Halberg and settled into the clinic. The X-rays that were a part of the pre-surgical examination showed that a large calcium deposit was pressing onto nerves connected to my brain, and also endangering a facial nerve. This deposit would have to be removed before the eardrum could be replaced. I immediately thought of Thelma, for it was a wonder my face had not become paralyzed already, as hers had been.

Since my husband had thought the examination and the surgery would all take place on the same day and we could be on our way west again, he became somewhat irate when Dr. Halberg told him I couldn't possibly travel for at least three more days. This was unsettling news indeed, for, as my husband reminded me, he and the children were staying in a motel across the road, and it was costing money. Three days later he came bounding through the doorway into the room, where I lay with a heavy plaster-of-Paris tiara around my skull, and said, "You've had your three days. Let's go."

I was hardly in a frame of mind for such a command. I had just learned that though the calcium deposit had been successfully removed and the replacement of the eardrum had gone well, there was not much hope of any improvement in my hearing, since the surgery had revealed that the stapes bone had crumbled. My hearing problems were the least of my husband's worries at that point, and he insisted that the doctor be called in to prepare me for the journey to Montana. I did not protest, knowing that once he made up his mind, there would be no stopping him.

The doctor must have sensed the urgency of the situation, for he responded to the nurse's call and came in at once. However, as he attempted to hack the plaster cast from around my head, I fell off the chair in a faint, causing the doctor to insist that I stay over yet another day. Even with a night's rest, I wasn't strong enough to go through the procedure sitting up, so I begged Dr. Halberg to work on the cast while I lay on my bed. The bandage thus removed, the ghost of Mother's stoicism came through again, giving me grit enough to avoid fainting while the doctor removed the stitches that held together the hole where the skin had been cut away to make my brand new eardrum.

Indeed, I felt her comforting presence all the way home to Bozeman, recuperating on the run, as it were, listening all the while to that voice from my childhood and daring to believe in the words that had seen us all through so many tough times: *It'll be all right again come morning, Love. You'll see!*

Those words echoed once more on August 17, 1959. We had barely gotten settled back into our old two-story home on West Lamme when an earthquake shook us from our sleep just before midnight on that fateful Monday. Registering 7.5 on the Richter scale, and the third strongest temblor to date in the USA, the quake's effects were felt throughout southwestern Montana, northwestern Wyoming, and central Idaho. In Bozeman the damage was immediately evident. Portions of Holy Rosary Church collapsed, neighbors reported cracked plaster and broken dishes, and several businesses and homes suffered considerable damage.

In West Yellowstone, just 90 miles or so south of Bozeman, residents were literally thrown from their beds by the force of the shock, and night owls coming out of the local taverns reported difficulty navigating the undulating streets. At Old Faithful Inn in Yellowstone Park, a beauty pageant had just drawn to a close when the building began to sway, stones shook loose from the fireplace and chimney, and more than 700 summer tourists were hurried out of the building to wait out the aftershock in their cars or in park buses. But as we tuned in to hear more news on the radio, we discovered that the tourists within the park had been the lucky ones.

All across Gallatin and Madison Canyons, dude ranches were filled to capacity, as were three Forest Service campgrounds in the area around Hebgen Lake. Many of the tourists had been outside their cabins or tents, enjoying the moonlight as they huddled around the glowing embers of their campfires. The full force of the quake rocked and tilted the lakebed, upending it like a saucer, and sending the sloshing waters roaring down the seven-mile length of the lake and forming thirty-foot waves that went up and over the earth-filled dam, which had sunk by more than nine feet in the course of the quake.

Six miles downstream, half of a 7,600-foot mountain broke loose and came crashing down, sending boulders the size of houses into the canyon, and burying a full mile of the highway and river to a depth of some 300 feet. We listened intently to Bozeman's KBMN reports from campers, for whom a mountain paradise had turned into hell. Hundreds of injured campers were airlifted from the canyon, and to this day twenty-eight or so remain unaccounted for and presumed dead. The story made national—and international—news. *Life* magazine ran a special earthquake edition on August 31, by which time the trapped waters from Hebgen Lake and what had been a six-mile stretch of the Madison River had begun to rise and form a new lake, the one known today as Quake Lake.

As traumatic as that event was for all of us, the children and I were so happy to be back home in Montana, surrounded by friends and familiar scenes, that even an earthquake couldn't keep our spirits down for long. In fact, for a brief while I thought that just being there in the house on West Lamme would be enough to ward off the depression that had begun to set in during our time in Madison. My husband was depressed as well, for returning home without the Ph.D. had dealt his pride a major blow. Being in the company of colleagues who knew of his failure meant he had to work all the harder to hide his disappointment.

Within the sanctuary of home, however, he handled his frustrations in other ways. He barked at the children, and a deep resentment glowered behind his eyes when he looked at me. He would look at other women, too, playing cat and mouse with my feelings by boasting of being locked in the freezer with the college secretary, for whom he had done a few favors. As a faculty member by virtue of his teaching in the lab, he also sponsored outings for women's events, like sledding parties high in the mountains, where I would sit in the lodge, keeping an eye on the children, while he enjoyed the outdoors and the girls.

In the face of such actions, I continued to keep despair at bay by filling every minute with busywork. Consequently I was fast becoming one of those persons my mother reverently called extraordinarily good women, whose souls and spirits were surrendered to endless extracurricular activities for the good of the children, the good of the school, the good of the church, the good of the community, state, nation, and world, just for the sake of "doing good."

In addition to burying myself in activities and hoping, as only a Hope can hope, that the pall would lift and I would find peace and new meaning in life, I dared to dream of doing something for myself. Though Dan had begun kindergarten classes, I still felt that I needed to be at home in the daytime, awaiting the children's return and monitoring their homework. But during the evenings, I reasoned, I should be able to leave them with their father, as long as I had them ready for, or already in, bed before I left to go anywhere. I wasn't sure where it was I wanted to go, so it seemed like a gift from the gods when the Little Theatre League invited me to try out for the role of an Englishwoman in their current play. I know I could have landed the part, since I was no stranger to the stage, and to be involved in drama again would have set me walking on air. But first there was my husband to consider.

I should have known better than to even ask his permission to join the drama group, for his answer was, as always, a negative one. And as always, I bowed to his wish in deference to my promise to love, honor, and obey. Reeling from disappointment, I tried to console myself with the thought that even if he had granted permission for my theatrical efforts, he would likely have made the experience a miserable one by accusing me of carrying on with male members of the cast. He had always been suspicious of my relationship with any man whose name I even mentioned, and I could only imagine the fuss he would have made over my taking on roles that would have put me into direct contact with male actors. Who knows what could happen when men get involved in the play-acting, eh? I know what that kind of thing can lead to!

The faults and fissures in my marital relationship were becoming harder and harder to ignore. In the face of such treatment, what does it take to keep on living? To keep on hoping? To try to keep on loving? Yet what reason did I have for complaint? After all, my husband had a good job, we had a comfortable home, and the children were obviously thriving.

Then, as suddenly and unexpectedly as the earthquake had come to jolt our idyllic world, came the news that my husband's position was in jeopardy. Governor Nutter was slicing the higher education budget, and Ray, being the youngest staff member in his department, would likely be the first one to be released. In early summer of 1961, the ax fell. In the scramble to find employment, my husband followed the dean's advice and accepted a position that paid well enough to make it worthwhile to move all the way across the state.

Once again we prepared for a long haul to a new town, and even though there were no guarantees that the job would be permanent, the house on West Lamme would have to be sold. It had been one thing to leave our friends behind knowing we'd be returning after the Ph.D. pursuit. It was quite another to think of leaving our home, our friends, and Bozeman most likely forever. By now the children were accustomed to being uprooted from familiar surroundings, but I knew from personal experience how difficult starting all over again could be. In fact, I've noticed as the years have passed, how much more difficult it is the older one becomes to find your own niche in a new scheme of things. And though youth is a time of remarkable resilience, at fifteen and thirteen, Haydn and Hope could not have looked forward to the prospect of once again seeking to find their place in a new town, a new school, and, as it turned out, a new environment. For this time we were bound for the eastern edge of Montana and the town of Glendive.

Part 4

Chapter 12

When a man points a finger at someone else,
he should remember that four of his fingers
are pointing at himself.

—LOUIS NIZER

*E*astern Montana was a far cry from the mountains we were leaving behind us. The long, blue line of sky as it met the horizon never budged, as mile after long, weary mile of travel took us closer to, yet seemingly further away from, our destination. The tiny towns we passed seemed virtually deserted, and the cattle we saw on over-grazed rangeland seemed too languid and despondent to move, hardly bothering to browse the sun-parched grass, and making no move toward the saline sinks that cried for rain. The only diversion on that entire trip was a lone eagle sitting atop a power pole, waiting to swoop down on some unsuspecting prairie dog foolish enough to leave the relative cool of his underground home and venture out in the heat.

Though the 370-mile, seven-hour drive was grueling. At least by the time we finally arrived at our destination, we were all so ready to be out of the car and looking for a place to eat dinner that apprehensions were momentarily forgotten. The people we met at the cafe were friendly, welcoming us to their town and offering all sorts of advice—from who might have a house or apartment we could rent until we were ready to buy, to where to buy our groceries and school supplies. Fortunately, that first impression of Glendive as a friendly town was an accurate one, for we settled down and stayed there much longer than I had supposed we might—eight years in all. I will never forget the friendships I made in that part of Big Sky country, as my husband worked in his new job as district sanitarian, traveling long distances between the small towns north and south of Glendive.

The children seemed to adjust easily to their new school situations, with Haydn entering his junior year at Dawson County High School, Hope in eighth grade, and Dan in first. They made friends quickly, and I found myself venturing out and seeking the company of others, too, breathing easier in this new place.

There was an environmental freedom in this land of wide-open spaces of eastern Montana—yet I missed the beauty of the Mission Mountains. There is beauty, yes, in this spacious land leading into Makoshika Park, and an almost other-worldliness invited me to explore the hills and valleys of this place that was once an inland sea. Now a spectacle of mud formations, these "badlands" as they are called, stirred up by wind and water, yield an occasional seashell to make today's child wonder . . . why? It is a place of learning for anyone who might find a fossil or two. At one time, this area was inhabited by dinosaurs, as evidenced by the many remains of Tyrannosaurus rex, Triceratops, and other inhabitants of that era, ancient creatures whose bones are now displayed in various museums across the state and nation. Today Makoshika is home to thousands of wildflowers and shrubs, birds, mule deer, and other wildlife.

I was so intrigued by the park that when we began to look for a house to buy, I chose one that overlooked a section of badlands outside the park itself, but just as wild and beautiful. The children seemed to enjoy the starkness of our new surroundings as much as I did. We had been warned about the rattlesnakes within those rocks and ridges, and Dan, who was soon old enough to take his dog Chauncey out for a run up the closest hills, would come back with reports of having seen a few rattlers. But we learned to accept those potentially deadly neighbors as part of our new world, and to respect their right to find a rock on which to sun themselves or a cliff under which to hide. Though I must admit we were careful to give them a wide berth.

It was there too, in my newfound sense of freedom and my new appreciation for a stark and barren beauty, that I recaptured some of my lost spirit. We had been members of the Methodist Church in Bozeman, but our lives began to revolve around the times we spent together at the Methodist Church there in Glendive. Wanting my children to be brought up in the church, and feeling it was my duty to see what they were learning within those hallowed walls, I'd taught Sunday school classes at the Methodist Church in Bozeman, but I'd always been keenly aware that these youngsters could have taught me much more about the presence of God than I could possibly teach them.

In Glendive things were different somehow. With my husband and children at my side, I felt a sense of fellowship within the church that I'd not felt before. Church had never been a part of my life at Mabel and Guy's, for though Mabel would sit at the piano and play and sing hymns for hours, to my knowledge they never attended any church at that point in their lives. Nor did my husband ever talk about having gone to church with them during his years of living in the house on the hill. Yet here we were, gathered as a family, listening to the words of a pastor whose views on life spoke to my heart, and we made close acquaintance with people who thought going to church should be a weekly Sunday celebration. The two older children were welcomed into Methodist Youth Fellowship (MYF), and I was soon recruited as a Sunday school teacher.

Not long after our arrival, the preacher had come to pay us a visit, and when he discovered that I'd had rather extensive experience as a secretary, he persuaded me that I was just the one he needed to fill the half-day position of church secretary. I accepted the assignment with newfound confidence that I needed no permission from my husband—perhaps because, after all, this was God's work I would be doing. God's work was often mundane: sometimes working to type up sermon notes on a Saturday morning, if the minister had been away and hadn't had time to dictate his message earlier in the week.

I was also the doorkeeper, in a sense. Anyone who came by to see the minister had to go through my office to enter his. And since he was often away on church business, I was left to deal with visitors in his absence. Our church was always left open in those days, and since Glendive was a bus stop and railroad town, transients often sought shelter there. Some of those persons I remember still.

I found her sleeping on the hard wooden bench by the front door as I came to work early one morning, and she jumped up, startled as I touched her shoulder. "They can't throw you out of a church, can they?" she asked. Her eyes, wide with apprehension, took me in from head to toe, along with the rest of the lobby and its furnishings. She had on a thin summer tee, tennis shoes, and a pair of over-worked jeans that couldn't possibly have kept her thin frame warm on a winter's day in Montana. The words tumbled out half-strangled from her thin, parched lips, and I learned she had been sleeping on the floor of the bus station during the night, until the caretaker found her and sent her on her way.

I assured her she would not be thrown out into the cold, then found a pair of socks and a cardigan in the lost-and-found box, and led her into the reception hall where there was a kitchen and a sofa. There were tea bags in the Women's Society cupboards, and a blanket was draped across a chair. In a few minutes, the hot tea had stopped the trembling, and she snuggled down in the warm cardigan and was asleep before I even had time to cover her up and tuck her in.

I had plenty of time to wonder what I could possibly do when she awoke. When the minister arrived, he suggested sending her to the welfare department, but I knew there would be no point in that. The way they handled transients—if there was sufficient money in the General Fund—was to buy the wanderer a meal and a bus ticket to the next closest town, where they might find assistance or they might be greeted with yet another "Sorry!" I saw no other alternative but to wait until she awoke and take her home with me.

She agreed to the plan, and while she took a bath, I found some clothes from Hope's closet that fit. Then we relaxed with a bowl of soup while her story unraveled. She had left her home in Minnesota, hoping to find instant stardom in Tinsel Town. Young, inexperienced in the ways of the world, and as naïve as I had been coming to Montana in the 1940s, with hopes of living happily ever after, she found her daydreams quickly turning into nightmares. Homeless and penniless, she walked the streets by day, seeking out a safe place to sleep on the sidewalks at night, until she decided to hitchhike back home to Minnesota, thumbing her way in stops and starts, because "there was nothing else to do."

How many cars she had hopped into, she couldn't quite remember. The one she wanted to forget was the car that took off, careening down the icy highway with her suitcase in the trunk, leaving her stranded by the side of the road at the top of a mountain pass. She shook her head and I knew she was too full of tears to tell the rest of her story. I almost said to her, "Never mind, Love, it will be all right come morning," but let a reassuring hug suffice. Her story finished, she blinked away the tears and rummaged in the plastic grocery bag she had picked up along the way, bringing out a slip of paper. Timidly, not quite certain she wanted to, she handed it to me. "Here," she said. "This is something I wrote. Would you like to read it?"

I nodded and looked down at lines written as poetry and titled "House in My Mind." As I began to read, she sat there at my kitchen table, twisting her hands. "I live in a house called Torture and Pain / It's made of material called Sorrow and Shame / It's a lonely place in which to dwell / There's a horrid room and they call it Hell." I risked a glance in her direction, but she quickly looked away. "From the faucets run tears that I've cried all these years." It was all I could do to hold back my own tears as I read her closing lines: "But the worst part to face / is I'll die in this place / . . . alone." I had no words to offer her, just a shake of the head that showed my appreciation and empathy. She smiled shyly as I handed the poem back to her, then pulled out several more pages, saying, "I want you to have these, too."

I let her sleep again while I phoned and made train reservations for her to go back home. The children came in, and we ate dinner earlier than usual, so that she could catch her train. I was proud of the way my children welcomed a stranger into our home, and of my husband, who was always willing to do a good turn if he thought it was necessary. He drove us to the railway station, where we put her on the train back to Minnesota.

I never expected to hear from her again, but one day, long after her time there in Glendive, the postman brought a letter telling me she had found a job, was doing well, and was reunited with her family. The envelope contained yet another poem! A gift indeed!

My hands wore gloves of fallen snow
My heart was made of ice,
I wandered through a frozen world
Where kindness had no name
And all around I only saw
Bitterness and pain.
But in the night I found a friend
  Who warmed my weary heart

. . . .

A friend who brought the sunshine
And took away the snow
A friend who let me in when
I had no place to go

Her final lines were those I cherish most, because I know in my heart that she has lived their promise: "I wish that I might someday be / A friend to someone I don't know."

Her name was Ardys, and I will never forget her.

Montana's cold winter months brought a barrage of bums traipsing into the church, begging for help or a handout. Since my husband's income was finally sufficient to take care of our family's basic needs, most of what I earned from my secretarial work was given to those poor souls in greater need than I—much to my husband's disapproval, since he had always had control over where I spent our money.

"You're a fool to be giving them your hard-earned money," he admonished. "They'll just head for the nearest bar!"

But what if they are really hungry, I argued with myself. I knew what it was like to be hungry, so I soon became pegged as a soft touch. Did I need a character reference from above, bearing proof of their need? It was standing right there before me: haunting, hungry eyes downcast with shame for the asking.

It was the day before Christmas when he hobbled into the office, obviously in pain. He wore an old army overcoat with all the buttons missing, but neither hat nor gloves, and as he walked over to the desk, I saw the reason for his pained expression. He wasn't wearing any shoes! When I questioned what he was doing on such a cold and snowy day without shoes, he told me that a buddy had taken off with his boots during the night, while they were riding the rails together. "Christ!" he blurted out, "Them boots were me bread and butter."

He said he had always worked for something to eat. "I just don't go beggin'," he said. He went on to tell me he had walked from the train through snow-packed streets, until he saw a shoe repair shop, where he stopped and asked to shovel the sidewalk for a pair of old rejects. The shoe man had quickly sidled behind the counter, closer to the cash register, and told him, "I shovel my own walks. Rejects will cost you ten bucks."

How on earth anyone with a heart could close their eyes on a pair of bare feet was beyond me, but I knew the owner of the only shoe repair in town. When I asked the transient if he thought he could walk back that far, he nodded and said, "You bet your boots I can walk that far," and he was too overwhelmed to realize the humor in his words.

I called the shoe shop owner and told him the man was on his way back to the store and if it wasn't too much trouble, to help him pick out a pair of decent boots, making sure they fit him well before he sent me the bill.

The rummage box produced a pair of socks that would fit his feet, and he was on his way. He stuffed the two dollars I'd put in his hand for a meal into his pocket, stood there uncertainly for a second, then said, "I'll never forget this place."

A waitress at the depot diner called later in the day to send a thank you from some bum who had "wolfed down a bowl of chicken noodle."

"Was he wearing shoes?" I asked.

"You betcha," she said. "Nice pair of boots he had on. He sure was proud of those boots."

Despite my husband's frequent reminders that with the children in school all day, I could have a real job that contributed to our savings account, I grew stronger and stronger in charting my own course. For one thing, his new job as county sanitarian necessitated his spending long days on the road, as he traveled from one small town to another, inspecting restaurants, checking water quality, and attending to other matters regarding the health and well being of citizens in the area. When blizzard conditions or below-zero temperatures made driving home hazardous, he would call and explain that he was spending the night and would either be home the next day or travel on to his next assignment. I enjoyed those hours of freedom, knowing I would not have to report my every move while he was away, yet ready with the answers should he ask.

My father once told me, "Trust everybody till you find them out, Love," and I have always done that, so rather than allow myself to foster suspicions of my husband carrying on behind my back, I became suffused in the work of the church and the peace I felt therein.

My fondest memory of Makoshika Park is of a cool Easter morning when we gathered in the darkness, anticipating nature's reminder of the miracle and the mystery of the risen Christ. At last the sun began to rise, sending shards of light and shadows through the heights and depths of the sandstone hills. And still we waited in silence, until its full glory spread across the natural amphitheatre in which we sat, and we rose to greet the sun with songs of praise and joy, our voices ringing loudly, echoing off the rocks and ridges of that hallowed hall.

I rose to the church's every expectation during the relatively few hours a day I was there, and I gave my all to assisting those in need. As I took on more and more responsibilities there, the church became my passion in life. Yet there was still a longing for something more, some truth I had failed to find either in the beauty of all outdoors or within this church that had come to mean so much to me.

But that which had been missing in my life came on yet another Easter Sunday, a rush of certainty, like a name on the tip of the tongue. It came like the comforting sound of voices after my surgery, assuring me I was still a living, breathing person. And it restored that sense of abandon I'd had as a child, too caught up in life's wonders to notice my feet were getting wet as I sloshed through the swamp to gather the wild orchids growing on the other side.

As I knelt at the altar that Sunday morning awaiting communion, the preacher was reading the Beatitudes, and I listened with a grateful heart as I had done so many times before. But on this particular Sunday, as I took the bread and ate, then reached to receive the wine, an overwhelming fear consumed me and the cup became so heavy, I needed both hands to lift it to my lips. Yet as I returned to the pew, the soul-stirring words of the Beatitudes still singing in my ears (blessed are . . . blessed are . . .), suddenly the dreadful fear was wiped away, and all the loves I had ever known welled up inside of me, like a dull flame quickly spurting into wildfire. The love of my compassionate father, his golden tenor voice singing me to sleep. The generosity of a beloved teacher, lifting me up and setting me down on her high desk to share our lunch, knowing I had nothing to share. The caring spirit of Mr. Nightingale, the Sunday school teacher who had carried me home on his shoulder when the big boys were making fun of the little girl in ugly glasses and the donkey fringe, who knew the correct answer to a question when they didn't have a clue.

I surrendered myself to the love I found at the altar of my church in Glendive that Sunday morning. I told myself that the search for beauty had brought me to this moment of truth. I wanted desperately to share what I had received, but there were no words that could possibly convey the overwhelming sense of joy I felt. Eventually I gathered courage enough to attempt to share my experience with the minister, but he kept looking down at his watch, and the miracle stuck in my throat and died there as he turned in his chair and began to study his appointment book.

How could a minister be so uncomfortable, so determined to end my attempted explanation of what I had experienced at the altar rail? How could the leader of the flock fail to understand that the love of God is not merely a few words of praise in private to some deity who has the power to grant our every wish, to watch over us and keep us safe from harm! It is an overpowering, gut-level, startling discovery of untamed passion that rushes into the soul, singing not from the wisdom of Proverbs or even the joy of the Psalms, but from the ecstasy of the Song of Solomon:

> *Let him kiss me with the kisses of his mouth . . . . Behold, he cometh leaping upon the mountains, skipping upon the hills . . . . My beloved spake, and said unto me, Rise up my love, my fair one, and come away. For, lo, the winter is past, the rain is over and gone; the flowers appear on the earth; the time of the singing of birds is come, and the voice of the turtle is heard in our land. . . . Arise my love, my fair one,*

and come away. . . O my dove, that art in the clefts of the rock, in the
secret places. . . let me see thy countenance, let me hear thy voice; for
sweet is thy voice and thy countenance.

But the Song of Solomon is considered by some as being strongly evocative—even provocative—writing, so it is understandable how any attempt to describe an experience parallel to Solomon's passionate embrace of "the beloved" can be dismissed as evidence of a passionate, even erotic attachment to someone rather than the One. And perhaps that was the opinion of the reverend after my attempt to share with him that soul-searing moment at the altar, when my heart seemed to break in two, the revelation lifting my soul to the skies, for a few mornings later I found on my desk a letter terminating my position in the church office, a letter written and signed by the reverend. He wrote that the good I thought I was doing for the church had been done in the name of himself, the reverend, not in the name of the Father. I felt like some snippet coming apart at the seams. He went on to say I had found my involvement in the church to be something to tide me over during a bad time. He said that perhaps I could use a psychiatrist.

For reasons I have yet to understand, he accused me of considering myself better than anyone else. And he accused me of crossing boundaries, saying there was obviously "something going on" between myself and another member of the church, a man who was one of his best friends, and so was often passing through the office where I worked. He had surprised and startled the two of us, he said, one day when he was coming out of his office and into mine. Again, words from Song of Solomon came to mind: "Jealousy is cruel as the grave; the coals thereof are coals of fire, which hath a most vehement flame."

Whatever the reverend's motives, the letter of termination was not enough to satisfy his need to be sure I would no longer have reason—or opportunity—to be in close proximity to him. He called a conference with my husband, who characteristically refused to tell me what was on their agenda, saying this was strictly a matter between the reverend and himself. Yet I would have been a simpleton had I not wondered what went on behind those closed doors in the sanctuary.

Was my former boss confessing fear of his own loving feelings toward me, feelings that became uncomfortably evident to him when I attempted to share my experience at the altar? In retrospect I am wondering whether I was wishing myself into heaven via the arms of this earthly figure, the reverend? Had I, in fact, spiritually embraced a human being as the object of my earthly search for gratification? If that was indeed the case, I take some comfort in the words of Charles Williams, whose analysis of the overall theme of Dante's works surmised: "Unless that which is false is followed, that which is true in the end cannot enter."

I sense the truth in that statement, but I remain convinced that my experience at that altar had nothing to do with the reverend, other than the fact that he happened to be there, perhaps as a catalyst, but certainly not as the center of the experience itself. Having searched for truth and beauty all my life, I experienced a glimpse of what I had longed for, a moment in which I stood alone in truth's reality. It is difficult to put such an experience into words even now. I only know that what I felt was too powerful a force to have been the idolization of a human being, for I remember looking up at the lighted cross above the altar and thinking I would die for the image hanging there. I asked myself if I might take his place, whispering, "Let me, let me!" I swear I wasn't speaking of or to the reverend, but I cannot deny that he must surely have been in the picture somewhere, somehow, on that long-ago day.

And so I wondered, as I sat at home waiting for my husband to return from the reverend's study whether my former boss was maligning my character, trumping up reasons for dismissing me from my job, as I had visualized Mabel black-balling me when my husband had stopped to visit her at the end of the war before coming home to his wife and newborn son. The telegram had specified the date of his arrival in Polson, but not the time of day, thus I had waited anxiously all day longing to see him standing in the doorway of the place I had come to call home—Geraldine's home! He had readily admitted stopping by to shoot the breeze with Mabel and Guy but refused to say for how long, or why.

This accusation by the reverend was déjà vu, that same scene of long ago, played all over again, in another town, on another day. Could that be the reason for the hateful look my husband shot at me when he finally came back from the church? Was the scenario from the first incident playing out in his mind all over again?

Or did the reverend feel some urgent need to confess to Ray that he was falling in love with his wife, and therefore had to let her go? Or, more likely still, had the reverend's wife accused him of philandering, and told him to get rid of me? That seemed—and seems—quite possible, since one thing I remember from his letter, indeed the only thing that spoke at all to any displeasure with my work as church secretary, was a line about his wife's having been upset over "the terrible work" I'd done on some personal typing job I had agreed to do for her. Excuses. Accusations. What was the reverend saying behind closed doors?

I was never to know, for after his meeting at the church, my husband came striding into the kitchen with hands up, palms backing me off as I approached him, and shot out the words that left me to wonder the rest of my life: "Don't ask! It's none of your business. My mouth's shut and I don't want to hear one word about it."

It was a devastating time for me, fearing what others were thinking about my dismissal, especially the board of trustees who knew the quality of my work, and my dedication and service to the church. They would surely have asked the reverend to explain his reasons for terminating my position. Without knowing what had been said, I never had a chance to defend myself against rumors and accusations. I was not, nor had I ever been, a tramp! I'd been a virgin until my honeymoon. I had never broken any vows made to the church or to God—or to my husband. Even during the most trying times in our marriage, I had not allowed myself to think of divorce—and that despite the fact that the reverend's views on divorce were starkly different from my own. If the shoe doesn't fit, don't wear it. Why suffer through something that isn't working? Had he come to that conclusion due to his own experience?

I was sick at heart. For one thing, the love I had tried to explain in my holy confession was a guileless love, untempered by wisdom, pure like a child's, nurtured in communion with those who likewise love. The love of which I spoke did not seek fulfillment for oneself but was a gift, perpetual, that kept on giving of itself. It was not a love in search of sexual satisfaction, but a love that sought only to satisfy the soul. Ironically, as I look back on that incident, I realize that Methodism is founded on the premise of circuit rider John Wesley's wholehearted belief that Christian Perfection is attainable in this life—and that in trying to explain my moment of revelation, I had ignored his warning that disclosure of that inner knowledge might cause one's sincerity and humility to be questioned by anyone lower than the angels.

In spite of everything that happened in the face of the reverend's actions—and in spite of all the trying things I have been through in the years since that glimpse of truth I was given at the altar, I have kept that love alive in my heart and treasured it to this day. I live in the knowledge that it will always be there, no matter how much of it I give away.

All this probing into memories of events so long ago has brought to mind a second act to the drama of this love triangle. Years later, seated at a table at a workshop in Great Falls, Montana, I was engrossed, head down, puzzling over an assignment I was writing, when I sensed a presence, as if someone were demanding that I pay attention. I looked up, at first not recognizing the gray-haired man who was saying, "I was sitting at the back of the room and I thought it couldn't possibly be you. I just had to come over to make sure it was you!" And there he was. The reverend. The man who had passed along to me at communion one day the passion of God's undying love, but had also turned me out of my office in shame.

That moment of recognition seemed—and still seems—like an experiential forgiveness, something that was just there, not contrived, not spoken, but deeply felt. And I wondered what my husband would have had to say about the demonstration that accompanied that outpouring of feeling. There we were, hugging one another right there in the middle of the conference room, holding onto each other as if to be sure of what was happening, embracing in the joy of reconnection and reconciliation, as if there had never been troubled waters or empty spaces between us.

"Time heals all wounds," so the saying goes, but time alone is not always sufficient to restore a sense of peace and appreciation after a traumatic event that threatens to overshadow all the good things that might otherwise have been remembered about a time and a place. Perhaps this moment of experiential forgiveness helped dispel whatever clouds still hung over my memories of Glendive, for I can honestly say that I harbor no grudges against the church, for I have many fond memories of the place that was my spiritual home during our years in Glendive.

But during that traumatic time, being dismissed from my secretarial job—yet expected to carry on supervising church school activities—had shattered any confidence I'd had in my ability to stand on my own feet and speak my thoughts. As a child I had never been afraid to take part in school plays, and as a young adult I had readily sought roles in drama and operettas. But those make-believe characters I portrayed weren't the real Irene Hope, the real me, who was expected to stand up, speak out, and fill my own shoes! At this dismissed-from-the-church crisis point in my long life story, I was becoming afraid to even stand up and teach my Sunday school class.

I know I could not have been the only person in the world to suffer those unholy fears. In one survey of adults, people were asked which of the two—death or speaking in public—was their biggest phobia. While only ten percent admitted to the fear of dying, ninety percent of those questioned admitted to fear of speaking. I had become one of those who would rather die than speak. Yet in the midst of my terror, I heard my father's persuasive voice coming back from the grave, saying, "Take yourself lightly now, Love. Your name is still Hope, you know."

With that gentle reminder ringing in my ears, I dared to become a Toastmistress. What an empowering experience that turned out to be—eventually. The first time I rose to my feet, sweaty-palmed, notes clutched desperately in my shaking hands, I wished the ground might open up and swallow me, relieving me of all obligation to ever speak again.

I made it through that introductory ice-breaker speech, not so happy about my delivery but overwhelmed by the faith expressed by other members of the group that I would be able to accomplish what I had set out to do. With their support and encouragement, I dared to venture through each step of the Toastmistress program, gaining not only confidence but friendships that would last a lifetime.

In recent years, friends have noted that surely during this time in my life my husband must have been proud of all I was accomplishing. My children were proud that Mom had finally ventured out and claimed a place for herself, especially in view of how depressed and defeated I'd been after being turned out of my position at the church. But my husband, true to form, belittled my efforts and was suspicious of what I might get into on those trips away from home.

I can't remember ever really thinking about having a career after I married, since the idea of living in that little rose-covered cottage, with a loving husband and beautiful children, was uppermost in my thoughts at that time. Not even my father's prediction that my Montana airman would one day cause my friends to walk away from me had prepared me for what lay ahead. I ought to have guessed there was more than fanciful romance attached to this ancient institution. My marriage preparation session with the vicar should have taught me that.

I had reason to remember that honeymoon experience on more than one occasion during our years in Glendive, for despite his faithful church attendance and the relative good manners he displayed to the reverend on Sundays, my husband was showing his less gentle side more and more often to others in the community.

As county sanitarian, his power over the owners of the cafes and restaurants he inspected was as great as his power over me, and he soon developed a reputation for badgering and browbeating them—even in front of their customers. He could be warm and pleasant to female colleagues on his own level, a veritable social moth, revealing his well-hidden social charms. Yet his paranoia, his belief that no one could be trusted and everyone was out to get him, led him to treat salespeople as if they were dirt under his feet. And his behavior whenever we were dining out remained as insolent and rude as it had been back in that elegant restaurant in our honeymoon hotel.

Such problems aside, the children and I managed to take advantage of all that Glendive had to offer. I was delighted when Haydn told me he had agreed to serve as an officer in the Methodist Youth Fellowship, and I was equally pleased by his modesty. The reverend had asked one of the other MYF members to speak from the pulpit during part of a Sunday service, sharing how the church had made a better person of him. When he asked my son to do likewise, Haydn refused, saying, "I would be a hypocrite to do that." He and Hope were both doing well with their studies, and Haydn was already setting his sights on college. Hope excelled in both science and math, and her experiment and demonstration on making plastic was awarded the Grand Prize at the Science Fair. Dan was making his way through elementary school in fine fashion, enjoying his friends and already looking forward to junior high, when he could don a uniform and participate in varsity sports.

Encouraged by my friends in the Toastmistress Club, I began to enroll in evening classes at Dawson County Community College, seeing at long last a route to obtaining the education of which I had always dreamed of that began in the old rocking chair by the hearth, where Father had read to me from *Tom and the Water Babies*, Hans Christian Andersen, the Brothers

Grimm, *Wind in the Willows,* and a children's story book called *Chatterbox.*

In those days children were taught to respect their teachers, and once I began my formal education at Evelyn Street Girls' School, I not only respected but loved all my teachers there. I can still see Miss George, who was Welsh, standing in the nature study room in front of the long, polished, wooden bench with the sink in the middle. She wore a simple daffodil yellow frock with a square neckline embroidered in richelieu. I knew it was the cutout kind of embroidery, because I had just learned to do that sort of fancywork in sewing class. The dress was sleeveless, and she wore a thick, golden snake bracelet on her upper right arm. Always, she was smiling, and I never took my eyes from her, unless it was to look at the brown china log planter on the bench. She had chosen me to plant the hyacinth bulbs so that the class could watch them sprout up from the black soil, leaning a little toward the light that came from the window. Their stately blue flowers filled the air with a little bit of heaven. It was Miss George who taught me to love not only the beauty of the flowers but the sound and sense of their scientific names, and it was Miss George who inspired me to create the pressed flower book that had helped Our Eve win a prize.

Miss Royal also came to us from Llangollen, Wales, where the River Dee runs through—and where I was later to spend my honeymoon. She would read to us from *Cricket on the Hearth* and *Wind in the Willows,* just as my father had, but in time she added the poems of Tennyson, Wordsworth, and Elizabeth Browning. Her readings were not simply for our pleasure, mind you. We were expected to write down as much as we could from the passages she read, and we were graded on spelling, punctuation, and handwriting. Dictation, she called this subject, and most of the class hated it. But such keen attention to the spoken word certainly made us aware of how the English language could and should be used.

Ultimately she provided us with a writing assignment based not on dictation but on our own creativity. We were to describe, as fully as possible, a day in the life of a monkey. This, like every other assignment we completed, was immediately read and graded at our desks by the teacher. There was no waiting for days to know whether your work had any merit. No homework was assigned or deemed necessary, unless you chose to do extra work in which you were interested. On that "Day of the Monkey," after fifteen minutes of scribbling down my thoughts, I placed my essay on my desk and waited breathlessly as Miss Royal started up and down the aisles, reading each paper in turn and assessing our level of achievement.

To my surprise, after reading only the first line or two, she actually squeezed into my side of the desk, sitting so close I could smell the faint perfume of lavender as she bent her head to finish reading my story: It was noon. High above me as I sat, swinging my tail in the topmost branch of a coconut tree, the sun . . . . As she came to the end of my page and a half, she looked up at me, her face flushed with what I hoped was pleasure, and said, "Excellent, Miss Hope," as she wrote a very bold A+. "Keep up the good work."

Years later as I enrolled for my first classes at Dawson County Community College, it was my unbelievable good fortune to meet a man whose love of the written word rekindled that burning desire to write that had first been ignited by Miss Royal's praise back at Evelyn Street Girls' School. This professor, known simply as Tusco, would read aloud to us from great authors, and his beautiful rendition of James Joyce's melodious prose fanned the flames of "Araby" into my own stream of consciousness.

Tusco had a voice worthy of the stage, and he used it to great advantage if his students cared to listen. His voice would toss aside with an air of disdain the words dripped so thoughtlessly from pen to paper, but those that had stayed with you through the night, the word, the phrase that sneaks into your dreams—pearls that you'd polished by candlelight and cradled in velvet, his voice would make of them a jeweled crown for you to wear, and you would know your worth! You would know your worth.

It was in Tusco's creative writing class that I wrote the piece that eventually became the prelude to this memoir.

Those years hold other good memories. Haydn had a glorious voice, (not tenor, like Father's voice, but a deep, resonant bass that echoed from the depths of his being), and I could hear Father's voice in harmony as the high school choir was singing "Send in the Clowns." All of us gathered for his graduation from Glendive High in June of 1963, and for his departure for Billings to attend college in the fall—a separation I was able to endure only because of my pride in his accomplishments, and my great pleasure in the knowledge that he would be able to obtain the education I had always dreamed of obtaining. Hope's high school career had featured commendable achievements in both math and science, and after her graduation in June of 1966, she set out for our old hometown of Bozeman to begin her studies in math at Montana State.

With only Dan left at home, I brought in extra income by working for the welfare office and busied myself with volunteer activities—until the spring of 1968, when my husband announced that one of the women who had worked with him for the past few years would be taking over his position there in Glendive, since he had just accepted a position as Park County sanitarian. Characteristically, this news was delivered as a matter of fact, not as a matter for family discussion. And, characteristically, he never acknowledged whether or not this move across the state was a voluntary or compulsory one. Had he worn out his welcome in Dawson County, or was the Park County offer simply too good to be passed up? Whatever the reasons for his transfer, I was happy at the thought of being back in the edge of the mountains, and moving to Livingston would mean Hope would be just half an hour or so away, at least until she finished her degree at Montana State.

Since uprooting Dan seemed unwise, with only a few months left until the end of his seventh grade year, I agreed to stay on in Glendive until school was out. The house needed to be put on the market, packed up, and sold, and "batching it" in Livingston seemed like a pleasant enough prospect for my husband. Once I arrived, we could start looking for a home—perhaps one we could count on living in for a long time, given the promised stability of this new job.

Chapter 13

Life is either a daring adventure or nothing.
—Helen Keller

nytime my husband would hear someone remark on the beautiful countryside, without fail he would reply, "You can't make a living off the scenery." Yet there we were on the move again, headed for Livingston, Montana—another small town in the mountains. He had been drawn to one after another of these far out scenic places in our nomadic existence. This time we had the best of both worlds, for we were moving to a spot more beautiful than I had ever imagined, my husband had a steady job, and we were looking forward to buying a home that we might well live in right through our retirement years.

The house we found was not only lovely but affordable—and was something of a local landmark as well. The moment I saw the McLaughlin home, I knew it was meant for us. At long last, my father's cherished hopes and dreams were about to come true, for there before me was my little gray home in the west, though it was not exactly little, and, being made of brick, it was more red than gray. It was a solid house with an historic pedigree. Sturdy white stone columns extended to the eaves from the red brick wall protecting the veranda. Were there geraniums in those big pots sitting there? I was already planting them in my mind, and made a mental note to buy a watering can. I would hang my swing in front of one of the big picture windows located on each side of the glass-paned, paneled front door. Glass-fronted, built-in bookshelves stretched the width of the wall on both sides of the brick fireplace in the living room, inviting me to fill them with my favorite volumes of the classics—my cherished Lamb's stories from Shakespeare, plus all the other books I'd won as a schoolgirl. Though we had not yet celebrated Thanksgiving, the mantle, with its massive mirror, was already crying out for Christmas, waiting for dark green boughs of evergreens and the growing covey of white-feathered doves with wings outspread that I had picked up over the years at Woolworths' after-Christmas sales. The house was full of hope for the future of my family, and after much persuasion on my part and Dan's, my husband finally agreed to buy the place, and we settled in and called it home.

Though there was nothing snooty or pretentious about its history, the house did have an aura of grandness. Jean McLaughlin McGrath, granddaughter of Angus McLaughlin, told me she remembered running through the house so she could make her grandmother's crystal tinkle. There had been plenty of love in this house, for Jean spoke with pride of the time when her grandfather Angus shaved off his moustache during a moustache-growing contest, just because grandmother said it tickled when he kissed her. Jeanette Ann McRae, the wife for whom the house had been designed and built, was descended from the Scottish McRae clan, whose motto was fortitude, meaning strength and impregnability.

Dan had earned a place on the junior high football team and was all set to win his first game of the season, which I wouldn't have missed for the world. I was there that afternoon, high up in the bleachers, standing tall and proud as the band struck up the first notes of our national anthem. Everyone around me sang those patriotic words with gusto, but I had to hang my head in shame, for despite all my excitement over becoming a citizen of my new country, I had never taken time to learn the words to "The Star Spangled Banner." Fortunately, the roar of the crowd as the home team stomped onto the field, and the thrill of the moment when I spotted my youngest son, left no room for embarrassment. There he was in the huddle with his newfound friends—Stevie Wedel and Ron Nemec. The coin had been tossed, the opposing team sprang into action, and there was the right tackle, my son Dan, plunging into that formidable line of helmets, and bringing down, arms encircling not one but two blockers. I could tell I had an athlete on my hands! Before the next game rolled around, I called a teacher friend, and she happily spoke the words of the anthem over the phone. An hour before kick-off, I was singing them in the shower, reaching hard for the high notes, but holding onto every precious word. It was a warm afternoon, the sun tossing its shine here and there along the deep waters of the Yellowstone. As I glanced up at the jagged, snow-capped peaks of the awesome Absaroka Mountains, it didn't take a lot of imagination for the fabled image to come into focus—an Indian chieftain silhouetted against the Big Sky, headdress and all, outlined clearly by those majestic peaks as if to reclaim once and for all the land that once belonged to him and his people. My heart sang louder than my voice ever could, "What so proudly we hail," and my spirit soared with the eagles to be part of this land of the free, this home of the brave.

Methodism still held me in its grip, and we transferred our membership to the Livingston church. Those were the liberal reform years of the early 1970s, when congregations were being urged to go ye therefore into the world and experience life as others were living it, in order to better understand why so many were turning a deaf ear when the church bells tolled on Sunday morning. It was a big, bold step and I was somewhat skeptical about the potential benefits.

I was invited to an experimental strategy workshop on this outreach project in Billings, and since my son Haydn was a student in the college there, I thought I might as well go out into the world and peek into the life of a former MYF officer while I was at it. He was happy to see me, and upon learning about my mission, he invited me to join him and his friend Bob Hiatt. Bob had just come home from Vietnam—severely wounded. I gladly accepted, for I found myself eager to hear Bob's opinion of that no-win war, in which so many of our young people were coming home in caskets, or in even worse shape than he.

When Haydn said, "We'll take you to Gramma's!" I thought of a smiling old lady. Imagine my surprise when I found myself not seated on an elegant chair in a lavender and lace sitting room adorned with cupie dolls, antimacassars, and aspidistras, but bellying up to a bar, eating peanuts and resisting the urge to throw their shells into the air and onto the sawdust-covered floor, as the rest of the noisy, beer-guzzling crowd were doing. Conversation was absolutely inaudible, given my ailing ear, the roar of the crowd, and the blaring boom-box band. I had imagined myself engaged in scholarly discussions with these college students, picking up knowledge of subjects I'd never studied—the theory of evolution, interplanetary space travel, or perhaps peace in our time, the futility of war, or why don't we study the consequences of past actions when planning a course of action today. I wanted to hear my son's friend talk about the consequences of war!

I looked around Gramma's hideaway at the young, eager college students enjoying life to the fullest, having fun without censure, yet every last one of them—including my son—willing, like Bob, to risk their lives for a country they were proud to call their own. Truth hit me like a thunderbolt as I realized I was staring into the eyes of freedom. They were free to do whatever they jolly well chose to do, including giving their lives, if necessary, to defend that freedom, and I had no business sticking my nose into their mug of beer. So when Haydn asked whether I might like a drink of water or something, I thought I might as well have a taste of that sort of freedom and answered, "Yes, please. I'll have what you're having!" Surprised and amused by my answer, he beckoned the waitress and ordered refills and an empty glass, into which he poured about half a cupful of beer from his own mug.

I was glad he had the good sense to ration my portion, for had I consumed a full mug, I would have forgotten to mind my manners!

As it was, that night-on-the-town-for-the-good-of-the-church ended up contrary to my expectations and those of the church. In addition to joining in the revelry, I took yet another step in the wrong direction—literally—and fell down the wrought iron stairway on my way out, sustaining damage to both my dental work and my dignity. I was more embarrassed than hurt, and I actually laughed at my close encounter with the devil—and the fact that Gramma had ended up converting me!

During that first year in Livingston, a Toastmistress Club was inaugurated, and I was invited to join. Many close friendships grew from that association, along with a new sensation of well being as I honed my speaking skills, winning contests throughout the Glacier Region levels of competition, and twice competing at the International level. I well remember the excitement of seeing those women from around the world, each in her native dress, plus the glory of the parade of flags. Here came the Canadian flag with its maple leaf, and the Union Jack, emblem of my homeland, following right after. China, Japan, Australia, India—how strikingly beautiful were the ladies from India—and the passing of Old Glory brought tears to my eyes.

Getting to know people from other lands on a personal basis opened my eyes to their ideals and beliefs—the things sacred to them that are so different from those we hold dear here in America. While the moment lasts, you begin to see through their eyes. We need more such moments if we sincerely wish to keep peace in the world today. But then I have always been a dreamer, sometimes dreaming of more impossible things before breakfast than the Queen of Hearts in Lewis Carroll's delightful story.

With or without my husband's praise, I continued to chase my dreams. I was greatly honored to be chosen as the keynote speaker at an inauguration assembly for Shirley Wareheim of Butte, Montana, the newly elected national president of the world-wide organization, International Toastmistress Clubs. My speech for the occasion was titled "Don't Let

George Do It All," and in those progressive days of feminism, I dared to suggest we further our cause for equality in a male-dominated society by keeping the brassiere out of the brazier and working harmoniously with men to win their trust and raise our status. I never did burn my own brassiere, perhaps because I still remembered "the thing" that served me as bra until I was fourteen and earning enough money to buy a real brassiere.

It is important to me that we recognize social progress by taking advantage of new opportunities. When women were finally allowed to enter the sacred ranks of the Toastmasters, I immediately availed myself of that so-called privilege by helping birth our town's first Toastmasters Club, which we named the "Livingston Last Word Club."

On one occasion, I was asked to speak to members of Bozeman's Masonic Lodge. There's no denying I love to talk, especially about America, and on this Fourth of July in the hallowed halls of the Masonic Lodge, I dared to demonstrate the extent of my belief in freedom, by defying the rule that members of the Women's Auxiliary must wear skirts at all Masonic functions. I tried to look nonchalant, the sleek lines of my black velvet pants making their own statement among all the bare legs and silk stockings of Auxiliary members who walked around the hall in short skirts, which shrunk even shorter when their wearers sank into chairs, forgetting to cross their ankles. I was so proud that night, not only because of the standing ovation I received for expressing my love of this country, its citizens, and the freedoms we all enjoy, but also because not one person there on that special Fourth of July celebration spoke out against my having broken a dress code as old as the Auxiliary itself.

There has been no more welcome gift in my life than the ability to communicate with an audience and to feel the rapport expressed in body language that needs no words to back it up. I began to be invited to speak at luncheons and formal occasions all across Montana and in surrounding states. Eventually I was accepted into the National Speakers Association as a professional platform speaker, having qualified for that honor through my past accomplishments, the recommendations of those who had listened to my presentations, and the income I'd already earned through speaking. By virtue of winning one of NSA's two annual "Speak to Me" spots, I was transported to Nassau, in the company of professionals who had already proven their worth in the arena of public speaking. Traveling across the waves on board the *Emerald Seas,* I felt honored indeed!

Despite my increasingly liberal attitudes concerning organized religion, somewhere along the way I earned a reputation as a lay speaker in the church. I don't really know whether my husband was serious or joking, but he began pressing me to start my own church. With my talents as a persuasive speaker, he said, I could make a fortune from radio and TV audiences. He would even buy my clothes. I held my peace and didn't remind him of the last time he made that empty gesture when I needed a special-occasion frock. At any rate, I would never have presumed to start my own congregation, for I would rather die than raise my voice "in the name of the Lord" for the sole cause of raising money.

At one time in my speaking career, I did have a sneak peek at what it might be like to be the head of one's own church—or cult, as some would have called it. Guru Elizabeth Claire Prophet, of the Church Universal and Triumphant (CUT), asked that I give a series of lectures to her disciples, who were headed abroad to carry her gospel around the world. I was glad enough to give more of my time to this endeavor, for the CUT members made a delightful audience. Highly intelligent, they were open to humor, and I used this to my advantage. The standing ovation they gave after each of my workshop presentations I took with a pinch of salt, knowing the respect and dedication Elizabeth's followers had for her, and I suspect that Mother, as they called her, had a hand-picked—as well as captive—audience waiting to applaud my efforts for her sake, even before I spoke a single word. One of the ladies on staff told me the church members were jealous, because Elizabeth was treating me as a sorority sister, carrying out my equipment for me after a lecture and inviting me to step into her study to see the priceless gifts she had received from nobles and notables around the world. I doubt any of her followers ever realized that she later asked me to critique tapes of some of her own lectures.

I learned sometime later that the Church Universal and Triumphant was on rocky ground and going through turmoil among the leadership. Shortly thereafter, I was sent a copy of a CUT publication, stating that Elizabeth Claire Prophet was a victim of Alzheimer's, and now that she was no longer able to lead her flock, new leaders with new goals had been chosen. Apparently she had been summarily closeted away, presumably in Bozeman somewhere—or in one of the cult's well-furnished, end-time "shelters." Her final fate remains a mystery. Was she sufficiently lucid to recall words from her own sacred text?

Birthless and deathless and changeless
remaineth the Spirit forever;
Death hath not touched it at all
dead though the house of it seems.

I could easily have made a friend of Elizabeth Claire Prophet, but not in her world. Not on her terms.

During my busy days as a speaker, Dan was completing his high school studies and preparing to move to Oregon and work for a year, so that he could acquire the residency requirement for in-state tuition payments at Oregon State University in Corvallis. Thinking how lonely I would be after Dan's departure, Haydn made a special trip home, arriving on the doorstep with an adorable St. Bernard puppy in his arms. "Here, Mom," he said. "You'll be needing something to love now that we've all gone. Her name's Christina!"

"Krissy," I murmured. And my heart opened up and took her in, oversized paws and all. She immediately took possession of her new home, not as a lady but as a romping bundle of brown and white hair, eventually tipping the scales at 210 pounds.

I found other ways to occupy my time, now that the last of my children had left the nest. Given my appreciation for the educational opportunities this country offered to all, I thought of running for a position on the Livingston School Board. I knew better than to consult my husband on the idea, so I asked Hope's opinion. She said, "Go for it, Mom!" I did and won, ultimately serving three terms in succession, spending almost ten years standing up for the right of children to receive the best education the system could afford to offer.

As a child, I had been too timid to ask teachers or even friends to speak loudly enough for me to hear, too sensitive to brush off the hurt when lack of response due to my hearing loss was presumed to indicate stupidity—yet rebellious enough to purposely break my spectacles when I saw that Mother was willing to buy new ones for my sister, but insisted I keep on wearing the hideous pair I had always worn. Thus I fought for programs that would level the playing field for those who were physically or mentally challenged.

I'd gone into the School Board race with the slogan "Knowledge taught should mean wisdom gained," convinced of the importance of encouraging our children to understand what they read and heard, so they might have the wisdom to improve their own lives and benefit society. I presented many requests that such enlightened approaches be considered by Livingston's teachers, but to my knowledge, those motions tabled so long ago are still gathering dust.

Familiarity breeds contempt, Mother had always advised us, and I might add futility breeds exhaustion. Thus, after nearly ten years of working for the right of every child to have the best education our town could possibly provide, I resigned from the School Board, too discouraged, disillusioned, and depressed to continue what I had decided was a losing battle. In the end my voice, so accustomed to swaying the opinions of those before whom I spoke, had dissipated into nothing more than a whisper floating around the football stadium.

Disappointed as I was concerning my inability to bring about more change in the local educational system, all three of my children went on to higher education, having benefited from a solid foundation laid by public school teachers who cared. I am proud of their accomplishments and thankful for the opportunities they've had for success. I am also thankful that their dreams of a college degree were not deferred as long as my own.

I was sixty-seven years old when I finally earned a bachelor's degree, a step I finally dared to take in order to add authenticity to my entry in the catalogue of the National Speakers Association. Friends advised me to look into a degree from Pacific Western University, an institution designed for older students, whose life experience and college or business school courses could be translated into college credits. The basic business courses I'd taken at Price's Business College in far-away Warrington—with hopes of being promoted to the position of Lever Brothers' Chemical Laboratories "retiring secretary"—all counted, as did the night classes in literature, commercial science, and German I'd taken at the Institute of Technology.

While all of these courses helped satisfy the core curriculum requirements, I was working toward a degree in English, and the writing class I'd taken with Tusco through Dawson County Community College was a treasured addition to my rapidly growing transcript, as were the credits I earned by virtue of my years in the Great Books course offered through that same college. A number of classes I'd taken at Montana State University added to the store, as did lectures I'd attended in Glendive and Livingston, plus experience gained during my years of public speaking. Communication and leadership credits came through my years of public speaking and my service as an officer of many organizations. Even my years of recording textbooks through the state's "Reading for the Blind" program counted toward my degree. I don't recall that birthing and rearing three children was considered an academic accomplishment, but my nine years of active participation on the School Board certainly was. I had also earned college credits for graduate courses taken alongside Livingston teachers, who were working their way up the school system's pay scale.

Even though my degree was from a California state accredited institution, my husband made some arrogant remarks about the superiority of four-year university programs and the importance of earning a master's degree. He was entitled to his opinion, but I have come to think it was somehow fitting that I earned my college degree in a rather unorthodox manner. I had always learned whatever I could whenever I could, taking advantage of every available opportunity that came my way. I have spent a lifetime learning for the sheer joy of learning, and I expect to go on doing so till the day I die—at which point I expect to go on to higher education!

With my bachelor's degree as my passport, I accepted an invitation to join the American Association of University Women, and the women I met through local and statewide AAUW events became some of my closest and most treasured friends. I had made many friends—men as well as women—over the years there in Livingston. In fact, my involvement in various groups and volunteer organizations, my years on the School Board, my accomplishments as a speaker and a lay minister, and as an employee of the Welfare Department and the county's Mental Health Center had all given me a relatively large support base.

It was this fact that prompted the committee chairman for the local Republican Party to ask me to run for the state legislature. The committee begged me to do so since no one else was willing to compete against the incumbent Democrat, a man who had been backed by strong teacher and railroad unions during all four of his elections. I wasn't a Republican at heart, but it was an opportunity to express my views on important issues.

Not many women in those days were being sought out to run for political office, but I always had dreams of standing in the shoes of fellow Montanan Jeanette Rankin, the first woman to serve her country in Congress. She was brave enough to speak out for peace, her voice rising to be heard above male voices clamoring for war. I admired her fortitude, but wondered how on earth she managed to survive her long hours in a legislative building designed by architects who saw no need to put in women's toilets! God bless such American women.

Even with a role model as steadfast as Jeanette Rankin, it was a daring step for me to even consider accepting such an unexpected challenge. I was amazed to think that people were willing to pay my campaign expenses to represent them in the legislature. All in all, I rather enjoyed the experience, even though I didn't manage to garner enough votes to beat the Democratic incumbent!

Surprisingly, what sunk in deeper than any other feedback I received from that venture into politics was a remark my campaign manager passed along from a would-be donor to my cause: "She must be either a saint, or stupid, to stay married to that . . . man!" Reflecting on someone else's opinion of oneself opens the door to a better understanding of one's situation. I gave little thought to the stupidity issue, having never doubted my intellectual abilities. But being considered some kind of saint was another matter altogether. Isn't saintliness generally associated with martyrdom?

While I am not, and never will be, sanctified for the life I have lived, someone very close to me has pinned that label martyr on me many times during my married years, with each jab of that pin digging deeper into my dignity. And though I never had the courage to break my vows—or my chains—my heart would answer each such comment with I am what I am, but I would much prefer to be recognized and referred to as a wolf in sheep's clothing rather than a sacrificial lamb.

Yet looking back I realize there were times I should have thrown off that wooly mantle and fought tooth and claw to defend my children, if not myself. I did so little to deflect the blows from those I loved and should have protected, but my attempts to defend them only enraged their father and resulted in even more severe punishment, especially for our first-born son. I was unaware of any kind of agency I could have turned to for assistance, and not a soul knew what was going on. All was kept hidden because of his warnings that *nothing* goes out of this house.

There were scenes I'd prefer to forget—like the afternoon when my husband came in and demanded to know why Haydn hadn't come straight home after his Cub Scout meeting. When I explained I'd let him go across the street to play with the neighbor's son, he stormed over to their apartment, burst through the door, and began kicking Haydn in the butt. I watched through our window the scene that was playing out in theirs, and suddenly, Hadyn was being shoved out into the street, my husband's angry shouts echoing the length of the housing complex. I held my tongue for my son's sake and later slipped out of the kitchen, in hopes of comforting him. But the door to the bedroom was closed and I had let the moment pass.

Like most young boys, Haydn never cared what his hair looked like—at least not until he turned thirteen and developed an interest in girls. But Ray's military training—and perhaps some half-buried memory of his own ill-kempt appearance during the days when he'd slept in the barn and hadn't even a comb to call his own—caused him to obsess over the state of his son's hair. Without a moment's warning, he would grab Haydn's arm, drag him across the room, then plop down on the sofa, while ordering Haydn to sit on the floor. Squeezing his shoulders between his knees, he held him in a vice-like grip, forcing him to keep still while he swept the hair back from his forehead with a wire brush more suitable for currying a horse than a boy. Ignoring Haydn's pleas and protests, he brushed his forehead red and raw, then shoved him away as if to show how little he—or his appearance—really mattered anyway.

He was a tyrant, and his word was law.

It was Haydn who bore the brunt of his anger, leaving me to wonder once more whether he had believed Mabel's spiteful insinuations concerning the circumstances of the birth of "his" first child. Hope came in for her share of yelling, but she learned to stay out of her father's way, acquiesce to his curfews and rules, and somehow continue to love him in spite of all his flaws. Dan also learned the advantages of staying out of his father's way. Haydn, like Our I, ended up bearing the brunt of a parent's anger, in this case the brunt of his father's anger at the world.

By the time we were living in Livingston, Haydn and Hope were already making a place for themselves in society, leaving only Dan at home. Yet we still managed to keep up the happy family image, at least in the early years. We were all seen in church together and at Dan's football games and PTA meetings. My husband was on the scene less often, but who could fault him for that, busy as he was with his work around the county. We must have been doing something right, onlookers must have assumed, for Dan was growing into a likeable, well-mannered young man. That rose-covered cottage, those rose-colored glasses. That shiny, bright plastic facade.

Yet underneath it all, those irreconcilable differences between husband and wife festering throughout our marriage had dug an even deeper ditch of longing—longing after all the beauty lost in this union, all the flowers trampled by my husband's unrelenting hold on my spirit. Out of this darkness arose the desire to make my own beauty. I longed to go posy picking again in my life.

Wildflowers of the mountains nodded acquaintance as the car was grudgingly brought to a halt, so I could slip out of the passenger side and admire close up the flaming glory of an Indian paintbrush growing behind the fence. I felt an intense longing to paint and capture forever the blood-red crimson of that lovely flower as the sun lit up its petals. A spark of determination welled up inside. I would make it happen! I reached my arm under the bottom wire of the fence, stretching as far as I could, but still finding the blossoms were inches away from my grasp. Before I could climb through the fence and reach their brilliant beauty, a long blast of the car horn summoned me back to the car, which then shot off like a horse at the starting gate before the door was quite shut. Another set-up for a let-down.

I held my tongue and kept a brooding peace the rest of the way home, the pain of such deliberate cruelty carrying me back to a similar experience in 1931. The headmistress of Bewsey Senior Girls' School had singled me out as the one pupil from our school to vie against the girls chosen from other schools for an art scholarship, and I was exhilarated at the thought of maybe becoming a famous artist one day, like Grandfather Hope, except that I wanted to paint landscape and flowers. Not little old ladies and beer bottles.

The building where the exam was to take place turned out to be a dilapidated schoolhouse, boarded-up windows shutting out would-be intruders and putting the damper on anyone's spirits, especially those of an imaginative ten-year-old intent upon creating an artistic masterpiece. Once inside the entrance, which was hidden behind overgrown Virginia creeper and spider-webbed ivy, its feelers groping for a foothold on the old bricks, it was comforting to feel the warmth of hot water pipes wheezing their presence in the classroom intended for the examination.

I squirmed in my seat as the monitor gave explicit instructions to take the ruler out of our attaché case, use it to underline where we were to write our name, age, school, and form before returning the ruler to our cases. He then described the assignment. We were to draw a stepladder, a bucket, a bar of soap, and a scrubbing brush. No flowers, not even a dandelion. My heart sank.

How on earth could all those items be merged into a masterpiece? I took heart from the fact that I had done my homework, including practicing geometric drawings, just in case they were called for. I had practiced and perfected my parallel lines till the vanishing point left the horizon, so I knew I could tackle a stepladder and those other inert objects that had neither heart nor soul to bring them to life.

The monitor was a somber, nasty-faced little man with a black handlebar moustache and scraggly eyebrows that were continually going up and down above his thick, horn-rimmed glasses, as if the handlebars were leading him impatiently up and down each aisle, nodding or grunting at a drawing here and there. And now, here he was, making his way down my row, tapping the pointer he held in one hand into the palm of the other, keeping time with the oscillating eyebrows in contemplation of his next plan of action.

I was confident I had a drawing in front of me with sufficient merit to earn a scholarship, to hear the words, "Good. Very good, Miss Hope."

No such compliment was forthcoming.

He lifted up the pointer and brought it down with a hard whack on my knuckles, which unfortunately were in plain sight on my desktop. From a faraway place I heard, "You drew those lines with your ruler!" This was not a question but a pronouncement. "You disobeyed the instructions to put away your ruler before you started your drawing. Cheating means you will be disqualified from the contest and your work will not be adjudicated."

I was too frightened by those dark eyes, made larger behind the thick spectacles, to deny his accusation. Children were supposed to be seen and not heard, as Mother had reminded me many times. "Hold your tongue now, young lady," she would say, if she suspected I wanted to join even the most commonplace adult conversations. As the pointer came down on my hand a second time that day, I never wanted to cry so much in all my life, and the words I wanted to say became tied up in my throat. All that I could do was put the pencil and the "no-good" picture in my attaché case, on top of the ruler—where it had been all along—and do what I was told to do: "Go home!" The tears started to flow as I saw the other girls swiveling around to gawk at me, so I pulled out the hanky from my gymslip pocket and blew my nose.

No use expecting my parents to speak out about punishment for a crime not committed. The rule at the Hope house was "teacher knows best." We were to take everything coming to us on the chin and without question.

Here in Montana in the Hedrick home, the rule was "Father knows best, with no questioning of his authority." Yet for one small moment, I had remembered what it was like to be among the flowers, and I resolved then and there that I would someday paint those flowers and bring them into my life again. That opportunity came within a year or so of our arrival in town. Eunice Nelson, a friend who'd earned a degree in art from a North Dakota College, dropped by to visit on her way back to Bozeman. As we talked about her artistic accomplishments, I confessed that I wanted to take up painting—if for no other reason than to turn out a few pieces to adorn the bare walls of our new home. Pleased by my interest and the thought of having more time to get reacquainted, she offered to come over on Sundays and give me a few pointers.

I became absorbed by her techniques—brushwork, use of color charts, contiguous flow—and was soon catching on to her purist approach to art. I loved what she challenged me to do, and before long she persuaded me to display my work beyond the walls of our home. Shortly thereafter my paintings appeared in other places around town, and I began to sell landscapes. When Jo Sykes, an accomplished artist who had a knack for encouraging others, urged me to hold my own show, I dared to do so and was gratified by the response my work received. Yet I never did feel I had earned the title of artist, since I'd never gone to a school of art or earned a degree in that field. Perhaps my lack of confidence as an artist had its roots in my childhood, when I was so severely and unfairly reprimanded by the man with the handlebar moustache and scraggly eyebrows.

A friend recently remarked that I seemed to have come into my own during those Livingston years, taking on all sorts of challenges, gaining some fame as a speaker, earning respect as a school trustee, obtaining my college degree. Yet I fought my way through Dante's *Inferno* in pursuit of those goals, and any pride I might have had in my accomplishments was tempered by my husband's jealousy over everything I did that brought one ounce of recognition. Each step was a threat to his ego. But even though he felt he might be losing control over his wife, he need not have feared that I would leave him, for I still clung to those pointless vows made as promises to keep. Still, I was determined to pursue once more the truth to be found in the beauty all around me, and determined as well to bring writing and art back into my life.

With the encouragement of Jo Sykes, I joined a writers' group there in Livingston. We met in each other's homes, gathering around kitchen and dining room tables, and reading aloud from whatever we happened to be working on at the moment. Jo was a published writer and an insightful critic, and under her leadership our little group flourished. Poems, short stories, even books were published with the encouragement and assistance we offered one another. One of our members, Gwen Peterson, drove over from Big Timber, even during the worst winter weather, bringing along chapters from what became *The Ranch Woman's Manual.* I was pleased when she asked for a few tips on public speaking, as she rehearsed the presentations she was giving all around the state.

My own writing improved dramatically over my years with the group, which had soon merged with Bozeman's Montana Institute of the Arts (MIA) group. I entered a couple of the MIA contests and was awarded first prize for an article written on a trip to England. The winning entries appeared in the MIA magazine each year, and I found myself drawn to the poetry of a consistent winner, Millicent Ward Whitt. She, like I, was a displaced person, an eastern native who had followed her husband west when he accepted a post at Montana State. Though she came to say of Big Sky country, "It's your place now / it's yours / it's you," she continued to see its landscape through the lens of her previous life: "I heard a diesel truck's hoarse throaty cry . . . a foghorn over sagebrush on a hill."

While I was exploring the world of artists and writers, my husband continued in his own world of restaurant inspections, water testing, and other duties assigned to him by the Department of Health. Tired of working for other people and convinced he could make a fortune on his own, he began a little moonlighting in addition to his work for the county. As his clients increased, he acquired an assistant, a young woman with a husband and several small children—and obvious and ongoing marital problems. She was an attentive assistant, ready and eager to travel long distances to help him evaluate the availability, reliability, and purity of water for prospective buyers of attractive lots in the high country. Getting to such faraway places took many hours, and many more hours were spent completing whatever they were doing together.

Early one morning he announced that they would be driving over to Cooke City and into the higher elevations to do their digging and pipe installations for percolation tests. I was watching from the dining room window as they loaded his shovels and other equipment into her truck. Glancing up at the window where I stood, he mouthed something to her and she instinctively followed his gaze, then the two of them burst out laughing, as if sharing a joke I could sense was at my expense. Though this was typical behavior for the two of them, I'd been seething since early morning, when he'd casually mentioned that they would be unusually late getting back from the job.

There was no doubt in my mind that he had deliberately scheduled this particular trip for the very day when the Hedrick clan—with all their kith and kin—were to arrive for their annual family reunion. Arriving was one thing. Departing was another. There was no predicting just when the various family groups would leave, and I might well be feeding and entertaining twenty or more people for goodness knew how long. This was by no means my cup of tea, but my sister-in-law, Helen, had just happened to phone to say it was our turn to host the reunion, not long after Mother and Joyce had flown over from England for a visit with us. "It's about time we entertained my family," my husband had declared, and there was no way out of the situation. Nor was there any way to persuade him to hold the "big do," as Emily would call it, in the church basement and have someone cater the event for us.

Having grudgingly attended a couple of these get-togethers years earlier, I had some idea of what I was in for, namely supervising the melee on my own, while he did as he pleased. Yet the nightmare was worse than I had imagined. My house became the Big Top, with all the performers dashing around madly from one mishap to another like clowns in a circus, while one child screamed for help as she pulled a sizzling palm from the red-hot stove burner. All bandaged up and still sobbing, she remained inconsolable, until I promised she could help me make the salad for which her mother had brought the recipe. They had all come prepared to make their own special dishes, in spite of the fact that I already had stocked the fridge and freezer to overflowing with dishes enough to feed an army, having spent the last week hurrying home from work and cooking until midnight. How could I be so furious about having help in the kitchen when I'd wished for the assistance of a caterer? I felt myself coming apart before the party ever started. I thanked God for a nice, sunny Saturday, and thanked him again the minute it was over and done with, for by that time I felt as if I might lose control entirely.

Morning came, no one made a move to go home, and I knew I could not, and would not, face one more day of this reunion business. I was the first to rise, and slipped out the back way, key in hand, to find safety at the home of a neighbor, who had entrusted her property to me while she was vacationing. Like a robot in a strange dream, I fell onto the first couch that met my eye and was asleep on contact. It seemed only seconds till I felt my shoulders being shaken and Helen's voice drifting over the waves of the Nile, "You have to come home now, Irene. It's nearly noon."

"I'm not ready to go home yet," I heard myself saying, "you'll have to take care of yourselves. Oh and don't forget to sign the visitors' book you brought me before you go." I made a shaky entrance to my own home hours later, feeling like a victorious conqueror after my tussle with fate. The house was empty!

Ray had been mulling over thoughts of retiring for some time but still hung on as sanitarian of Park County along with the monkey business with his young partner. As the year sped by, I resigned myself to having him around the house again by the following June when he would retire. Imagine my surprise when one of the commissioners came into my office a month or so before then, after a Board of Health meeting, to tell me Ray had found a good replacement to fill his shoes, and that he, the commissioner had found a nice apartment for her to begin her training with Ray before his retirement! Did I hear correctly? Did he say *her?* The commissioner's next words confirmed my fears. Apparently this was the same woman the Dawson County commissioners had hired—on my husband's recommendation—to fill his position in Glendive when he had left for Livingston. Apparently they had met at a Sanitarians' Conference years before and had kept in touch. Oh, to be in England, now that April's here! Shouldn't tit make up for tat, I wondered? Where had all my male friends been hiding through the years? Shouldn't a wife have equal opportunity to enjoy such relationships with the opposite sex? That possibility had never been mentioned on the day we knelt at the altar.

They were sitting at the kitchen table, snacking, when I arrived home from work the day after my awakening. Their heads were together, pouring over some manuscript as if it were their future together they held in their hands. After brief introductions (and I didn't even care to remember her name), she looked at me with a rather supercilious smile and said, "What happened to the food I put to cool in your refrigerator? Ray helped me buy stuff from the delicatessen for my dinner tonight, and there's not a crumb left." I pretended innocence, but I knew what had happened to whatever she had placed there for her own consumption, because Haydn had called me earlier, saying he had helped himself from the fridge as he was passing through on a quick trip to Bozeman. He just wanted to send his compliments to his mother, the chef, for the elegant lunch.

I held myself together and asked the intruder point-blank, "Didn't the commissioners tell you they had an apartment waiting for you?"

My husband spoke up for her, giving the lame excuse, "Oh, she didn't like that place, and I assured her she could stay with us until she can find what she wants." The muscles in my whole body tightened, as if to ward off something unconscionable, like being tossed into the Black Hole of Calcutta. But I didn't have the courage to let her see my disapproval, at the risk of receiving a browbeating from her sanitary partner.

Evening approached and her stay-over became a certainty, as they sat with their heads nearly touching, perhaps scrutinizing something from a previous conference they'd both attended. They ignored my presence entirely, just as Mabel and her brood had done as they continued their pinochle game under the bare bulb of the house on the hill. With no tolerance for their arrogance, I separated myself from the cozy scene and said, "I'm going for a walk!" I stayed out walking for as long as I dared, before returning home to find both back and front doors locked! Another shutout! The third in a lifetime: once by my own mother when I was a teen, then by a pseudo mother-of-sorts, and now by a husband inclined toward promiscuous behavior, despite the vows he'd made so long ago.

"Oh," said Ray when he finally answered the ringing of the doorbell, "I thought you'd gone to bed."

I drew in a deep breath of courage, stared at him for a second, and then turned to face his guest. "Oh I'm just about to retire, dear, and you, young lady, had better be gone, bag and baggage, by the time I get up in the morning." Oh yes, Mother, everything will be all right, come morning.

Thereafter my husband and I tolerated each other as best we could, with no attempt whatsoever to cement a cracked relationship. His retirement party came and went without much ado, and he found plenty of excuses to keep in touch with his trainee, at the same time cutting ties with his business partner by turning over the moonlighting business to her, lock, stock, and barrel—assets and all—without a word to me.

I began to envision climbing into the car and taking off for parts unknown—an impossible dream, since I still had no driver's license. The occasional Sunday afternoon driving lessons my husband had offered over our years in Livingston had been as traumatic as the one he'd given me before he returned to college into Bozeman, but at this point I was determined to do anything necessary to gain my license. I studied the manual, passed the written test, and endured enough of my husband's "lessons" to pass the driving test. I was seventy years old.

There was another obstacle to my going wherever I wanted, whenever

I wanted. In my memory lurked the scene of Our Dot lying in the roadway, having been struck by a lorry. I was petrified that I might hit a child, a dog, or a deer. And there was yet another reason for my fears. During the long-awaited driving test, the examiner had remarked, "Irene, your depth perception is way off the mark!"

Over the next several months, I began to notice that the top edge of my teacup looked more like a child's Crayola drawing of waves at sea than the perfectly level edge from which I'd long been accustomed to taking a sip. At first I blamed the sight problems on eye strain, preferring to ignore the situation rather than face my fear of blindness that had haunted me ever since the day I deliberately broke my ugly pair of glasses.

When I realized the right side of the road kept disappearing from view every time I got behind the wheel, I finally had to admit that my right eye was virtually useless, and I drove over the hill to see an ophthalmologist in Bozeman. A careful examination revealed that my right eye had developed a hole in the macula, and nothing could be done about it. With the encouragement of my children, I had the doctor send an angiogram to a specialist in Salt Lake City, and to my alarm, he reported there was also a slight "window effect" developing in my left eye. My constant prayer was that I would be able to keep the sight in my left eye, so that I could go on painting the beauty all around me.

By that time my husband was a constant presence on the home front. Once his almost daily "training sessions" with his replacement ended, he found himself bored with retirement. He had been a member of the Masonic Lodge for many years and was a Shriner. He also loved to help the ladies on their "cooking for the men" nights at the Lodge. One woman had the temerity to tell me they all called him "The Little Colonel." Still, cooking with the Women's Auxiliary was better than moping around at home, and outside of his Masonic activities, he seemed lost for something to do. He read very little, didn't appreciate art or music, and whenever I persuaded him to go dancing, he literally dragged his feet and obviously didn't care to learn. I decided he was enjoying his misery and that his mind was shrinking up from lack of use.

Out of the blue one day, he said he wanted to go back to England to visit his old supply depot at Burtonwood Base. I couldn't let the chance of a visit home go by, especially since I wasn't sure my diminished vision would allow me to go to England alone anymore, so I took vacation time and went along.

Back in the 1940s, most of the country roads in England were country roads, and merely meandered from place to place. I had left the old country to fend for herself, and that she had. Roads from north to south had been transformed into major motorways and carriageways fit for a king to speed along post haste. I had traveled very little by car during my growing-up years, the family never having owned one, and so wasn't too familiar with road-sign language. My poor vision often meant I failed to see and read signs in time to be of much assistance, and I often misunderstood the phrasing on cautionary signs as my husband pushed the speed limit. We had planned to explore Scotland, but after one day of my confused attempts at directing, he decided to take a side road to the west and into Wales.

Once we were off the motorway, the trip became a beautiful, leisurely drive, reminiscent of the olden days when people stopped to smell the country air. Stone walls stitched a patchwork quilt of green and golden fields, dotted with black-faced sheep. Bracken on the hills had been turned to bronze and amber by the chilly October nights. Along the grassy lanes, milk cans here and there seemed in no hurry to be picked up, and from the distant church spire, white against the darkening sky, the glorious sound of Welsh voices rose in evensong.

As the sign Llangollen welcomed us back to our honeymoon hotel, I was back in time, being greeted in the lobby with the same royal welcome, the same reverence and respect for dignity. The same aura of constancy and purpose surrounded the palms and aspidistras still stuck in the same porcelain plant pots dividing the stuffed sofas from the overstuffed chairs. The

Welsh lamb was as delectable as it had been way back when. The River Dee still made its way around Llangollen, and we rowed a boat again where horses had once pulled barges through the water along the river's edge. The royal atmosphere had not changed one iota since the day I had said I do.

The trip overseas had put the spark of life back into my husband, and it wasn't long until his unspent energy turned to thoughts of going back to work. "Where?" I asked. "Oh, I thought maybe out to Oregon. We could go to Corvallis where Dan and his family are living. Or to Bend, where Hope's living now."

I loved my home. I was happy right where we were, having many friends and interests. And I was by no means as confident as he was that he could get a job at his age. His eyesight was failing, and his fuse was shorter than ever. One evening when I tried to express my concerns, he began an angry tirade and I walked into the kitchen, saying I was going to call Hope and tell her I'd like to go to Bend to think things over. Before I could finish dialing, he charged into the kitchen, grabbed the receiver from my hand, and yanked it so hard that dial box, handset, and a chunk of plaster were torn off the wall.

He had his way, of course. The house was put on the market, and I discovered what it takes to sell a home. A stream of realtors, hand-in-hand with prospective buyers, paraded through, met by shining windows, polished floors, flowers from the garden, and a cup of coffee and warm apple pie. As we waited for a buyer, I held a garage sale to hopefully clean out the conglomeration of stuff that hadn't seen daylight for years. In the process I discovered that Ray had become a collector of pens that didn't work anymore, pencil stubs, unrecognizable objects from his various jobs—you name it; I couldn't. When he said, "Don't touch any of my things," I heaved a sigh of relief and hoped they would become lost in storage.

I tried to make a party of the affair, with free lemonade and homemade cookies, which didn't last since the sale dragged on to overtime. The first lady who came looked as if she belonged there, and I guided her to an item that I'd marked as a freebie. When she came back to me, she opened her bag to show me she was taking every single item I had marked with a no-charge label. The sale ended with something like $1,200 in my pocket, and since none of my husband's belongings had been for sale, I kept it there.

While hunting through my personal cache of special items, I was fortunate to find a program from a writers' workshop I had attended, which had been organized by Gwen Peterson from Big Timber. There on the workshop program, written in ink, was the name and phone number of Linda Peavy, who had published poetry and fiction, as well as a number of books on women's history that she'd written with her coauthor, Ursula Smith. At Gwen's invitation, Linda had come by to meet the presenters and visit with those of us who'd attended the workshop, and soon the two of us were talking about my writing—and my experiences as a British war bride. "You should write a memoir," she said.

"I wouldn't know where to start," I protested. "And I don't have anything worthwhile to write about." She smiled and told me I could start by writing to my typewriter! "Talk to it," she urged. "Tell it anything you want to. Just keep on writing!" I placed that precious program back into my treasure box and dashed into our bedroom, with one thought rushing through my mind. My memoir, those few precious pages—ten or twelve—I'd scribbled down when my husband wasn't home. I'd deliberately written by hand to make them harder for him to read, and I'd hidden them under the mattress to share with Linda, should our paths ever cross again. I dared not leave them to be found when the bed was taken apart and loaded onto the truck, so I pulled them out from under and stuffed them into my handbag.

As I did so, I was swept by a longing to start writing again. Suddenly I could hear the words of my headmistress, Miss Norman, of Evelyn Street Girls' School: "You'll write your own book one day, Miss Hope!" With those words echoing in my ears, the longing to write flared into a determination to resume work on my memoir as soon as we reached Oregon. I couldn't wait to start afresh on the Xerox electronic typewriter—with its seven pages of memory—that I'd bought to replace the old Royal portable Hope had taken with her to college.

I felt like a new woman at that moment in my life.

Some books from my library collection I had sold at the garage sale, but I couldn't part with others, such as the Great Books series and the leather-bound, gold-leaf selections of literary masterpieces published by Eaton Press. They will stay in the family, with the stipulation they get dusted off once in a while and read for all they're worth. I had also held onto my books from childhood, planning to pack them all up with care and make sure they were in a safe place in the truck.

Though my husband didn't cotton to the idea of my giving directions during the move, he seemed overwhelmed by even the simplest tasks and couldn't manage to get the whole picture in his mind's eye. I asked him to help with only two chores during the packing, and the first was to find several large boxes to hold my treasured books. "No room for that stuff," he replied. "I plan on taking the books I'll need when I find another job. Yours will have to go into storage."

The second thing I asked of him was to deliver a pile of books to the AAUW book sale being held downtown. His answer was to work himself up into such a frenzy that he began jumping up and down and stamping like a spoiled child in a temper tantrum, finally kicking the stack of books through the open door, out onto the porch, and down in the yard.

So much for new beginnings.

"Our Night Out" student wives activity on the Montana State campus.

At home on West Lamone in Livingston with Our Krissy.

Finally speaking my mind.

Two-year-old Haydn.

Haydn and Hope at student housing.

Dan, our Montana cowboy.

Earning a Ph.T. at Montana State.

Skipping rocks below the cabin on East Shore.

Chapter 14

To halt each plunging day,
Each avalanching night,
To snatch at sliding time,
We write.
—MILLICENT WHITT

*I*n the spring of 1992, after all my years of city, county, and state involvement stemming from my fervent desire to repay Montana for what she had given to me, we were leaving Big Sky country behind and heading westward-ho to Oregon, perhaps to find a new home near the Pacific Ocean. Hope had volunteered to drive the Honda since the sight in my right eye was by that time greatly diminished. I could only pray that my husband was capable of driving the truck full of our belongings. His sight was stable, thanks to his new prescription glasses, but what about his temperament?

As we gathered speed on the interstate, I glanced in the rear view mirror to make sure the truck was close behind and found it a little too close for comfort. And the driver was obviously unaware that the ropes tying down the tarp protecting our belongings had already torn free, leaving the tarp flapping in the breeze as we headed over Bozeman Pass. I turned to Hope and she agreed that considering his present mood and knowing how he hated to stop for anything once he got behind the wheel, there was no point in signaling him to pull over and batten down the hatches. I could only hope the only thing that got bounced out would be his precious hoard of dried out pens and pencil stubs.

Though he usually chose to drive straight through to his destination, this time there would be a deliberate detour, for he had timed the date of our departure to coincide with the date of the family's annual reunion. We were headed for Burns, Oregon, and the home of his sister Inez. Though I was not in the least looking forward to being part of that gathering, there was nothing I could have done to change his mind. The trip was pleasant enough, because my husband and I were not traveling together. We were barely speaking by the time I sold the house in Livingston, held the garage sale, and packed for the move. I had been cheated by the realtor, I'd given things away at the garage sale, I'd expected him to be my slave and on and on and on with all his accusations reverberating in my ears, weighing me down and reducing my tolerance to the minimum.

I had come to the end of my rope, and I asked Hope to pull over to the side of the road. He was closing in behind us and I warned her that he knew I was unwilling to turn off the highway in the direction of Burns and that I would inform him we were going on to Corvallis. I found strength enough to do that, but it was a difficult situation, wondering what the outcome would be. However, I stuck to my guns and did as I intended. He stomped off to the truck, a black cloud hovering over his head, Hope moved the car forwad and he followed—the rest of the way to the home of our son Dan and his wife Leslie.

I closed my eyes, trying to relax in the Honda, remembering the gathering of the clans in Livingston last year—the circle of folding chairs on the patio where the beer and champagne has inspired reminiscences and laughter over incidents only the Hedrick family would find humerous. "Hank, remember the time you shot a hole in the living room ceiling with Pa's gun, just about killing us all?" "Oh no, couldn't of been me would do something like that. Just have been you, Raymond!"

"Weren't you just a tyke Hap when you struck a match and put it to a newspaper just like Hank taught you, and couldn't put the fire out when you were supposed to trample on it? Burned the barn down didn't it? Was Pa ever mad!!"

Remember . . . remember . . . remember when . . . ?

By the time we arrived at Dan's home that evening I was feeling much like I'd felt after straying away from the safety of my mother's hand in the butcher shop—lost and scared, worrying about leaving my husband to fend for himself and what on earth would happen next.

Details are not quite certain on any part of this journey from the starting point, since my mind was in turmoil, but move to Corvallis we did, with the help of my daughter, and by the time I awoke next morning my husband was gone, along with the truck. I had no doubts about his destination, so later in the day I called Inez's number and was told, "Yes he was here, but he left and we don't know where he went!" Two days later, he showed up at Dan's door shouting, "Keep her away from me!" I slept on the living room floor that night.

The next few weeks were a nightmare, especially for Dan and Leslie. She put up with more than any daughter-in-law should have to endure as we spent four long weeks in their beautiful home. They were more than hospitable, though Ray was becoming increasingly forgetful with each passing day. To make matters worse, the skin problem he'd acquired years before had returned with triple-pore vengeance, and skin flakes were evident all through the house. He insisted on driving, dodging accidents whenever he was behind the wheel. Then came the day Dan took his car keys away. Ray's depression deepened. The anger surging inside him threatened to explode, and I found myself searching frantically for a house, any house, not the home of my dreams, but the refuge in my dreams.

I eventually claimed title to a small three-bedroom that reminded me a bit of Father and his little gray home in the west. Though my heart reached out to the trees and flowers surrounding the grounds, wild though they had grown without care from loving hands, the interior of my little gray home was somewhat foreboding. Shuttered windows perhaps installed to evoke the image of a quaint English cottage—though not quite succeeding—created an aura of darkness. There was no point in consulting my husband on such projects as skylights and bay windows to let in the sun, but I managed to scrape up enough money from my retirement fund to have those items installed, and the house began to look like a home, though it really wasn't.

My husband had grown up believing you'll never get ahead in this world unless you have a job, and even at the ripe old age of seventy-four he became desperate enough for employment to take a job bussing tables at Burger King. When that venture didn't work out, he seemed to be falling apart, accusing me of stealing his "things," yet when I managed to help him find them, he would accuse me of putting them back where they belonged while pretending to look for them. At least he still enjoyed walking, and I joined him in doing that, but soon that wasn't enough for him and he decided he would run, leaving me behind to find my own place there in Corvallis.

Corvallis! What a beautiful city. I felt immediately at home among the apple, plum, and cherry trees, each blossoming in turn, the magnolias shedding their petals along the campus sidewalks. I imagined myself scurrying along to my next class, backpack hunching my shoulders, enjoying a host of Wordsworth's golden daffodils transplanted to this very spot. As the roses began to bloom in my new neighborhood, I could see myself standing on a Portland street with Gerry all those many years ago, part of the crowd assembled to pay their respects to that city's favorite flower, and I longed more than ever before to paint all that beauty.

Happily, the art supplies I'd had to leave in storage arrived safely, and I began by capturing in oils my beautiful Mission Mountains and the stark and lovely Absaroka range, tangible memories of my years in Montana that hang on the walls of my home in Oregon. When I had to abandon oils because of allergies, I turned to solar art, using colored inks on wet watercolor paper. I was delighted to find that these paintings, along with computerized prints and cards I made from the originals, sold very well at art shows and in local shops.

Art that brought in money was one thing, but my husband never understood or approved of my taking advantage of the many opportunities for taking courses and workshops in art and other subjects through the university. Ultimately, it was not his disapproval but my deteriorating vision that thwarted my ambitions. I could no longer distinguish shapes or colors with my right eye, and my vision was so poor in my left that I could barely see at all without a magnifying glass–a great hindrance and doubly frustrating since I was taking a delightful university class called "Reading and Writing Women."

Even with limited vision, I was determined to keep adding to the few pages of the memoir I had started with Linda's encouragement. As the pages began to mount up, my husband became increasingly paranoid about what I was writing and began hovering about, trying to read over my shoulder. Pretending to give up entirely, I hid the manuscript away in the daytime, yet kept on writing, scribbling thoughts onto paper in the dark, under the covers, as my husband snored beside me. Living in fear of being found out, I once again found comfort and inspiration in the words of Millicent Whitt.

When loss of sight became too severe to be ignored any longer, I sought the opinion of an ophthamologist, Dr. Hufsmith, who immediately discovered a hole had now developed in the macular of my left eye—just as the specialist in Salt Lake had predicted. Dr. Hufsmith recommended a new procedure called a vitrectomy in which the surgeon removes the vitreous matter behind the eyeball and fills in the hole, after which he replaces the removed substance with a gas bubble that dissipates over time as the natural liquid of the eye replaces itself.

The most amazing thing I experienced during the mending of the macular was actually being able to see the gas bubble behind my eyeball and watching it slowly shrink day by day until it became the size of a pinhead, then disappeared altogether. It was almost magical and kept my idle mind busy wondering how on earth that poor damaged macular could possibly reverse the process of sending messages to my brain from the outside in, so that I could see what was happening inside my own eye!

The convalescence was harder to bear than the operation, for it necessitated sitting, standing—even sleeping—with my head in a downward position. I persevered with this inconvenience rather grudgingly, but I will be forever grateful to Dr. Hufsmith and Dr Servais for two more years of 20/20 corrected vision in my left eye. After those two wonderful years of enlarging and enriching the hide-and-seek memoir, that eye required yet another vitrectomy, which I again chose to risk—at the same time a second surgeon was replacing the cataract-damaged lens with a plastic one.

Knowing this second surgery would likely be the last spurred me to return to my memoir as soon as I had recuperated sufficiently to sit at the computer once again. I was working feverishly, writing as if every word would be the last one I would be able to see. It was a relief when my husband said I should move to another bedroom. Hoping he wouldn't sense my eagerness to do so, I moved out in a fit of faux pique.

I don't usually bore people with my surgeries, but the whole process of recovering my sight had been miraculous and I shall be forever grateful to those Drs. Hufsmith, Servais, and Berzins. I could see! See not only well enough to write and paint but also well enough to realize that my husband was showing more and more signs of senility and behavior akin to schizophrenia. Sometime between our departure from Livingston and our settling in at Corvallis, my husband had become a bull with clipped horns, yet he remained ready to challenge the world at the slightest provocation.

Looking back to more pleasant times, I think of our first Thanksgiving in Corvallis. The celebration was held in Dan's home, with all of Leslie's family traveling many miles to be there, along with Hope and Gary from Bend, grandson Dan from Portland, and granddaughter Molly, who was working as an intern in a master's degree program at a behavioral school for troubled children close to the university at Eugene.

The holiday dinner was a two-turkey affair with accompaniments galore. My contribution to the feast was to be the rolls, six or seven dozen of them, since they had become a must item for every special occasion. They were there in plenty of time, ready and warm for the family—and for the guests who had already heard how my bread had won a ribbon once. The same number of Mother's famous mince tarts, jollied up with the prerequisite spot or two of Grand Marnier, went up the hill to Dan's house and were gone before the tables were set.

One of the long tables already held the Irish linen cloth I'd packed in the V-2 and brought across the ocean in 1945. With hundreds of embroidered names already sewn the length and breadth of it—family, friends, dinner, lunch and tea-time guests who had signed their names for me to embroider—it was ready for Leslie's family to add their names on this Thanksgiving Day.

I've gone on many a solitary trip through time as I've washed and ironed the cloth through the years. Sliding past the names of my parents and sisters and the friends and co-workers from my days in England, I steam across the Atlantic and on to Montana, where I am surprised all over again as I see the names of the many young women who honored me with a bridal and baby shower way back in 1945. Lora Mae Biggs' name was there, right beside Gerry's who had helped organize that wonderful party especially for me and who would become my dearest friend during that first lonely year in Big Sky country.

Even Mabel's signature is there, for she signed the cloth the day she asked me to bring it out so Guy's relatives, who were visiting from Minnesota, could add their names. Near one end I see the unmistakable penmanship of Carol Thomas, my dear friend from Bozeman. She and I won many a jingle-writing contest during the days our husbands were at M.S.U., hers as a professor, mine as a student. Through the years as we have moved from place to place—Roswell, Glendive, Livingston—many more names have been stitched into my cloth, keeping people and places alive in my memory.

A cherished reminder of joys and sorrows shared, the cloth has been a means of many mental trips back home for me and has helped bring to life for my children and grandchildren their British history and heritage. As I slather a warm roll with butter, I share once more stories about the privations of the war years when even necessities became hard-to-find luxuries that cost precious coupons, along with cash. What we didn't have, we simply had to do without. Some things were missed more than others.

Through the early days of my childhood, Mother had always insisted on using "best butter"—Danish—which became nonexistent during the war. I don't believe she ever forgave the enemy for the fact she was forced to eat margarine for six years. And we were allotted only four ounces of margarine, or sometimes lard, per person, per week, and considering what Mother needed to cook with, that didn't leave much for use at the dinner table. If mother decided we had hoarded enough sugar from our four ounces each per week, she would scrape up enough margarine and use the family's egg allotment, to treat us with a Victoria sponge cake—like the ones I have made and served so often to those who have gathered around a table spread with this linen cloth.

My children and grandchildren had heard all these stories before, of course, for the cloth had always been a conversation piece within our family circle. I remember Hope caressing the silken stitches that spelled out "Martha Knight," my grandmother who had been kept home from school to help raise her many younger siblings and had never learned to read—and yet could write out her name and add up a long list of numbers in her head without an error. When Hope sighed and said, "I wish I had known her" I told her about our trips in the charabanc Granny would hire to take us to New Brighton.

I can see her even now, dressed to the nines and looking every inch like a duchess as she reclined on the back seat of the charbanac, her brimmed, black velour hat tilted a little forward to avoid contact with the edge of the vehicle's canvas top that was folded down behind her. I always felt sorry for the poor bird whose plumage was wrapped around the hat's brim, but the silver fox fur slung around her shoulders was a constant source of fascination to a small girl looking at life. How I loved to sit beside her, stroking the fur around her neck while trying to keep my finger out of the fox's "mouth," a hinged device intended to keep mouth and tail joined in a circle around her shoulders. Yet she would always manage to catch me unawares, open up the creature's little jaws, and snap them shut around my stroking finger, bringing howls of laughter from everyone else aboard the bus.

She would twiddle her thumbs as we rode along, urging us to join her in round after round after round of a chorus, and I never did tell her how much I hated singing those silly songs along with her. Especially the one called "Knees Up, Mother Brown." Haydn, who was waiting to get a word in edgewise, pointed to the uneven scrawl in the very center of the cloth. How old was I when I wrote that, Mom? He'd been only five, and he'd loved the color red, even at that early age. Dan, pointing a finger at my name, looked up at me with a twinkle in his eye. "Remember the time you pitched to me out on the lawn, trying to turn me into another Pete Rose?"

I knew where he was going, since I'd been broadsided by that memory more than once. But feigning ignorance, I said, "Ah, yes! Those were the days!"

Waving his fork for emphasis, he corrected me. "No, Mom! Not days, but day! That was the one and only time I ever practiced my hitting with you. You were so determined to make a pro out of me you gave it everything you had. Most of the pitches went flying into the hedge, but I suppose you've forgotten all about the one that didn't get away."

I deliberately gave him a befuddled look, letting him have his moment in front of my wide-eyed grandchildren.

"You know the pitch I mean, the one when you hollered, 'Here comes the fast ball!' The pitch that smacked me right in the teeth. See . . . ," and he gave me a big grin, exposing a front tooth that was still slightly chipped after all those years.

Everyone laughed—but Ray, who had sat in silence throughout the meal, eating his dinner slowly, occasionally looking up to smile around the table, yet not really being there. As we stood to take the dishes out to the kitchen, he ambled into the living room, even then maintaining his unaccustomed silence.

After Hope and I had dusted the crumbs from the tablecloth and folded up those precious memories, I placed the cloth in Hope's hands. "I can no longer see well enough to embroider the names, Love. And since I've always known this would be yours one day, you might as well take it now and start keeping your own memories safe forever. I taught you to embroider, didn't I?"

Chapter 15

*I*t had never occurred to me that I would one day become a nurse, but my course was set the day the oncologist asked if I would tell my husband he had prostate cancer, since Ray refused to listen to anyone else—not the urologist, the oncologist, or the nurses. He also refused to follow doctor's orders even after the diagnosis had been made. Instead, he insisted on purchasing his own brands of medicine and vitamins, wasting hundreds of dollars and filling his bathroom cabinet with useless and possibly harmful drugs, which Dan would take out and dump, all the while trying to persuade his father to take what the doctors had prescribed. He would agree, but at the first opportunity, he would sneak out to the mall to replenish his stock. When I would give him his prescription medicine, he would take it and put it into his mouth with a smile, but the next second I would turn around to see him spitting it across the room.

During most of our married life, his belligerence and his eccentricities had marked him as being antisocial, provoking, intimidating, antagonistic, and just plain mean. I'd grown accustomed to thinking of his violent and irrational behavior as no more than an exaggeration of his natural disposition, and even after we'd moved to Corvallis, I found myself looking for ways of excusing his actions to others and myself. Gradually I began to suspect he might be schizophrenic, but it was months thereafter that I gathered the courage to suggest perhaps he'd like to see someone who could offer counseling and medications. But no. He was his own physician!

His paranoia became more and more pronounced—the house was bugged, the neighbors were spying on him, and I was providing information on his finances, his comings and goings. I was plotting to kill him or, worse yet, to "put him away somewhere with all the other old geezers." I turned at last to my children. Though I'd done my best to hide the worst of his behavior from them, they'd obviously become more and more concerned about their father's safety and my own. Fortunately our daughter-in-law, Dr. Leslie Clautice, had managed to win his confidence and persuade him to see Dr. Elizabeth Waldron.

It was Dr. Waldron who convinced him to undergo tests, which were performed by a gerontologist known for his expertise in mental disorders of the elderly. When the specialist confronted my husband with the diagnosis of Alzheimer's, my heart ached for him.

I felt I should have suspected something was wrong, and so could not help but feel guilty for failing him in his time of greatest need. But there was no time for regret and self-recrimination. I held back my tears, knowing I needed to put up a brave front in order to help him handle this devastating news. I remembered all too well how difficult it had been for him to accept the oncologist's diagnosis of prostate cancer, how powerless he'd felt in the aftermath of his first heart attack, and how he'd warded off the pain by remaining an island unto himself, as my father had predicted so many years ago. If he continued to wall me out, how could I be of any help to him? And how could I expect any change in his behavior now that Alzheimer's was eating away at his brain? I found myself wondering where that fine line was between love and pity, and whether the pity I felt would even be enough to get us through.

Strangely enough, only when I could hide my husband's behavior behind a name—Alzheimer's—could I finally stand up and say, "Yes, he belongs to me." There was no longer any need to hide behind the menu over his behavior toward waiters and waitresses, or look the other way when he launched verbal attacks at salesmen, grocery clerks, or anyone else who thwarted his wishes. After all, he had Alzheimer's. And since we were living in a new town, where virtually no one knew how similar his present actions were to his habitual ones, observers responded with pity—and even understanding. Pity alone would have sufficed; for at long last people were no longer questioning why I had continued to stay married to such a seemingly monstrous man.

On the other hand, the knowledge that my husband's behavior had a verifiable physiological cause meant I had more reason than ever to stand by my vows and stay with him until the bitter end, a task that was far from easy.

I awoke one mid-summer morning, wondering how many words I would need to tiptoe through before it was time to set the table for a quiet lunch. Or which words from yesterday would be forced back down my throat. The lawn mower had already gone roaring through the grass, and now the snap of shears confirmed my fears that my husband was once again disfiguring the beautiful Japanese maple. I dared to go out on the deck to see for myself, and hurtling shears landed at my feet before I could say good morning. All because I was "interfering." I made sure I stayed out of his garage and his bedroom the rest of the day.

He had a very green thumb and plantings sprang into bloom at his bidding, only to struggle for breathing space under that same thumb. Pansies grew profusely for him, but during his days of darkness, after we had moved into our little gray home in the west, those floral fantasies weren't allowed to show their pretty faces to the sun very long. When it wasn't raining he used the garden hose, with the might of Thor striking with his ham-mer. No gentle spray for those little beauties. He would pelt everything in sight, hard enough to batten them down into the ensuing rivers of mud, and there they stayed, struggling to rise and seek the sun. Until, of course, it came time again to take care of the flowers.

He took the upper hand in every situation that came along, and I allowed him to take advantage of me rather than fight back. But keeping my silence was not always easy. One afternoon I walked in and saw on the kitchen table my beautiful pieces of Royal Doulton Glamis Thistle china, pieces I had collected bit by bit for years, an entire collection built around the one tiny cup and saucer Grandmother Hope had given me to pack into one of those two allotted V-2s bound for America. The dishes were not set out for company, but strewn willy-nilly across the tablecloth. He came into the house, pointing wildly at them, and said something almost unintelligible, "You say one word . . . and I'll smash every last one of them!"

I had promised myself I would keep him at home until the day he didn't recognize me, but that day never came, not even when his physical condition deteriorated to the point that he could neither bathe nor dress himself. He became angry at having to use protective garments to take care of his incontinence, and I'm sure his anger stemmed from shame. There were many accidents, necessitating a constant run of cleaning floors and clothes and bodies. I was scrubbing up one day, when I realized the washer had started to hum, and I ran to check out the problem. There was my poor husband standing before the open lid, in the nude, his freshly soiled Depend garment swishing around inside, along with a pile of not-so-dependable items that had been waiting for washing day. He had become so ashamed of his accidents, he would hide the soiled garments in all the secret places he was sure I would never find.

My heart still ached for him, but he wouldn't allow me to love him.

He would leave the house and become lost, and I would have to track him down time after time. He had been hospitalized once with a heart attack since our arrival in Corvallis, and I feared another one was looming.

My fears were realized one day when he had went for a walk, which turned into a nightmare. I called all the places in which I had previously caught up with him, and was pushing telephone buttons for police help when the door banged open and he fell into a heap on the rug, covered in mud and feces, twigs and pebbles. He was breathing heavily as I cleaned up the mess, but I managed to piece together his story. Had it not been for some Good Samaritan who had found him in the street, picked him up, and helped him into his car, along with the mud and feces—and the frightened eyes of a lost child who couldn't find his mother—he could have died there, alone.

This kind stranger had kept on driving until my husband recognized our street sign and assured his rescuer that he could see his house and walk the rest of the way. Dan and Les came to my rescue, and I relaxed in their strength. I have been so thankful that our home was close enough to theirs to afford a comfort zone, and in such times as this, they were always there, reliable as the Rock of Gibraltar.

By the time we arrived at the hospital that day, my husband was being prepped for surgery, having suffered through a second massive heart attack without one admission of pain, even as he lay in a heap on the asphalt in the solitude of his lone island, while the heart was being robbed of fifty percent of its muscle power. Having regained consciousness and a sense of himself in the hours while he awaited surgery, he kept the surgical staff at bay, fighting them off, saying there was nothing wrong with him.

Those were the times I wanted to hate him, wanted to run away to some Elysian Field to lay my head on someone else's shoulder in my misery. It is so much easier to hate than to pity an abuser, so very hard to honor one who breeds ill will. A love that is tied to obedience dies before it is permitted to breathe, yet I had no wish to spite him for my frailties. Instead I sat there wishing I could die and take his misery with me. All I had ever wanted for him was to find a life that he could *live* in good conscience, and with a merry heart. A heart I was afraid wouldn't last through this long, terrifying day. I wanted to be there, in surgery, sharing the ordeal, though unable to assist those whose expertise could keep him alive. Instead, I made my way to the surgical waiting area, heartsick over his misery and loss of self, his hopeless fight to regain control, a dictator and derelict caught in an antagonistic relationship with life.

It had been a terrifying morning after a sleepless night, and I spent an interminably long afternoon in the waiting room. Almost drugged by the antiseptic atmosphere of hospital efficiency, I laid my head back and stretched out in the comfortable chair in the waiting room, surrounded by families anxiously waiting, like me, to hear the comforting words, "You can go up now!" The hours crawled by and still, we waited and wondered and worried. And I let the fancy roam . . . .

Ever let the fancy roam.
Pleasure never is at home.
. . . .
Thou shalt, at one glance, behold
The daisy and the marigold;
White-plum'd lilies, and the first
Hedge-grown primrose that hath burst
      —John Keats

Red haws are taking over the hawthorn trees, as the days of their flowering pass into yet another season, and there are daisy chains scattered on the path where I sit and slit the flower stems with my fingernail and twine them together into a pretty ring. I smell the sweet, fragrant violets of springtime on the steep railway bank, holding onto their roots as the trains streak by with the wind. The anemone and water crowfoot hide their startling white beauty in the shadows of the woods. I pick the weed we called the mother-die, then throw it over the hedge, remembering Mother's warning, "Don't go bringing that stuff in the house, now. Throw it away, this minute!" Those gray-white petals trembling under my fingers in my reverie,

I want to cradle that world of fragrance in my arms again, and the feeling comes rising up, the ecstasy that is there, waiting to be plucked from nature. Half asleep, I heard a mother chastising her crying child and settled back with my eye on the clock. Would the waiting never end? As the weary mother issued yet another warning, my thoughts slipped back to instances when Mother had chastised me. The water lily saga trod the stage of memory. One morning when walking home from Sunday school, by way of a short-cut through fields filled with tiny white daisies, I saw the color of sunshine here and there on a patch of round, green leaves floating on the surface of a pond. I had never seen water lilies in Warrington before. In fact I had never seen water lilies ever before that day, but I had read about them and marveled at Monet's interpretation of their beauty. I had dreamed of finding one to press into my books.

The temptation was irresistible. Leaving my shoes and socks in the grass, the new Bible I had been awarded at Sunday school alongside them, I plunged in. The water was deep, and my new crêpe de Chine dress with gold square buttons down the front, which Mother had made out of one of her own dresses, clung to my chest. That lovely yellow lily was tough and resistant, even when I tried to coax it up in the name of its family, nymphaeaceae, learned from my nature study teacher, Miss George. But the stubborn stem finally broke loose, sending me backwards into the water, lily and all. The golden treasure mine at last, I happily put shoes and socks back on my feet, wrung out the water from the skirt of my dress, and picked up my Bible, hoping Mother wouldn't look at the kitchen clock when I finally got home.

I was in such a rush to get there I almost missed the rabbit, so tiny that my poor eyes saw him as just a twitch on the side of the road. There was no sign of a mother as I looked around, and I thought he's probably lost. If you, as a child, ever saw a scared, trembling baby rabbit, without a mother, what would you have done? I undid a few of the square gold buttons of my dress, picked up that trembling bundle of soft fur, twitching whiskers and all, and made room for him inside, trying not to think of what Mother would say. After all, that baby rabbit didn't have a mother, poor thing.

I wish you could have seen Mother's face as I walked into the kitchen with a rabbit's ear sticking out the front of a wet, Sunday-best dress—which was now showing more of my thighs than it should have—a wilting lily in one hand, and clutched in the other my Sunday school prize, the St. James Bible earned for good attendance.

Lucky for me, Mother did sometimes have a sense of humor along with all her other senses, because I must have looked so comical that she laughed out loud and led me over to the bureau mirror to look at myself. I felt more like crying than laughing, but to hear Mother laugh was such a rare treat, I let myself be caught up in her merriment, and we laughed together until my sobbing brought the moment to a sudden halt. After the crying was over, she let me take the bunny to a friend who had a rabbit hutch. "One more won't make that much difference to a rabbit mum," she said.

When I got back from the rabbit hutch, Mother had wrapped the tough-stemmed water lily in a tea towel and had run it through the big rolls of the mangle all ready for me. "Go stick it in your album now, before you forget!"

How I loved Mother that day!

But then again came that voice chastising a child, followed by the words I had been waiting for.

"Well, he came through with flying colors," the white-coated man was saying. "I've never worked on such a fine physique, but this second attack has severely damaged an already ailing heart."

The fancy roamed for a few more days and nights spent at my husband's bedside, leaving his room only to eat my meals at the cafeteria.

My three children were gathered around me in the hospital lobby, persuading me to make out a living will for my husband and myself. This was a difficult decision to make, but I understood the reality of my husband's inability to make decisions for himself, and the possibility that I, too, might someday need loved ones to make life or death choices for me. Ray's own choice had always been that he would definitely not want to linger on in a vegetative state of helplessness.

The hospital staff told me that he had already used up his allotted hospital Medicare stay and advised finding a place for him. Yet I had promised myself I would never put him in a caring place until he could no longer recognize me. Even after this traumatic ordeal, he still recognized me by name, but spoke to me as a hostile stranger with schemes to "do away with him." My children begged and pleaded with me not to take him home. "Mother," they argued, "You can't do this anymore. It's an impossible task caring for him at home. How many times has he strayed away and become lost already? You can't go on this way!"

In 1945 I had traveled many miles alone so that my family could be born and raised in this great land of freedom and opportunity, and my children have all encouraged me to keep faith in my own dreams. I look back on the steps they urged me to take along the way: Supporting my work as an artist and a writer. Encouraging me to earn a degree at the age of fifty-nine. Giving me confidence enough to run for the local school board and the legislature. I would never have made it alone, without their support. Now they were saying, *You have to get away from it all, Mother. You have to go. You need to take care of yourself!* Oh, how I wished I could have just gone far away and left it all behind, but the children were offering wise and loving counsel, and I had to tell them that they were right. I could no longer manage their father on my own, with eyes too dim to differentiate between a parking meter and a perambulator. Their concern for us both was evident. How could I ignore their loving counsel?

The task of finding a safe place for him to live in harmony with other patients became a difficult assignment, when one after another facility refused admittance because his hospital records characterized him as "antagonistic" and "hard to control." We eventually found a new "locked facility" that leased out suites at an exorbitant cost, with expenses for medications shooting the moon. The only other alternative would have been the state mental institution, and I would rather have died than do that to him!

It was a sad day when we moved him, along with his furniture and personal belongings, into a place behind locked doors. When he said, "We'll stay in this hotel overnight then, and fly back home tomorrow?" I didn't have the heart to correct him. I just responded, "We'll see," and wondered how many more excuses I would need to dream up and still hold onto that thing called integrity. I wondered too if I could muster the strength to go back there the next day. But I did, and again the next day, and the day after that, until I felt like the mother of all those poor souls in Regent Court.

It was so easy to make friends with people who so desperately needed the love and comforting presence of someone who might be there to take them home again. Not to the place they wouldn't recognize when they got there, but to the warm, safe place of belonging they used to know. To the rightful place of personage they once had, to the selfhood so rudely snatched away from them, as they hopelessly reached out in a dark underworld that had slammed the door of understanding in their faces.

Pity was tinged with fear every time the phone rang. I had given permission to the aides for him to call me at any time, and time after time I would hear the ring and think, "There it goes. Oh no. Not again." But yes, it would be my husband yet again, and my heart would sink to a new low. "Irene, come on now," he would say. "Let's get on the road! We have a long way to travel tonight and not much time to get there."

Where we were going I didn't ask, and again and again I used the old cliché about his heart being too weak to allow him to leave so soon. He insisted that we owned three houses in town, and since I didn't want him anymore, he would take the one that was furnished, for he was quite capable of taking care of himself. Each time I searched for another bit of logic he might accept for staying where he was—he wasn't strong enough to go home yet, the doctor would probably release him tomorrow, he had to consider his heart—he pooh-poohed my excuses away. Eventually I had to be firm and tell him he wasn't going anywhere with that kind of attitude. "Oh, all right. We'll start packing tomorrow then," he'd say. And I wanted to run away. Far, far away where I could hide my face from the world and curl up like a caterpillar, just sleeping it all away inside my chrysalis. Yet I knew I would not run away. I knew I would go back again tomorrow. And tomorrow. We would make clay pots with the rest of the residents. He would sit beside me, rolling his ball of clay into a nothing, while I showed him how a pot should look in different stages of its growth. He would sit for a few more minutes, put his chin on his chest, and go to sleep. The moment he woke up, he would ask, "Are we home yet?"

Or we would sit in the makeshift chapel, mostly wheelchaired rows of pews, listening to a visiting preacher tell them about the good life ahead. I tolerated the sermon because he seemed to enjoy the piano and guitar that thumped out the hymns, but he would soon fall asleep, whispering, "Take me home." Each nap was short. He'd awake with a start. "Is this the bank?" And when I'd answer, "No," he'd say once more, "Then why don't you take me home?"

The rest of the time we sat on his bed while he pleaded with me to pack up his bag and take him home. Outside on the patio bench, he would hold my hand and cry, begging me once again to take him home, and I would cry along with him, squeezing his hand, despairing. Forcing a strained smile, he had once whispered hoarsely through his tears, "Well then, if you'll buck up, I'll buck up, and we'll work things out together when we get home."

I promised to stay until after dinner one day, and we sat in his usual place at a table with two other residents. There wasn't much talking except when Richard, a neighbor across the ward from him, started to choke on a piece of meat and spat it out, along with his teeth, onto the tablecloth. I helped him separate the two, and we somehow got his teeth back inside his mouth. He looked up at me and said, "I have been very sick, and I love you." This beautiful soul, wheelchair-bound, barely able to hold up his head, had once been a prominent judge, and from my acquaintance with him in Regent Court, I knew his judgment in the court over which he once presided would have been upright, honest, and meted out with due consideration for all parties. There was much sadness in that place those suffering people could never call home. Alice had pushed her walker over from another table to complain that yesterday Frances, her neighbor, had been begging Alice to take care of her because nobody else would. "Nobody comes to see me any more," she said. Alice, being somewhat forthright and opinionated, had told her, "No! I have enough to do to take care of myself." Whatever else might be troubling her on any given day, Alice would move into her familiar lament: "They put my husband in a different home, and they won't listen to me when I tell them we should be together."

Frances, on the other hand, thought she deserved the hugs I gave her every day, reminding me, "Because I'm half deaf, people think I'm stupid." I told her I had the same problem, and that if she said, "Please speak up. I'm nearly deaf," they would understand that she was certainly not stupid but quite intelligent. Among the residents of all four divisions at the Court, Alzheimer's ran rampant and confusion reigned. Bill, who'd been a colonel in some battalion or other, lived across the hall from my husband, and usually ate at his table. One night I noticed Bill was sitting at a different table, and I soon learned why. My husband, who frequently misplaced his glasses and was nearly blind without them, had mistaken Bill's room for his own. Having spotted him just as he disappeared through the doorway, Bill had come charging into his room, fists up in front of his face, ready to challenge the thief who was rummaging around in his stuff. Raised fists from anyone, colonel or no, would raise anybody's dander, and my husband, the sergeant, took the challenge right back to the colonel in the form of a karate kick and an angry order to get out of *my* room! Details were hazy, since they had been lost in a flurry of pent-up emotions.

After dinner that evening I bided my time till the dreaded third act, the goodnight scene, hoping this time to escape with a kiss, since my husband had been readied for bed and seemed in a somewhat vacant state. That hope vanished as I saw the colonel coming on like a cyclone, flying through the room and trashing everything in his path. Ray shot up from the bed, fists upraised, shouting, "Come into *my* room will you, you s*6^@ b." The colonel's reply as I stood between them, warding him off, was "Let me at him. I'll take him on any time." I was crying out for help, pushing with my hands against two pairs of fists making their mark in all the wrong places—on my body—when one of the aides arrived to help me disentangle myself and finally persuade the colonel to go for a cup of tea.

The goodnight kiss did nothing to settle Ray down that night, but I had to catch the last bus, even though I knew he would be hurrying behind me as I headed for the outside door, which, of course, was locked for good reason. As usual he tried to see and remember the numbers I punched in—the code that would guarantee his freedom. I made my exit in the two seconds the door gave me leeway, listening to him cry, "Take me with you!" I knew I had to go back there again tomorrow, and the next day, and all the days after—never knowing exactly what I'd find when I arrived.

A young aide met me at the door one Sunday. "Before you go in to see Ray, would you like to hear a funny story?" I waited and she went on, "We lost Ray last night!"

I wasn't too surprised, since my husband had a habit of roaming around the corridors in the night, and would wander through any open door. Nor was I too alarmed, since obviously this story had a happy ending.

The aide went on, "When I found him missing on a routine check after 'lights out,' I alerted the rest of the staff. We all went off looking in different directions, and when we couldn't find him, we went to his room to decide what to do."

My husband's room was connected to another by a shared bath. The second bedroom, unoccupied at present, had been decked out as a showroom for Alzheimer's caretakers looking for cozy quarters for the loved ones they were leaving behind. I immediately asked if they'd checked the empty room.

"That was the very last place we looked." They had already started out into the hall, when the aide happened to glance into the other room. "There he was, sleeping like a baby in that lovely bed." She'd shaken him awake and pulled down the bedclothes. He was naked as a newborn baby, his clothes all neatly folded on the table beside him. "Ray," she'd said, "What on earth are you doing in this bed? This is not your bed!"

"I know it's not my bed!" he'd said. "It's my wife's bed and I have every right to be here."

At the close of yet another visit, I heard him calling, "Wait for me! Pleeaase, wait for me. I hate it here!" And he kicked and screamed and threw himself against the locked door with such force that I feared for his heart and his bones. And still I did not turn around, afraid to let him see my stiff British upper lip quiver. Suddenly I was swept by memories of the day a professor had read aloud a poem in which a horse was being beaten. To everyone's amazement, including my own, I found myself screaming "Stop! Stop! Stop!" at the top of my lungs. And now, as my husband's pleading followed me home, my heart was screaming those same words.

I wanted it all to end. And soon. The visits to Regent Court were bringing up memories of visits to my dear father lying in a cot outside an English sanatorium, crying to "go home to his girls." He died, shivering and breathing in that cold air of no hope, everyone believing his isolation and outdoor treatment were for his own good, when he was really suffering from lung cancer and not tuberculosis. I still wish with all my heart that we had known his true condition, for I know Mother would have brought him home to die. And I could not help but ask myself over and over during my husband's days behind locked doors, dare I take him home with me?

Sunday's visit had gone well that week, with the two of us listening to a guest play the music of his favorite '40s songs on the piano in the sitting room. But Monday morning began with an early call from Regent

Court. "Irene, we have taken Ray to the hospital. He isn't responding." My wonderful neighbors, John and Debby Gremmels, answered my call for help as they always did, and at the hospital the staff explained that my husband had suffered a transient ischemic attack, a stroke that does not paralyze the body. His body was obviously in working order, since he was once again fighting those whose help he needed most, shoving the nurse away from the emergency room gurney and cussing out the doctors trying to restrain him. As I came into the room, he sat up with his fists raised, saying, "And you . . . you!" The doctor by my side held my hand and whispered, "It's hard, isn't it?"

I waited until Ray became calm enough for me to take him back to Regent Court. He put his hand on mine and said, "Did they tell you I died and came back to life this morning?"

Home again at last, I tiptoed around his garden, momentarily bending to the winds of his will as gracefully as the branches of that beautiful maple tree, as I considered the child that he was and the man he had become, a man filled to bursting with the bitterness that had festered from his earliest years, when he'd had to work for nothing. Up with the dawn, rising from the hayloft to milk the bellowing cows before he ran for the school bus; hurrying home in the evening to milk them again; performing the dreary after-supper task of washing the milk separator; then going through the remaining evening routine of the farm on the side of the hill, until bedding down with the cows again that night. The source of his bitterness and anger was clear. Less evident was the source of his occasional acts of kindness—like giving his prized possession, his 1929 Chevrolet, to his sister Inez, so she and her sweetheart could run away to be married.

Gifts of kindness. As I stood watching the maple branches sway in the wind, my heart ached once again at the memory of the few gifts I'd received from my husband over the years—the turkey leg he brought along on our first date, a broom on one Christmas, a set of steel bowls on another, always something to stamp me as a hard-working wife. One

Christmas he surprised me with a ring—but I was later told he'd held it back for a year because I hadn't earned it yet. And yet now, in the midst of his tirades, there were occasional moments when he seemed content, and one such moment came on a day when he agreed to go to an art show where I'd set up a booth. Always glad to be allowed time away from Regent Court, he had smiled in my direction as people stopped to purchase the pieces I had on display, and he had enjoyed the sunshine, strolling about the grounds with his children, and eating something other than institutional food.

Since that outing had given him such pleasure, Hope and I decided to surprise him with a Labor Day weekend picnic in Avery Park. There he sat, surrounded by his children, his grandchildren, the chicken, the potato salad, and all his other favorite things—including a cooler of Coors Lite. As his eighteen-year-old grandson, who'd flown in from Montana, played his own compositions on his guitar, Ray sat in a spot of sunshine, sipping a beer and smiling. We reminisced and laughed and ate ourselves silly until dusk arrived, a little too early.

"We'll drive Grandpa back," the children said as we packed up to leave. And I breathed a sigh of relief that I would not be going through the escape routine that night. Afterward they said that when they walked him through the entrance to Regent Court, he first asked if they were going to the bank, and then, still smiling, he shouted to all the residents who were close enough to hear, "This was the happiest day of my life!"

It was to be the last happiest day of his life.

I was awakened around 10:00 P.M. the next night with the words coming out of the phone: "Irene, Ray just died and we need to know the name of his funeral parlor."

What a harsh, cold message so close to a happy family reunion. What an impersonal way for any loved one to receive such tidings, although the matter-of-fact delivery seemed in keeping with the way my husband had lived. Even so, he was my husband of nearly sixty years—and the father of my three children. Surely I deserved some show of respect in recognition of even the slightest iota of bereavement I might be feeling at his passing. My indignation turned to sorrow, for though it was not entirely unexpected, the news of his death came as a stunning blow that robbed me of all reason and left me running about the house, crying, "No! No! No! Oh, No!"

I had asked the caller to contact my son Dan, who lived close by, and he took over from there. We drove to Regent Court and I asked to see my husband. He was stretched out on his back on the bed, with his head turned sharply away to the left in a pose of resistance, almost of defiance. When I bent down to touch his face, he was far, far away on his lone island. He would not turn around. He wouldn't turn around to recognize me. And I knew he was dead.

God alone can put a measure on the amount of love we give and receive in this life, and God alone will ever know how much of it I tried to give. My only consolation will be in never looking back with regret, if I can help it, on whatever I did in good faith.

My eight-year-old grandson sat beside me at the military funeral September 5, 2001, holding my hand, holding back his tears, and glancing up at me now and then as if to be sure he was behaving like a gentleman. He had loved his grandpa, in spite of his harshness.

A salutation of shots rang out, fired by men who had courageously lived through the Second World War, the war in which Ray had fought. And the poignant notes of the trumpeter playing Taps resounded among the tall, stately evergreens guarding the graves in that quiet place. The Honor Guard in formation, they began to fold Old Glory with such dignity and respect for what it meant to have served under that beautiful flag. I had forgotten it would be presented to me to keep in honor of his service. They asked if I had anything to say, and I assured them I did. Not to those present, but to my husband, lying in the coffin ready to be covered with the cold, black earth. I stepped up to the grave and read a letter I had written to him, and these were the words I know he heard.

Memories of a Big Sky British War Bride

On a September day almost sixty years ago, I stood beside you and we said, "I do," and so we did. We have striven to stick together through thick and thin for all those years since that day in 1943, holding onto the promise, 'till death do us part. The road may have been rocky in spots, and the ice too thin to skate upon, but you never seemed to notice the bumps, and I kept on hoping for that life of freedom and happiness you once promised.

Though all our dreams were not realized, I thank you for the security you provided me as a stranger in a foreign land. I thank you for your love of your country and your belief in the value of hard work. And I thank you for our children, who have lived those values and passed them on to our grandchildren.

You suffered much in your lifetime, yet you never acknowledged your pain and never reached out for the love we had to give. Yet I know you felt our love for you at the picnic we shared that day in Avery Park, a day you described as "the best day in your whole life." Knowing you found peace on that sunny afternoon, I can celebrate your passing, certain that you have been given up to an even greater love, where there will be many more such picnics in the park.

Your wife,
Irene

While my closing words might seem to imply a traditional belief in heaven, I find little comfort in the words one hears so often: *He's out of his misery now. He's in a far better place than this one.* I nod my head, a silent yes intended to move the speaker beyond that topic, for though there was a time when I too believed in a better place, my search for truth has led me beyond the tenets of organized religion and altered my perspective on the hereafter. I no longer think of eternal life as a second Eden, stretching peacefully to the far shores of eternity with no earthly adversity to break the monotonous perfection. I am no longer able to imagine taking pleasure in such a hereafter. There would be no balance between joy and sorrow in such a Paradise.

"You would know the secret of death," says Kahlil Gibran, "but how shall you find it unless you seek it in the heart of life?"

I think of Krissy, our beloved Saint Bernard. We buried her in Livingston one early spring day, alongside the patio, under a bush that had never given us the pleasure of one single bloom. On a late June morning, as the weather was warming in Montana, I thought I spotted a splash of red outside the kitchen window. But a light mist rising up to greet the sun swallowed up the bit of color I'd imagined. My curiosity lingered, and a few minutes later I took a second look. The mist had cleared and our Krissy tree was ablaze with deep pink blossoms.

My stoical mother, Our Em, was one of the few people I knew who could speak of death with resonance and confidence, and not in whispered fear. When my youngest sister, Our Little Dot, learned that the doctors could do no more to stop the progress of the cancer that had metastasized throughout most of her shrunken body, she pleaded with Mother to take her home to die. And Mother set about the task of making her comfortable in her last days, setting up a bed in the parlor so there would be no need to climb the stairs, preparing all her favorite childhood foods, and cradling her in her arms while whispering in her ear, "It'll be all right in the morning, Love." But not even Mother's third eye could bring her daughter through this final crisis.

It happened on Christmas Eve, according to the letter Mother wrote me from so many miles away. She had rocked Doris to sleep before putting her back into bed for the night. A short time later she heard her cry out to my father, who had been dead for over twenty years. Hurrying back into the parlor, she saw not the shrunken, wizened body that the curse of cancer had shaped, but the beautiful thirty-year-old woman who had been her youngest daughter. Doris was smiling, with no sign of the pain that had haunted her for so long. As Mother reached her side and took her hand, Our Little Dot closed her eyes and was gone. "It was all so strange and a little frightening," Mother wrote. "It was as if she was ready to start her young life all over again!"

I was not with my husband when he died, and so I cannot say with certainty what he'd have done had I reached out a hand to him. I have at least the memory of that moment in Avery Park, when he sat in sunlight, smiling over something known only to himself. There were so many things he chose to keep inside and never share that I can't help but think it would have been his choice to die as he had lived—alone.

Chapter 16

Hope is an empty teapot, awaiting fulfillment
from the kettle singing on the hob.
—I. HOPE

*D*eath happens. We just don't take it out of the closet often enough to make it a part of our everyday lives. We let it sit there, rattling its bones among the family skeletons, convincing ourselves *it will never happen to me.* Only when death comes close enough for us to turn around and speak our mind to it, does its stark reality come home to us. And yet, even with my husband's coffin lying in the ground, even with the last clods of dirt being shoveled over his remains, the full reality of what the end of his life had to do with mine did not sink in. Only now, almost four years later, can I say I am a widow. A part of my life has been snatched away by death. Death has unquestionably touched my life. I have lived with it. It's inevitable, and it's my turn next.

The caterpillar puffs his ring of smoke into the air, asking once again, *Whoooo aaaare youuuu?* And even having faced mortality, even after all the retrospection apparent in these pages, I still have no answer to the question floating in that puff of smoke. Having searched the heart of every living soul I've met, seeking the truth that's hidden there, I realize I haven't really searched my own.

I have found nothing closer to truth than the lone poppy in a field of wheat, its scarlet petals aflame in the sun, a warning flag for the child who dared to pluck and take it home to keep. I had never heard the word trespasser as I thrashed through that waving grain. I was a will-o'-the-wisp, floating in a heavenly place, intent on picking a posy for my wildflower book, a bold and barefoot tomboy assuming all the beauty in the world was mine for the plucking.

Anything seemed possible, given my father's unconditional love. I took advantage of every opportunity to prove myself worthy of such love, yet not from any sense of fear or obligation. My adherence to his unspoken code of behavior was a matter of free choice. There was no fear of reprisal if I failed to live up to his expectations, only a renewed resolve to do better next time. Under his guidance I began to know myself as an individual, a free spirit let loose on the world. Yet that invitation to be me was countered by my mother's determination to force me to conform to her sense of what was right and proper. Given the many times I was reminded of and punished for my failings, I found it hard to believe that Mother counted me as one of her blessings. And yet without her unselfish determination to get us all through the hardest of times, where would I be today?

Tomorrow comes too quickly now, as the years add up to eighty-five, and I tend to forget there ever was a yesterday. Yet writing a memoir is an invitation to explore those yesterdays in an attempt to make sense of a life, to balance the joys against the sorrows and to come to accept sorrow as a crucial part of any meaningful existence. Sunshine and shadow. Laughter and tears. Only through darkness do we learn a full appreciation for light. But what if the darkness is tied to a single moment, when one has made a vow that sets the wheels of destiny in motion so there seems to be no turning back?

I think of Whitehead's assertion that "Apart from blunt truth, our lives sink decadently amid the perfumes of hints and suggestions," and I wonder how many memoirists have felt the sting of that statement and closed up their laptops for good. Blunt truth. How can one who has spent so much of her life in a search for truth hide behind hints and suggestions?

Yes, there are still some things to be written, but they are things not easily confessed.

I wrote with relative ease the letter I read at my husband's graveside service, but it was not until three years later that I gathered the courage to write a second letter to the grave: I hope you hear me, Ray, wherever you are, because I will never rest in peace until these things have been said. Words so long unspoken erupted onto page after page after page.

You have to listen now that I am free to stand up for myself!

Obedience be damned!

I had begged him from the first to talk to me about his childhood, hoping to find the key that would open his heart to trust and love again. Yet in all those years we spent together, he revealed nothing at all about his family, not even those things he must have known I'd hear from others. You never spoke one word to me about the time your mother went to the house on the hill and accosted Mabel with a butcher knife, Ray. Our lakeside neighbor brought that news—she'd watched them come and take your mother away. And she made sure I understood the problem was "nothing that could be passed along to the children." Our children, Ray, your mother's grandchildren, the little ones she never saw, never rocked, never gave a horsey ride on her knee. Your mother died in a mental institution, Ray. Was that why you were so terrified of being "locked up with the other old geezers"?

On and on I wrote, delving into the darkest secrets of his family relationships, revealing my true feelings about our physical relationship, recounting the many ways in which his behavior in the presence of others had made me want to run and hide, talking freely and openly about any and every thing that came to mind as sixty-five years of pent-up emotions spilled out onto paper, all in direct defiance of his cardinal rule: "Everything that happens in this house stays in this house!"

Well, this house isn't yours anymore, is it, Ray?

And there is nothing you can do to silence me.

At the time I wrote that letter, I assumed it would have a place in this memoir—perhaps a chapter all its own. But I've come to realize those words have served their purpose. Having had my say at last, none of those old hurts seem to matter quite so much anymore. Yet there are times when I still hear you creeping around the house, and wonder if you have come back in the night to frighten me or to look for something left behind.

Fear is not always rational. In the days before sound was introduced, and the words in the silents appeared underneath the action with every flip of the screen, my mother used to have me accompany Granny Knight whenever she wanted to go to the pictures, so I could read the words for her. Granny's favorites were the horror stories, and though I tried to keep my eyes glued on the words she wanted me to read, every now and then I'd dare myself to squint up at the pictures.

The night I saw the club-footed man, I started to shiver, and it wasn't even cold. He was dressed in black, a cape hugging his shoulders, his top hat nearly falling off his head as he slouched across the screen, dragging his lame foot behind and feeling his way along the alleyway, his silver-handled cane poking between the cobblestones.

"What's he going to do now?" Granny asked. And I had to admit I didn't know, since I hadn't read on cue.

Walking Granny home after the pictures was a nightmare in itself, and I was always glad to see the lamplighter walking down the street ahead of us, his ten-foot pole lighting up the globe on top of each lamppost. Granny hung heavy on my arm, and her girth slowed me down considerably as I tried to hurry past the alleyways, where the cats were doing their prowling and yowling, their luminous eyes betraying them in their furtive pursuits.

I usually enjoyed sleeping at Granny's house on "picture nights"— once we'd made it safely through the door. That night, though, I asked her for a safety pin, hoping she wouldn't ask what it was for. When she did, I had to tell her I needed to pin my nightie to the sheets, so I wouldn't be able to get out of bed and sleepwalk and find myself out in the alley with the cats and the black-hearted villain with his silver-tipped cane. Grandmother did her best to comfort me, yet all those horrible images stayed with me long after the gas jet over the mantel had been turned off and grandmother's heavy footsteps were echoing down the hall, a chill, club-footed reminder that there would always be a next time.

I could blame Granny Knight for taking me to horror shows at such an early age. I could blame my mother for forcing me to read the words my Grandmother could not. In fact I have blamed my mother for a good many things in my life, and since a memoir is a time for analysis and forgiveness—of oneself as well as of others—it is time to take another look at the one person whose example helped make me who and what I am today.

Whoooo aaaare youuuu? The question comes again and this time I am ready. I am the daughter of Emily Knight Hope, a woman who never told me what faith was, but showed me through her actions. Whatever problems she encountered, she managed to rise above, largely because of her unfailing belief that everything will be all right come morning. Only through this examination of my life have I come to understand that her words—and her example—enabled me to hold onto my hopes and aspirations, even in the darkest of times. Yet only with the wisdom of age have I come to remember what she was more than what she did.

Perhaps that is understandable, since she did so much to keep our family clothed and fed and cared for, through strikes and wars and daily calamities. Like the moon and the sun, she was always there, and I never doubted her ability to carry on. Yet there were times when I doubted her love. I longed for some show of affection from her, though I think I realized even as a child that love was just taken for granted in our household. We were supposed to care about each other, including the dogs that followed Father home, old Tom the cat, and the two budgies, the pair of talking birds Father hung in a cage from the clothes rack in the kitchen.

Love as a matter of course was not enough for a little girl hungry for some show of affection. Yet, had I sensed how much in need of love my mother was herself, and how much of it I had to give, things might have been very different between us. I want her to understand that, even now.

You never knew how I held those tea-leaf readings to my heart when we had a cuppa tay together, did you, Emily? You would tell me wonderful things about the future, things that only you could see rising up from the bottom of the cup. I treasured those brief moments, yet how I longed for you to say "I love you, Our I." I'm sure I would have said, "I love you back, Mother." But it's never too late to make amends, and I say them now.

"Mother, Emily, Our Em, Me Mam! I love you now and I loved you then!"

And, after all these years, I've finally come to understand how she could rush to save me from Reggie's life-threatening grip, even while scream-ing for all to hear, "What did you do to make him choke you like that? What did you do?" She saw my shame and confusion with those eyes in the back of her head, assumed the worst, and was too disappointed, too angry, and too proud to get to the truth of the matter.

I can forgive her for that deep hurt, only because I have lived long enough to learn that no matter how much a mother loves her children, there are bound to be times when she fails them by choosing not to take their side out of fear, or pride, or whatever. And I have lived long enough to feel a need to say to each of my own that I am sorry for those times when I failed to stand up for them.

Was that what you were trying to say to me, Mother, as I sat beside your hospital bed in the moments before you died, and you beckoned me closer to whisper over and over, "I'm sorry, Love . . . I'm so sorry . . . for that time when you were little and . . ."

You couldn't finish. You couldn't say it even then, Emily. But if it's any comfort to you, there is no longer any need to apologize. It's all been neatly put away and taken care of. And whatever events have shaped my days on earth, life goes on, doesn't it, Mother? It is undeniably perpetual as long as the will is there to make the best of it, or what is left of it for me.

I stand in my kitchen doorway this gray November day, looking out at the Japanese maple, my head swaying in rhythm with its bare branches, rejoicing with them in their freedom. The rain-soaked tree stands black against the lightening clouds, its characteristic white markings wending their way in brazen contrast up and around the bark until they vanish, out of sight, among the twigs and branches. If sun and rain make peace together, next spring these branches will be laden with leaves casting their dancing shadows on the deck, and I suppose I will need to do a little trimming myself then.

I breathe a sigh of relief, remembering the crew cuts those draping branches suffered year after year after year, harsh prunings that never allowed the tree to reach her full beauty. "It'll grow back," he always insisted. But there was never enough time for full recovery before the sun went down on summer. And even today, with his harsh prunings but a memory, the old survivor stands and waits, holding her breath till spring comes shearing 'round again.

Epilogue

*M*other had been sitting in Father's rocker for days on end before that very special Christmas Eve in our little cottage on Gatewarth Street, her crochet hook poking down through another hole in the sequence of stitches, and pulling up yet another stitch as the tiny dress took shape before my very eyes. As she finished that garment, she started a second one, until there were two of everything—dresses, booties, and bonnets—all of which she placed gently in the linen drawer of the bureau in the kitchen.

I asked, "Who are those for, Mother?"

"Oh, I'm just making them for someone's new baby."

"Will the baby be that small?"

"Maybe." The tone in her voice said that's enough questions now, and I gave the matter no more thought.

Christmas morning always came early at our house, the excitement bubbling and occasionally spilling over into tears for one reason or another. My tears that morning were permissible.

I had awakened to find on my bed the most beautiful baby doll I had ever seen, cuddly rag body with china limbs and a beautiful, smiling china face. She was wearing a crocheted pink dress and matching booties, and as I picked up my brand-new doll, I knew before I ever looked that the eyes peeping out from the matching crocheted bonnet would be big and blue, and the long black lashes would open and shut.

I had never loved anything more, but in the rush to share my good fortune with the world, I ran out of the room so fast I slipped on the landing, falling head-over-heels down the stairs, bouncing against every one of those wooden steps, and shattering the smiling face of my new doll.

Unable to stand my tears, Our Eve said, "Here, you can hug mine for a while, but I want it back!"

I kept glancing at her to see if she was about to snatch it away, but she left it with me for a long time.

Meanwhile, Mother rubbed a little bit of butter on my bruises, and Father found a pot of glue and tried to put the pieces of my doll's head back together. But she wasn't truly beautiful after that.

I held her anyway, my tears dropping over lashes that remained shut and lips that no longer seemed to be smiling.

Mother, always one for making the best of things, said, "Never mind, Love. You can put her in your doll hospital with Our Ike's Golliwog, and you can go see them every day."

Everything will be all right come morning, Love. You just wait and see!